EDWARD GIBBON

A Biography of the Author of *The Decline and Fall of the Roman Empire*

by D. M. LOW

Excerpts from leading English reviews of this book:

This biography is just the sort of book which we have hoped for. Mr. Low's admiration for Gibbon is not idolatrous. He knows that for most of us, without the chance of talking with Gibbon and being directly impressed by his knowledge, his thought, his "facility and elegance of talk," it is impossible, it always was and always will be impossible, not to smile at the droll little figure that we know from the portraits (and Mr. Low has done his share in making them known), and at the self-complacent sage revealed by contemporary accounts and by his own letters. Mr. Low himself can smile. The difference between the grandeur of Gibbon's work and the fussiness of his person and his little ways is perhaps the widest in all the history of authors, and it leaves him unfairly vulnerable. But though Mr. Low's book will not cause the smiles to die upon our lips, it should put a stop forever to easy sneering at the great little man. In love, in soldiering, in politics, in all his personal relations, Gibbon is here seen to have had candour, dignity and worth.

EDWARD GIBBON

EDWARD GIBBON

After an oil painting by Sir Joshua Reynolds

EDWARD GIBBON

1737—1794

D. M. LOW

1937

RANDOM HOUSE

NEW YORK

MADE IN GREAT BRITAIN
BY R. & R. CLARK, LTD.
EDINBURGH

To

CHARLES

By the Same Author

GIBBON'S JOURNAL

Novels

THIS SWEET WORK

TWICE SHY

Contents

The dates of chapter v refer to the entire first residence in Lausanne, not merely to the house mentioned. Chapter viii carries the narrative to 1763 although the Militia service ended in 1762. Since chapters xiv, xv, xvi do not cover the whole of their respective titles, only the commencing dates are given.

Illustrations

From a Wedgwood plaque in the possession of Dr. John Thomas.

This was no doubt made in 1787. One other copy is known to exist. A poor reproduction reversed, with the consequently necessary alterations to the coat, appeared in the *European Magazine*, 1788.

From a contemporary drawing by Brandoin, lithographed by C. Constans.

It shows Gibbon seated in his garden at La Grotte and belongs to the last decade of his life. The original belonged to a friend, the Rev. Professor David Levade, but has not been traced.

From the original autograph in the British Museum.

Written probably in the last five years of Gibbon's life. It illustrates Lord Sheffield's remark that the historian's beautiful hand improved with the course of years; compare the earlier specimens reproduced in *Gibbon's Journal.*

PREFACE

MATERIALS for a life of Gibbon are copious but widely scattered, and even some modern books of the first importance are not readily procurable; while in addition to the great collection in the British Museum, his and other relevant manuscripts are preserved in half-a-dozen different countries. A number of Gibbon's letters are included in the present work, which are either unpublished, or if printed lurk in such remote quarters as to be virtually unknown. In addition there is included a number of letters or portions of letters, nearly all unpublished, from members of his family or his friends. Their style, so often in humble contrast to the historian's virtuosity, illuminates the background of his life. For letters are to a biographer what dialogue is to a novelist.

A collection of Gibbon's letters, to rank with those of the other great English letter-writers, is indeed a very big desideratum of English scholarship. Lord Sheffield's editorial methods came in for much criticism when Prothero's two volumes appeared. They were a great advance. But the text in them is by no means perfect, and there are some strange omissions even from the avowedly limited material that was drawn upon. A rich harvest could be gathered of other published and unpublished letters.

To avoid overburdening the text with footnotes, it has been assumed that the reader who wishes to verify the narrative will know his way about the obvious biographical sources, such as Gibbon's own writings and those of his important contemporaries. Explicit references, however, are given to these authorities in support of crucial points; and where the signposts are less precise, it is hoped the reader will not mind being advised, in the words Gibbon himself used of Herodotus, that 'it will be a pleasure not a task to read' those inimitable works.

The following works are referred to by short titles:—

The Decline and Fall. *The History of the Decline and Fall of the Roman Empire*, by Edward Gibbon Esq[re].

The method of citation here is as follows. For Gibbon's notes it is only necessary to give the chapter and the number of each note; for the text the chapter is given in Roman numerals followed by brackets containing the volume and page. These are given from Smith's Milman's edition, 1854 etc., still probably the most widely diffused edition. There is a serious objection to giving references to Bury's great edition. References to the notes there would not tally with other editions since the editor's additional notes have been most unfortunately combined with Gibbon's in a new numerical sequence.

Misc. Works. *The Miscellaneous Works of Edward Gibbon Esq.*, edited by John, Lord Sheffield, the 2nd edition, 5 vols. London, 1814.

Prothero. *Private Letters of Edward Gibbon*, edited by R. E. Prothero. London, 1896.

Murray. *The Autobiographies of Edward Gibbon*, printed verbatim from hitherto unpublished MSS., edited by John Murray. London, 1896.

Birkbeck Hill. *The Memoirs of the Life of Edward Gibbon*, with various observations and excursions by himself, edited by George Birkbeck Hill. London, 1900.

Gibbon's Journal. *Gibbon's Journal*, to January 28th, 1763. My Journal, I, II & III, and Ephemerides, with introductory essays by D. M. Low. London, 1929.

Meredith Read. *Historic Studies in Vaud, Berne, and Savoy*, by General Meredith Read. London, 1897.

A number of the documents quoted in this book,

generally in translations from the French, are still preserved. But those which the General mentions as having passed into his possession are understood to have been destroyed by fire in a Paris repository shortly after his death.

M. et Mme. de Sévery. *La Vie de société dans le Pays de Vaud à la fin du 18me siècle*, par M. et Mme. de Sévery. Lausanne et Paris, 1912.

Brit. Mus. 11907, dd. 25 (1) and (2). *The Sheffield Papers used for the editions of Gibbon's Miscellaneous Works*, 1928. *Collection of unpublished papers once in the possession of Mrs Dorothea Gibbon*, 1936.

These are typewritten calendars prepared by Messrs Birrell and Garnett. Cited by the press mark of the British Museum copy.

Boswell. *The Life of Samuel Johnson LL.D.* by James Boswell. References are given by dates, so that it is not necessary to specify a particular edition.

Boswell Papers. *Private Papers of James Boswell*, from Malahide Castle in the collection of Lt.-Colonel R. H. Isham. Prepared for the press by Geoffrey Scott, etc. Privately printed. 1928–34.

Other works are referred to in the footnotes as they occur.

In the forefront of many obligations incurred in preparing this book, it is a pleasure to put the names of M. and Mme William de Charrière de Sévery. The grandson of Wilhelm de Sévery, whom Gibbon regarded as an adopted son, M. de Sévery cherishes the relics and traditions which have come down to him, and it is not only in their delightful books that he and his wife keep alive the spirit of that old Lausanne which so completely won Gibbon's heart. Invaluable information over topographical questions was received from M. G.-A. Bridel, whose knowledge of the past and zeal in preserving its survivals are alike inexhaustible. Great thanks are also expressed to M. F. Dubois, Director of the Cantonal Library in Lausanne, and to M. H. Perrochon.

Grateful acknowledgment for permission to reproduce portraits or documents is made to the Earl of Rosebery, Captain G. C. Onslow, and Dr. John Thomas; to the firm of John Murray (for illustrations Nos. 7 and 8) and to the Trustees of the British Museum; for permission to use letters or other documents, to the Marquess of Bath, Madame Grenier-Brandebourg, the Honourable Sir Montague Eliot on behalf of the Earl of St. Germans, Magdalen College, Oxford, Miss J. E. Norton and Captain Onslow. The late Sir John Murray gave the author permission to use Gibbon's unpublished Journal, and thanks are further due to the firm of John Murray for permission to quote from Gibbon's letters and those portions of the Memoirs which are still in copyright.[1]

Among many others who have given valuable help the author wishes to mention Mr Percival Boyd; Miss Belle da Costa Greene, Director of the Pierpont Morgan Library; Mr H. M. Hake, Director of the National Portrait Gallery; Mr C. A. Howse, Head Master of Kingston Grammar School; Captain C. M. H. Pearce, Mrs Charles Tyson and Professor C. K. Webster.

January 1937 D. M. L.

[1] Quotations from the Autobiography are chiefly made from Murray's edition, including those parts which had already been published by Lord Sheffield; otherwise from *Misc. Works*, vol. i.

Chapter I

PORTRAITS

THE contrast between the portrait by Reynolds, the frontispiece of this book, and the small work by Walton which quizzes the large canvases of his contemporaries from its corner in the National Portrait Gallery, is in a way the contrast between the text and notes of *The Decline and Fall*.

Walton's portrait, done in 1774, is one of a series of four friends, each of whom probably had a complete set.[1] In it Gibbon appears as the genial clubman and *bon viveur* ready to amuse and be amused. It was natural that Lord Sheffield considered it the best likeness of his friend.

The Reynolds portrait on the other hand is *The Decline and Fall*.[2] We discern the full onset of learning and intellect in the great forehead and the steady, unflinching gaze; the round resolute mouth, petulant rather than sneering, is ready to mould the rolling period and the swift decisive phrases. The coat, though not a uniform, is very properly red; for 'in England the red ever appears the favourite and as it were the national colour of our military ensigns and uniforms'.[3] It is a subtle

[1] Four copies of the Gibbon are in existence. The reproduction facing p. 4 is from the copy in Capt. G. C. Onslow's possession. The other sitters were G. Wilbraham, Godfrey Bagnall Clarke, and Booth Grey.

[2] The reproduction of it in *Misc. Wks.*, 1814, vol. i., appears to be an amalgam, in the interests of dignity, of Walton and Reynolds.

[3] *The Decline and Fall*, c. lvii. n. 18.

reminder of a school of experience to which the historian was proud to be indebted.

Romney's portrait, painted in 1783, is a mild affair. The boldness and the humour are gone. Yet Hayley, who had commissioned it, claimed that the artist had brought out Gibbon's social qualities even better than Reynolds. In a number of drawings and caricatures of the historian there is always the same frank and steady look mellowing in a rapidly ageing man to a round-eyed invitation to be shocked, a delightful pretence in one who had nothing to learn about our weaknesses, amiable or otherwise.

Personal beauty, Gibbon remarks, is 'an outward gift which is seldom despised, except by those to whom it has been refused'.[1] Most of his contemporaries held that it had been refused to Gibbon without reservation, and the man's vanity added a piquancy to their amusement.

When he ventured to use Reynolds' portrait for the frontispiece of his second volume he doubly delivered himself into the hands of the irreverent. For impressive as this portrait is, it did not pretend to conceal the features which most moved the wags. 'Those Brobdignatious cheeks' Fanny Burney called them, and she was but one among a dozen ready with more offensive adjectives and comparisons.

But the best complement in prose to this picture comes from the German poet Matthisson. His testimony is valuable because unprejudiced; it confirms the observation of others but goes far beyond them. It was written some ten years after Reynolds had painted the portrait.

'His face', says Matthisson, 'is one of the most singular spectacles in physiognomy on account of the irregular proportions of the individual parts to the whole. The eyes are so small[2] that they afford the strongest contrast

[1] *The Decline and Fall*, c. l. (6-219).

[2] This remark by no means agrees with the portraits.

with the high and splendidly arched brow; the rather snub nose almost disappears between the extremely prominent cheeks, and the large double chin hanging far down makes the already elongated oval of the face still more striking. In spite of these irregularities Gibbon's face has an extraordinary expression of dignity, and proclaims, at the first glance, his deep and sagacious thoughts. Nothing can surpass the intellectual fire of his eyes.' [1]

Gibbon never alludes to his looks except once when, on sending his portrait to his stepmother, he says that whatever she may think of his face, she knows his heart is sincerely hers. That is not much to build on. A slight sketch of himself must, however, surely be concealed (it was Gibbon's way) in the portrait of the early Renascence scholar Barlaam.

'He is described, by Petrarch and Boccacce, as a man of diminutive stature, though truly great in the measure of learning and genius; of a piercing discernment, though of a slow and painful elocution. For many ages (as they affirm) Greece had not produced his equal in the knowledge of history, grammar and philosophy; and his merit was celebrated in the attestations of the princes and doctors of Constantinople.' [2]

Gibbon was in fact under five feet in height, and Lord Sheffield remarks that although he became extremely corpulent in later years, his bones were small and finely made. Fanny Burney gives a vivid confirmation of this. She met Gibbon for the first time in 1782 when she was in the first flush of fame from *Evelina*. 'His neat little feet are of a miniature description and with these as soon as I turned round he hastily described a quaint sort of circle, with small quick steps and a dapper gait,

[1] 'Nichts geht über das geistvolle Feuer seiner Augen', *Briefe von Friedrich Matthisson* (Zürich, 1802), p. 43.
[2] *The Decline and Fall*, c. lxvi. (8-108).

as if to mark the alacrity of his approach, and then, stopping short when full face to me, he made so singularly profound a bow that—though hardly able to keep my gravity—I felt myself blush deeply at its undue but palpably intended obsequiousness.' [1]

Fanny Burney also had occasion to note 'the slow and painful elocution'. For after this elaborate preliminary Gibbon said nothing at all. The girl thought that he did not know what to say to her—for she could not believe that Mr Gibbon had heard of *Evelina*—and that he was embarrassed because all eyes were upon them. It is however probable that Gibbon was going to pay an elaborate compliment on the book which Sir Joshua said he had read in a day, had not Fanny's attention been diverted to her hero Burke. Sir Joshua later ascribed Gibbon's unusual taciturnity on that occasion to his fear of being put into Fanny's next book.

Miss Burney found his look and manner 'placidly mild, but rather effeminate,' and his voice when he talked with Sir Joshua 'gentle but of studied precision of accent'. Most witnesses agree on his deliberate and rather affected manner of speaking, and Suard says he spoke in a falsetto tone.[2] Moore records a rare instance of repartee. Dr. Tissot and Gibbon were rivals for Lady Elizabeth Foster's attention. The doctor said to Gibbon rather crossly:

' "Quand milady sera malade de vos fadaises, je la guérirai." On which, Gibbon drawing himself up grandly and looking disdainfully at the physician, replied: "Quand milady sera morte de vos recettes, je l'im—mort—aliserai". The pompous lengthening of the last word, while at the same time a long sustained pinch of snuff was taken by the historian,

[1] Mme d'Arblay, *Memoirs of Dr. Burney*, ii. 224.
[2] In Guizot's introduction to his edition of *The Decline and Fall.*

EDWARD GIBBON

After an oil painting by Henry Walton

brought, as mimicked by Spencer, the whole scene most livelily before one's eyes.'[1]

With age he gave increased attention to his appearance. In the year after his appointment as a Lord of Trade he had a tailor's bill for £145 14s. 10½d.[2] His taste was loud even for that colourful period. We can still read of his 'Burgundy coloured cloth frock with orange shag velvet waistcoat, laced with gold and silver lace', etc. Quantities of lavender water, pomade and powder were no doubt not exceptional, but it is difficult not to smile at his using *bandeaux* for the hair at night.[3] He wore his own hair in later years. A lock preserved in the British Museum is of a deep red colour with few signs of grey.

[1] Moore's *Journal*, 21–22 September 1844; J. Russell, *Memoirs of Thomas Moore*, vii. 374.
[2] *Magdalen College Papers*.
[3] *M. et Mme de Sévery*.

Chapter 2

THE HOUSE AT PUTNEY

IN the year 1720 the South Sea Bubble was pricked; in a moment of time the nation's speculative frenzy changed into a vindictive clamour against those upon whom a few hours previously they had been pressing their anxiety to share in certain and unlimited wealth.

The facts were obscure and of unprecedented complexity, and it was only clear that there was no help in the law. This was nevertheless instantly felt to be one of those major calamities in the midst of which legality is silent, and Parliament took upon itself the task of interpreting the country's moral indignation. If some people could be made to smart, everyone would feel better. There were members of the government such as Lord Sunderland or Mr Secretary Aislabie upon whom the blow might have fallen as well as on any, but the chosen victims were the members of the committee of the South Sea Company. They were held under arrest for a time, they were compelled to make sworn returns of their property, they were forbidden to alienate any part of it, and then a Parliament—whose own prolonged existence was of doubtful validity—sat to consider what was to be done to each culprit. They were to be punished severely, perhaps reduced to beggary.

Prominent among these scapegoats was Mr Edward Gibbon, a successful army contractor, a member of the Board of Customs in Queen Anne's last administration, a man of Tory convictions and suspected Jacobite sympathies. His fortune had been declared at a sum above a hundred thousand pounds, and after Parliament had exhibited every mood from justifiable concern to the most reckless spite and puerile levity, the vote on him decided that all was to be given up with the exception of ten thousand pounds.

But one of whom Bolingbroke had remarked that he had never conversed with a man who more clearly understood the commerce and finances of England was a match for the country gentlemen's assembled wisdom. By settlements which were secure in law, whatever moral judgments might be passed on them, he had already safeguarded a great part of his fortune,[1] and while his grandson, the historian, remarks that by his skill and industry and credit (which appears to have been little damaged) he created a second fortune not inferior to the first, it must be noted that the great part of the landed property, which he was to bequeath eventually, was already in his possession before the disaster of 1720.[2] In fact, when the dust of the battle subsides, he is discerned established at Putney in a fine house with ninety-two acres of land.[3] There he reigned for the remaining

[1] A fact suppressed by Sheffield. See *Murray*, pp. 16, 109, 215, 391.

[2] *The Particulars and Inventory of Edward Gibbon, Esq.*, 1721. 'The freehold estate at Putney, the manor of Lenborough and farm, the manors of Buriton and East Mapledurham, the reversion of Moon's farm and 1/36 share in the New River Water were in pursuance of marriage articles dated 28th-29th March 1720 settled and conveyed to my late mother Hester Acton and Francis Acton and their heirs in trust for my wife's jointure and other uses.' But Mr Gibbon had married in 1705! His personal property was sworn at £75,072 15s. 2d. and real estate £35,970 10s. 4d., a total of £111,043 5s. 6d. Allowing for debts and an interest in his late mother's estate—she died in 1721—the net amount was £106,543 5s. 6d. His furniture and plate were valued at £1208 3s. 4d. Being in Black Rod's custody cost him £130.

[3] The house at Putney was subsequently known as Lime Grove. The details given in *The Particulars, etc.*, show it to have been a considerable place. It stood in the angle to the north of Upper Richmond road and to the east of Putney Park lane and the estate extended up to the Common. The house faced the Pleasance. I. Rocque's map, 1744, in Add. MSS. 14411.

sixteen years of his life a tyrant to his family, as we are told, and the oracle of his neighbours among whom he was the oldest, richest and wisest.

Gibbon tells us that whereas his grandfather had received his education in the rough school of affairs he prepared his son for the considerable fortune which should come to him by sending him to Westminster, where he might become an elegant scholar and would certainly mingle with the highest ranks of society. It would be wrong, however, to infer from this that Edward Gibbon the first was a man of no education or too humble a position. For the greater part of his life Gibbon was remarkably ignorant and indifferent about his family history, and confesses that for all he knew his grandfather might have been a cottager's son or a foundling. The truth of the matter was very different.

Matthew Gibbon, the historian's great-grandfather, was the son of a landowner at Westcliffe in Kent, whose grandfather had bought the property in Queen Elizabeth's reign. The family was believed to have been well established in the Weald of Kent long before that, and it is therefore possible that Gibbon may after all be descended from the Gibbons of Rolvenden, though not by the line which he claims in his Autobiography.[1]

Matthew was one of several children, and coming to London in the second half of the seventeenth century, is said to have made a fortune as a linen-draper in Leadenhall.[2] At the age of twenty-five he married Hester Abrahall of All Hallows, Barking. Of his five children the two daughters made good marriages and one son, Thomas, went from St. Paul's School to St. John's, Cambridge, and became Dean of Carlisle.

[1] See Appendix I for genealogical tables, p. 353.
[2] He also retained some interest in the Westcliffe Property by the law of gavelkind. See Egerton Brydges, *Lex Terrae*, Note UUU, pp. 267 *sqq*.

It is not improbable that Edward also went to St. Paul's.[1]

Matthew must have died fairly young, for his widow married again. Her second husband was Richard Acton, a younger son of Sir Walter Acton. He was in business in London. The alliance with this old Shropshire family was further strengthened. Hester's daughter, Catherine, married her husband's nephew, Sir Whitmore Acton, and her son Edward married Richard Acton's daughter by his first marriage.[2]

That was in 1705.[3] Edward Gibbon was then in a position to spend £500 on his bride's jewellery.[4] In the following years he prospered steadily and was worth £60,000 in 1716 before he embarked on the luckless South Sea scheme. This fortune came largely from profitable contracts for supplying the armies in Flanders. He figures there during the years 1711–13, sometimes as Captain Edward Gibbon, sometimes just Mr Gibbon, but always in connexion with considerable transactions.[5] He had other interests at home, and over these, it is said, during his absence his mother watched with ability and success.

In the normal evolution of an English fortune this

[1] Gardiner, *Register of St. Paul's School*, gives an Edward Gibbon who was at the school under Dr. Gile, *i.e.* 1672–97, and was a Steward of the Feast in 1701. There was another son, Matthew, who was 'not right in his head'. Gibbon appears aware of only two sons and one daughter. He does not seem to know that his aunt Catherine married her first cousin, since Edward Elliston's mother was Matthew's daughter Hester.

[2] In the common text of the Autobiography Gibbon states that Matthew Gibbon's children both married Richard Acton's. Those who are impressed by the fact that these two families produced two great historians should note that Lord Acton did not descend from Sir Whitmore. Thus Gibbon had Acton blood but Acton had no Gibbon blood.

[3] The husband is described as thirty years of age in the marriage licence. He was born therefore in 1675, not 1667 as Gibbon says. Gibbon has confused the date with that of his great-grandparents' marriage.

[4] *Particulars and Inventory of Edward Gibbon, Esq.*

[5] Hist. MSS. Comm. 14th Report, Portland Papers, iii. (v) pp. 152, etc. Thomas Gibbon appears in the same correspondence as an aspirant to the deanery of Carlisle. *Ibid.* vii. pp. 156 *sqq.*

Edward Gibbon might have returned with honours to the country life which his father had sprung from. The South Sea crisis was a set-back, and the old financier was to get no further from Crosby Square than the pleasant riverside of Putney. But he could hope and plan for his son and grandsons to take up the pleasures and duties of country gentlemen on the landed estates which he had bought farther afield. They should be squires and magistrates, members for borough or county, attaining to the government perhaps, and ending quite possibly peers of England. Meanwhile it remained to be seen what could be made of his son.

The widower's family—his wife died in 1722—consisted of Edward born in 1707, Hester born in 1706 [1] and a younger sister Catherine. A strange light hovering between truth and fiction plays round these children owing to their association with William Law.

Law was no ordinary tutor. He may have come to teach young Edward after his brief career at Westminster and he certainly accompanied him to a residence at Cambridge which was either about as brief or phenomenally long.[2] But he remained with the Gibbons in what is clearly a privileged position for the best part of twenty years, leaving a year or two after his patron's death. He was only eleven years younger than his patron and there was probably something more of common interest between the two men than their official relation. It was not merely that Law appealed to the Tory as a non-juror, a man who at the age of thirty-four

[1] Gibbon exaggerates his aunt's age when he says she was eighty-five in 1789. *Murray*, p. 216. He would have blushed to suggest that she could have been born before 1706. She died 1790, aged eighty-four.

[2] Law is supposed to have joined them about 1723. Gibbon's father was at Westminster, 1717–20, and boarded with Mrs Playford (*Particulars, etc.*). Probably he was withdrawn in the hour of crisis. According to *Alumni Cantabrigienses* he entered Emmanuel in 1723 as a pensioner and became a fellow commoner in 1727. He was certainly in residence 1729–30. He did not take a degree.

was doomed to a life without preferment in the church whose outward privileges he had so ably defended; he was commended as well to the business man by qualities which his biographer summarises as 'the thorough reality of the man, his ardent piety, his clear and logical intellect, his raciness, his strong and vigorous common sense, his outspokenness, the very bluntness and abruptness of his manner'.[1]

Gibbon himself speaks with some pride of the fact that his family had made of so sincere and able a man an honoured friend and spiritual counsellor. Candour and clarity of mind and style were qualities that always won him. Nor is it without relish that he reminds us that Law had drawn a damning picture of the difference between the professions and practice of Christians, and adds, in a sentence which Sheffield did not print, 'it is indeed somewhat whimsical that the Fanatics who most vehemently inculcate the love of God should be those who despoil him of every amiable attribute'.[2]

Gibbon's praise of *A Serious Call to a Devout and Holy Life* is just and discerning. But the irony of things is revealed by one brief patronising word. 'Mr. Law's master work', he wrote, 'the *Serious Call* is still read as a popular and powerful book of devotion.' Law's book was destined, for a long time after these words were written, to be one of the most widely influential books in that religious revival which would have been so surprising to many philosophers could they have survived to see it. 'That Law indeed was the great forerunner of the revival . . . and did more to promote it than any other individual whatever; yea, more, perhaps, than

[1] J. H. Overton, *William Law Non-juror and Mystic*, p. 81. But did Law ever show Mr Gibbon his copy of an edition of Thomas à Kempis, published in 1722 and '*Dedicated to the Unhappy Sufferers by the great National Calamity of the South Sea*'?
[2] *Murray*, p. 27.

the rest of the nation collectively taken', was the judgment of Wesley's biographers.[1] Both John [2] and Charles Wesley visited Law at Putney. Charles was even there in August and September 1737 and may well have seen or more probably heard the new-born historian.[3] These are coincidences, but they have acquired a significance of their own in the course of time.

Law 'is said to have been a tall thin bony man of a stern and forbidding countenance, sour and repulsive in his spirit and manner'.[4] That may be an enemy's portrait. But he was clearly rather formidable and hardly the man to bring a temperate atmosphere into a family whose head, as we may gather, was sufficiently stern. He was a man of scholarship, but had revolted against the powers of reason with which he was so well endowed. His great vigour of style is lost for us in common oblivion with the topics he trounced or defended, and even in his greatest book he appears less apt to mould characters than to denounce them.

Relying on family tradition and his own observation so far as his father was concerned, Gibbon tells us that the two sisters and their brother are portrayed in *A Serious Call* in the characters of Miranda, Flavia and Flatus.[5] This identification must be received with some caution. In some of the biographical touches reported of these characters the author may have been prudently seeking to conceal his debt, since they do not harmonise with the known facts of the supposed originals. Of the sisters Miranda and Flavia it is said that their parents were dead and they had been in enjoyment of their own fortunes for some years. But this is not true of Hester

[1] Coke and Moore, *Life of Wesley*, p. 7.

[2] John Wesley's first visit to Putney was in 1732. H. Moore, *Life of Wesley*, i. 190.

[3] Overton, *op. cit.* p. 89, and T. Jackson, *Life of Charles Wesley*, i. 112.

[4] Jackson, *Life of Charles Wesley*, i. 112.

[5] Miranda and Flavia are sisters but Flatus is not said to be their brother.

and Catherine Gibbon. So when we are told that Miranda was an unwilling participant in routs and balls and the folly of every fashion until by her mother's death she was able to give herself to devotion, we must beware of assuming that this mother is sketched from Gibbon's grandmother. Yet a gay and worldly strain came into the family somewhere. And it is undeniable that these characters do depict the essential truth of the three children of Edward Gibbon. This is so plain of the portrait of Flatus that Gibbon, seeing the difficulties of identification, especially on the point of age, nevertheless concludes that 'the prophetic eye of the tutor must have discerned the butterfly in the caterpillar'.[1]

Hester took after her father in the manly vigour of her understanding, and in a certain rigidity and even moroseness of temper. She became an apt disciple of Law's religion without relaxing her grasp on the affairs of this world. People spoke of her as a very good sort of lady but looked on her as a little mad. She was an undoubted Miranda. The little we know of Catherine Gibbon is not inconsistent with the character of Flavia. She was akin to her brother's spirit and followed him into the society of such people as the Mallets after their father's death. She married her cousin Edward Elliston. Shortly after that John Byrom came to visit Law at Putney, and a comment in his diary that it was such an absurdity to come to communion with patches and paint as no Christians would have borne formerly, is clearly intended for her.[2] Neither she nor her husband enjoyed their world for long, and their daughter Catherine, after

[1] *Murray*, pp. 47 and 383. Gibbon refers to the 2nd edition, 1732, but the portrait of Flatus appears in the 1st edition, 1729, when his father was only twenty-two. Gibbon never knew his aunt Catherine and only met Hester Gibbon in middle life. For Miranda, Flavia, Flatus, see *A Serious Call*, cc. vii., viii., ix. and xii.

[2] J. Byrom, *Private Journals, etc.*, Chetham Society, xxxiv. p. 619.

their death, lived with her uncle till her marriage in 1756 with Edward Eliot.[1]

Flatus is not a wicked man. The root of his character is inconstancy. He is healthy, wealthy and young. He has run through foppery and all the pleasures of the town and turns to the country. From hunting he comes to the solider but not less expensive joys of farming and building. He invents new dovecotes 'and has such contrivances in his barns and stables as were never seen before'. But next year he is away to his horses again. Then he goes abroad, but soon comes back because foreigners are so impertinent. He gives a year to Italian in order to understand the opera. At last he is brought to a stand and is reduced to reason and reflexion only to determine which of his old ways he will resume. 'But here a new project comes in to his relief. He is now living upon *herbs* and running about the country to get himself into as *good wind* as any *running footman* in the kingdom.' If this last is a vice it was one which his son at any rate—if Flatus be Gibbon's father—was never guilty of.

Of his general disposition we read:

> 'Flatus is very ill-natured or otherwise just as his affairs happen to be when you visit him; if you find him when some project is almost worn out, you will find a peevish, ill-bred man; but if you had seen him just as he entered upon his *riding regimen* or begun to excel in sounding of the horn, you had been saluted with great civility.'[2]

We must turn back from the butterfly to the caterpillar who appears in the pages of John Byrom's diary. Byrom is a kind of flat Pepys. He was a Cambridge scholar and wit, poet and also hymn writer and teacher of shorthand. In the course of frequent journeys about England he kept a diary which deserves to be better

[1] See Appendix I.

[2] *A Serious Call*, c. xii.

known for its quiet yet colourful picture of England and for its skill in reporting the talk of such men as Law. He had long admired Law from a distance, and at last in March 1729 had the courage to go with a friend to Putney. Law came to them while they were fortifying themselves with mutton chops at the Bull Inn and took them to Mr Gibbon's house, where they saw the gardens and the library and then 'sat in a parlour below with Mr Law and young Gibbon who left us after a little while over a bottle of French wine'. They talked of Malebranche and Butler. Young Gibbon was then twenty-two; his son at the same age would hardly have left the room.

The scene shifts to Cambridge towards the end of the same year. After some playing for him Byrom has secured Mr Law's pupil for a course in shorthand. But he is elusive and unpromising. He writes wretchedly and is terribly slow, which is a pity for Mr Law's sake. Besides he is seldom to be found. Either he has been playing at quadrille, or he is at the Westminster Club or gone to Huntingdon. At best Law is able to fetch him out of the Combination Room. Finally we learn in March 1730: 'Mr Gibbon went to London on Wednesday last, I think, without telling me and a gentleman of his acquaintance gave me five guineas at the Music Club'. More puppy than caterpillar.[1]

Soon after this the young man set out on his travels accompanied by a young Acton kinsman who was a physician.[2] He does not appear to have gone further than France and gained an imperfect knowledge of the language which he subsequently largely forgot. By 1735 or earlier he was back again, and settled down—if we may use the phrase—to a life of pleasure tempered

[1] Chetham Society, xxxiv. pp. 337, 411, 421-6, 435.

[2] Edward Acton, great-grandson of the second Bt. Walter, by his second son Walter. Vide *Birkbeck Hill*, p. 276.

by such responsibility as there was in being elected one of the members for Petersfield in the general election of that year.[1] He was now approaching that step in his life for which his father could least forgive him.

If this Edward Gibbon might be the model of Law's inconstant man he nevertheless showed himself courageously true where above all constancy is prized. His son tells us that he had long admired the youngest and handsomest of three daughters of a neighbouring family, and neither dissipations nor absence abroad let him forget his purpose. From old Mr Gibbon's point of view Miss Judith Porten was an unsatisfactory choice.

The Portens were going down in the world.[2] They had nothing else to be ashamed of. They were of Dutch and German descent, and in the course of less than two centuries in England had prospered and been connected with another German family, members of which had attained to higher civic dignities than had so far fallen to the Gibbons. On their plate they engraved the arms of the Hamburg family von de Porten,[3] and though it does not follow that they had a right to them, the fact does show that they claimed a foreign origin. Several men of this name came from Friesland at the end of the sixteenth century and from one of them no doubt descended Gibbon's great-grandfather, Daniel Porten, a merchant of the Parish of St. Catherine Cree. He married Thomasine Stanier, the granddaughter of David Stanier who had come from Cologne in the last

[1] His father had bought 'a weighty share' in the borough in 1719. Edward Gibbon II sold it to the Jolliffe family in 1739. See Appendix in *Birkbeck Hill*, p. 276.

[2] The name is pronounced with an accent on the last syllable and is often spelt Porteen in old records. I am indebted for the information which follows to Captain C. M. H. Pearce. Genealogical table, Appendix II, p. 357.

[3] See J. B. Rietstap, *Armorial général*, ed. Rolland, 1921, plate lxxxiv.

years of the sixteenth century, had received his certificate of denization and resided in England till his death of the plague in 1625. One of Thomasine's brothers was Sir Samuel Stanier, a merchant of Bishopsgate, who had an estate at Wanstead, Essex, was a colonel of the Blue Regiment of militia and crowned his career by holding the Mayoralty of London in 1716, the year of George I's coronation. Stanier always remained a favourite name in the Porten family. If the Portens were less distinguished than the Staniers, the possession of plate and books mentioned in their wills indicates that they were people of substance and culture. They are believed to have been engaged in the Levant trade. Daniel Porten had another son who was more successful in life than Gibbon's grandfather James. Francis was an alderman and was knighted in 1725–6 when he was Sheriff. He was also a Director of the Bank of England.

Of James Porten we know that like his uncle Samuel he was a colonel of the Blue militia. That he was established at Putney indicates a certain degree of prosperity at one time. He had married in 1703 Mary Allen, daughter of a Putney resident, and of his children, a son Stanier survived to have a career of some distinction in the public service; a daughter Mary had married Robert Darrell in 1724, and their fortunes rose steadily. But twelve years later, through the merchant's failing credit, his youngest daughter was not considered good enough for the heir of the whilom Director of the South Sea Company, who might come into near one hundred thousand pounds. In fact she brought her husband only fifteen hundred pounds.

Obstructions were put in the young couple's way from both sides. For pride compelled James Porten to follow his richer neighbour in disapproving of the match. But Pyramus and Thisbe in Babylon, Mr Gibbon and Miss Porten at Putney, the beginnings of such affairs are much the same. There were clandestine meetings; in after-years Catherine Porten used fondly to dwell on her part in them. A packet of tender letters still survives.[1] Mr Gibbon's opposition was in vain. He could only alter his will, and he did. His son and Judith Porten were married on 3rd June 1736, not at Putney but at St. Christopher le Stocks. The marriage was by licence and the ceremony was performed by William Law.[2] The participation of his chaplain indicates some sort of resignation on Mr Gibbon's part. Perhaps Law had taken a hand at reconciling the parties. If so, it was not the first time he had done this sort of thing. Once previously the son had been turned out of the house, apparently for smoking, and Law, who had been accused of setting them at odds on the question, claimed to have brought about a reconciliation.

Edward and his wife were received to live in his father's household. It must have been a very uncomfortable beginning to married life. Yet Gibbon tells us that his mother by her beauty, goodness and understanding was in a fair way to win over her father-in-law's hard heart, and he was confident that could the old man have lived to see his first-born grandson, he would have altered an unjust will. That was not to be, however, for Edward Gibbon the eldest died and was buried at Putney on 31st December 1736.

The grandfather's will was not so unfavourable as Gibbon subsequently tried to make out. He had already made settlements for his daughter Catherine. To Hester he left six of his eleven shares in a copper-mine in Glamorganshire, his real property at Meething and Plomp-

[1] In the possession of Captain G. C. Onslow.

[2] Why St. Christopher le Stocks? It was not a run-away wedding; apart from Law's presence it may be noted that the Gibbons had some connexion with this church. Two years previously the Rev. Edmund Tew had been married to Barbara Gibbon of Putney there, Law again performing the ceremony.

ton Piddinghoe in Sussex, all upon trust, with remainder to her children. If she had no children the property was to go to his right heirs.[1] He also left legacies of £500 each to Hester and to Williams Gibbon. Fifty pounds to William Law and two other small legacies. All his plate and household effects at Putney went to his son. The residue of his personal and real estate was to be held on trust for his son, with remainder to his sons and grandsons, and with powers to make jointures for his wife or wives up to £100 a year for every £1000 he received.

It does not seem too bad, yet no doubt his son was dissatisfied and passed on his discontent to *his* son, who expresses it both directly and also in oblique references in his History. He describes wills 'which prolong the dominion of the testator beyond the grave' as 'this last use or abuse of the right of property', and records 'that the simplicity of the civil law was never clouded by the long and intricate entails which confine the happiness and freedom of unborn generations'.[2] The law and lawyers in the eighteenth century were formidable enough and Gibbon had tiresome experiences of them, but he had reason on the whole to be thankful for the law of entail.

Meanwhile young Mr Gibbon had succeeded at Putney and the last glimpse that Byrom gives of him does not suggest that he was overcome by grief or disappointment. Byrom arrived just as dinner was going up, and though he had not dined said that he had, and the hospitable young man pursuing the matter, Byrom lied and said 'on the other side the bridge'. One can see the easy smile of the emancipated pupil with his next enquiry as to how shorthand went on.

[1] P. C. C. Wake, 5. There was a charge of interest on £1000 on the above property for his brother Matthew as prescribed by his mother Hester Acton's will.
[2] *The Decline and Fall*, c. xliv. (5, 308 and 310).

'I said', replied Byrom, 'that more persons were desirous to learn. After dinner I sat to the table and drank a few glasses of champagne. Mr. Law eat of the soup, beef, etc., and drank two glasses of red wine, one, Church and King, the other, All friends; Mr. Gibbon fell asleep.' [1]

That was on the 13th April 1737. Somewhere in the house must have been Mrs Gibbon awaiting her first confinement.

[1] Chetham Society, xl. p. 104.

Chapter 3

EARLY YEARS

1737–1752

A FORTNIGHT later, on Wednesday, 27th April (O.S.) 1737, Judith Gibbon gave birth to a son. He was baptized Edward on Friday, 13th May, an apt date for enemies of superstition. 'There were great doings', Byrom recorded, 'at the christening of Mr Gibbon's son.' [1]

Very probably William Law performed the ceremony. But the holy and profane elements of this household did not hold together for long after the old despot's death. Law is believed to have stayed on for two or three years. By 1740 he had retired to his native King's Cliffe. Three years later Hester Gibbon joined him there in the company of a widowed Mrs Hutcheson. Leading together a life of devotion and charitable works they sought to realise the precepts of *A Serious Call.*

Law did not lead his disciples into a Thebaid. They lived sparingly but not miserably on a joint expenditure of £300 a year. During the week they studied and the ladies wrote spiritual exercises. Miss Gibbon played the organ. On Sundays after church Law and Miss Gibbon rode out on horseback accompanied by a

[1] Chetham Society, vol. xl. p. 158. He continues: 'Our landlady says that his lady had no fortune, but was a young lady of good family and reputation, and that old Mr Gibbon led her to church and back again'. Old Mr Gibbon was undoubtedly dead at this time, as both the landlady and Byrom must have known. The phrase is misleading, but cannot refer to the christening.

carriage which contained Mrs Hutcheson and 'The Honourables the Misses Finch Hatton'. In her rare appearances in society she was like the resurrection of the last age. So her nephew said, and if it is true that she was human enough to go into yellow stockings after Law's death, imagination may construct *ex pede* a fantastic figure. But apart from one or two rare interventions the worldly half of the family at Putney were left to work out their own damnation.

Gibbon had two reasons to complain of his father's behaviour during these next years. He was neglected in infancy and his inheritance was embarrassed. Yet his comments on his father are not without a certain gusto:

> 'His spirit was lively, his appearance splendid, his aspect cheerful, his address polite; he gracefully moved in the highest circles of society, and I have heard him boast that he was the only member of opposition admitted into the old club at White's where the first names of the country were often rejected.'

He was equally at his ease in different extremes of society, with lords or farmers, citizens or fox-hunters, and was accepted everywhere for his goodfellowship rather than for any brilliancy. But popularity is expensive. His home was too near London, and 'acquired the dangerous fame of hospitable entertainment'. He gambled too, of course. Moreover, he was far from displaying either his father's attention or competence in business. Within three years of his succession losses were incurred over some contracts with the Court of Spain. The Spaniards defaulted; no one could help that. But 'several undertakings which had been profitable in the hands of the merchant became barren or adverse in those of the gentleman'. Yet a gentleman must go on; money must be found. That is always certain.

Nor was his incursion into politics more impressive. He had been a member for the borough of Petersfield since 1735. But in 1739 he disposed of his interest,[1] and at the election of 1741 he stood with Peter Delmé in the Tory interest for the County of Southampton. They were elected; the victorious opposition overthrew Sir Robert Walpole in 1742. But 'after a short vibration the Pelham government was fixed on the old basis of the Whig Aristocracy'.[2] Hopes were disappointed and the election had been expensive. When Parliament dissolved in 1747 Mr Gibbon's wife was dead, his fortune impaired and he had no inclination to continue this unpromising career. To become an alderman was another way of serving his party which had less appeal, and after a short tenure he resigned in 1745 at a time when he was among those perplexed Englishmen of Jacobite sentiments who had no appetite for a rebellion. But he had acquired the title to fame that he would least have coveted. When his son came before the world Horace Walpole chose to recognise him merely as 'the son of a foolish alderman'.[3]

In all his dissipations and diversions this Edward Gibbon remained constantly attached to his wife, and she to him, to the detriment of their family. In her desire to please and to restrain her husband she suffered herself to be dragged through his fashionable follies. During a married life of less than eleven years she bore six more children, none of whom lived a year. Her eldest child was neglected. He hardly knew her. The only memory he records—it remained vivid—was driving

1 Woodward's *History of Hampshire*, iii. 320. He sold the manor of Petersfield to John Jolliffe, M.P. *Victoria Hist. of Hants*, vol. iii. p. 116.

2 *Murray*, p. 30.

3 Gibbon says (*Murray*, p. 31) his father became an alderman 'in the most critical season' and 'resigned his Gown at the end of a few months'. But his father, who was a member of the Fletchers' Company, was made Alderman of the Vintry Ward in 1743. His resignation was accepted 18th June 1745. The Court of Aldermen was never anxious to accept resignations. The reasons in this case must have been convincing although they are not stated in the record. Information given by the Record Office, Guildhall.

with her across Putney Heath to Dr. Wooddesdon's school while she told him that he was now going into the world and must learn to act and think for himself. He certainly learnt the lesson. He was nine years old then. That she could have given her son much more cannot be doubted. Her faithful sister Catherine never wearied in after-years of enlarging on her charm and merit. But all Gibbon could claim was that he had a faint personal resemblance to her.

In this tragic record of waste, Gibbon's own life was deemed so precarious, he tells us, that as his other brothers were born they were successively christened Edward too, in order to secure the name. The registers at Putney do not bear this out. There only one brother is called Edward. He was baptized in August and died on Boxing Day 1740, and perhaps we may infer that Gibbon himself was despaired of at that time. But this brother was also called James, as were two others, while another was called Stanier. The daughter was called Judith.[1] There seems therefore to have been more concern to perpetuate the Porten family names.[2]

The young Gibbon was indeed more of a little Porten during those early years. It was Miss Porten who sat by his cot when his life was despaired of, and became 'the true mother of his mind' when he was better. It was in his grandfather Porten's home—an old house near Putney bridge—that he spent his happiest hours of childhood and in his library first had the free run of books.

Catherine Porten has her secure place among the world's perfect aunts. Perhaps she is beyond compare. The indomitable nurse who had conquered death might have sought to rule her nephew's life. She never did, but passed with miraculous smoothness into the posi-

[1] Baptized November 1743. Buried March 1744.

[2] *Gibbon's Journal*, p. xxix.

tion of an equal and sensible companion. When he was eighteen Gibbon was calling her 'dear Kitty', a phrase which gives warmth and substance to his eloquent praises of her in his Autobiography. Less familiar, more spontaneous, though not more genuine, is the account of his infancy in a letter to Lord Sheffield at the time of his aunt's death:

> 'To her care I am indebted in earliest infancy for the preservation of my life and health. I was a puny child, neglected by my Mother, starved by my nurse, and of whose being very little care or expectation was entertained; without her maternal vigilance I should either have been in my grave, or imperfectly lived a crooked ricketty monster, a burthen to myself and others. To her instructions I owe the first rudiments of knowledge, the first exercise of reason, and a taste for books which is still the pleasure and glory of my life; and though she taught me neither language nor science, she was certainly the most useful præceptor I have ever had. As I grew up, an intercourse of thirty years endeared her to me, as the faithful friend and the agreeable companion. You have seen with what freedom and confidence we lived together, and have often admired her character and conversation, which could alike please the young and the old.' [1]

In the pertness of youth Gibbon recorded a less gracious opinion of her powers. 'She is far from wanting sense but it is friendship, gratitude and confidence which contribute chiefly to attach me to her.' [2] Later he wrote of her 'clear and manly understanding'.[3] Both the judgment and sentiment of the older man may have been truer. She was well read in English, her only language, enjoyed religious discussions and was sometimes puzzled by the theological conundrums which her nephew, like any clever child, propounded. He is said to have offered to kill her, since she was so good that she was bound to go to heaven; while if she went on living, she might become wicked. She had a partiality for

[1] *Prothero*, ii., letter of 10th May 1786, p. 144.
[2] *Gibbon's Journal*, 18th January 1763, p. 202. [3] *Murray*, p. 117.

Shaftesbury's writings, not a great sign of orthodoxy. But her will is markedly religious in tone and her nephew cannot have imbibed any scepticism from her. He says he believed implicitly when he went to Oxford. She has the enviable fame of being the first to kindle his imagination with Pope's *Homer* and the *Arabian Nights*. They were lasting influences.

The tale of his sufferings is long and curious. Besides the accidents of being starved by his nurse and 'bitten by a dog vehemently suspected of madness', he tended towards consumption and dropsy, was subject to violent fluctuations of temperature, suffered a contraction of the nerves, and had a fistula in one eye. Smallpox he escaped, thanks to inoculation, his parents or aunt being themselves immune from the current religious and even political prejudice against it. Every healer from Sir Hans Sloane and Dr. Mead to less regular practitioners such as Ward and Taylor was called in,[1] and to the end of his life his body was scarred with the cuts and burns of their treatment. A particularly serious bout of illness in 1750 put an end to any plan of regular attendance at a school. But within three years of this his afflictions lifted unexpectedly and he was henceforward to enjoy a remarkable regularity of health, with a corresponding growth in mental vigour. It is not surprising therefore that he fell in with his admired Buffon's opinion that the child is little or nothing until the age of puberty is reached.[2]

It would seem probable that these miscellaneous symptoms are to be accounted for by infantile rheumatism.

Influenced then by his theory of mental and physical development Gibbon does not linger over memories of childhood. It was rendered a disgusting topic by his many sufferings. Moreover, he would not attempt to

[1] In the vulgate text the contrast is spoilt by the reading 'from Sloane and Ward to the Chevalier Taylor'.

[2] *Murray*, p. 35, and extract from Buffon there quoted; also p. 97.

distinguish between things that he actually remembered and those which he might fancy he remembered although they had been actually told to him later. His earliest recollection went back to his fourth year, to a whipping he received then and to his revenge taken in shouting out the names of his father's opponents in the election of 1741. He had a pleasant memory of his infant sister who died in 1744, and always regretted that this relationship with a contemporary of the other sex, the only truly platonic one, had been denied to him. He claimed, what is scarcely credible, not to remember when he learnt to read and write, and records that his prowess at figures was so good that they might well have made a mathematician of him.

After some instruction at home and at a day school, his education began formally at the age of seven under the care of the Reverend John Kirkby, another non-juring parson, who appears to have taken Law's place as chaplain and tutor at Putney. He was a man of some originality—too original to succeed either in his profession or out of it. He ruined his chances of preferment by a pamphlet, and lost his tutorship by forgetting or refusing to include King George's name at prayers.[1] In this man's brief reign of eighteen months Gibbon learnt some arithmetic and the rudiments of Latin.

The next experiment on this feeble body was Dr. Wooddesdon's school at Kingston. This was not a private school as is sometimes stated, but an old foundation known to-day as Kingston Grammar School. But it had been purged of its vulgarities by a successful headmaster,

> 'and consisted of members of aristocratic families alone, who not only claimed none of the privileges of the school as a Free Endowed School, but in the only case in which those privileges were claimed, so maltreated the unfortunate youth whose father

[1] Compare *Murray*, p. 40 with p. 221.

> had the temerity to seek those advantages that he was *mercifully* removed, and thus the intentions of the Royal Founder were for a time entirely frustrated'.[1]

Nevertheless it was a severe change from a luxurious home to the bleak status of a boarder and insignificance among a crowd of seventy boys whom the rod, and perhaps the rod alone, impartially coerced. That was the order of the day, and if the price of Latin was blood and tears, that does not imply unusual brutality. Wooddesdon is said to have been liked. For the rest, Gibbon was too puny and too shy to join the boys' play: but he could not avoid the abuse and cuffs that were aimed at a young Tory in the year after the '45.

In a short time another change was brought about by two events which happened in the space of a few months. Mrs Gibbon died in December and her son was then finally withdrawn from Kingston.[2] In the following spring James Porten became bankrupt and absconded.[3]

Father and son were not drawn together by the mother's death. They did not meet until some weeks afterwards. The scene then was never to be forgotten.

> 'The awful silence, the room hung with black, the midday tapers, his sighs and tears; his praises of my mother a saint in heaven; his solemn adjuration that I would cherish her memory

[1] Biden, *History and Antiquities of Kingston-upon-Thames*, p. 75. Wooddesdon was headmaster 1732–72. His success necessitated hiring another house. This was Hertington Combe or Hert Combe Place at the foot of Kingston Hill on the right from London, *op. cit.* There is no direct evidence, however, that this was where Gibbon boarded. Hayley, Steevens, the Shakespearian editor, Gilbert Wakefield, Edward Lovibond and other men of some distinction were there. See references in *Murray*, p. 43, n.

[2] Gibbon is very uncertain about the dates of this period of his life and the wrong ones were incorporated in his Autobiography. His mother died December 1746, was buried January 1747; his grandfather's failure was in 1747. He entered Westminster January 1748. *Putney Parish Registers; Record of Old Westminsters; B. Hill*, p. 278.

[3] He did not disappear altogether. He died in 1750, and is recorded in the Putney burial register as Colonel James Porten. See also Appendix II.

and imitate her virtues; and the fervour with which he kissed and blessed me as the sole surviving pledge of their loves.'

The husband's grief was genuine in its characteristic extravagance. His zest for pleasure was broken, and after some half-hearted efforts to resume the old gay life he retired to the rural interests of Buriton. Economy too, his son hints, was on the side of grief in this renunciation. But he could appeal to his son's sentiment without making a burden of his own obligations to the same memory, and his were much greater obligations. It does not appear that he spent much time or thought on his son. For some nine months during the year 1747 Gibbon was living in his grandfather's house by Putney bridge. After the old man's disappearance the library that had been hitherto kept locked was left open, and while his elders were distracted with their troubles the child 'rioted without control' in it, helping himself to any volume that caught his fancy and reading widely in English poetry and romances, history and travels. His mind was plentifully nourished and grew rapidly.

His father now determined that he should go to his own old school; his aunt made so bold a step possible. At the age of forty she had been suddenly faced, by her father's ruin, with the necessity of making a living.[1] Some friends came to her aid, and she staked her resources on a boarding-house for Westminster boys. This was mainly for the sake of her nephew, who became her first inmate in Great College Street in January 1748.

Instead of seventy boys it was now a matter of over

[1] Gibbon speaks of her as 'destitute'. This is perhaps too strong. She had a small annuity and could always have found a home with the Gibbons, to whom she was indispensable. But she had and saw an opportunity of serving her nephew. The house she took had belonged to Vincent Bourne, who had certainly taken in boarders. She took none over from him, but started, as stated in the text, with Gibbon alone. Her enterprise was rewarded. In time she had forty to fifty boys, moved to the house on the terrace of Dean's Yard which was lately the Church House, and retired with a competence.

three hundred. They were taught in the babel of one room by two masters and about half a dozen ushers. Yet the chances were that if Gibbon's health had been better he would have been happier there than at Kingston, and he would have attained to that finished scholarship which he was destined to envy at a distance. He admits rather grudgingly that he could not rise to the Third Form without improving his knowledge of Latin.[1] He did not begin Greek. He took no part in such games as there were, but a cryptic note to Memoir F,[2] contrasting the 'margent green' of the Thames of Gray's Eton with the barges and carpenters' yards of the Westminster riverside, suggests that he sometimes went down to watch his fellows, 'the idle progeny', swimming or rowing.

From what he saw of it Gibbon could not take the English public school very seriously. It had its advantages, mainly social, for those who were strong enough to stand the life. It could produce scholars, but turned out the average boy entirely ignorant of the world of affairs. A school in general he judged to be 'a cavern of fear and sorrow'. The pupil worked in continual fear of the inevitable rod, and was devoid of the finer sensibilities which came with manhood. He was a captive mentally as well as physically, and for Gibbon freedom was always a blessing second only to health.

A brief friendship with Lord Huntingtower was thought worth recording, the first perhaps of those rather impulsive leanings towards young men of his own age which he manifested later on. After his return from Switzerland he tried to pick up the threads. But the young peer did not respond, and Gibbon was too proud to persist.[3] In the school with him were a number of men whom he was to meet here and there when he returned from Switzerland. Westminster at that time

[1] *Murray*, p. 115. [2] *Murray*, p. 59. [3] *Murray*, p. 53.

pretty well divided the fashionable world with Eton. His brief stay at Westminster may have given him some footing in it, but it is doubtful.[1]

Early in 1750 his health was worse than ever. On the advice of Miss Dorothea Patton, whom his father was later to marry, he was taken to Dr. Joshua Ward and gained relief. He did not return to Westminster again except for a brief and unsuccessful trial in the following year. There followed an aimless period during which he was taken about the country partly in search of health, partly on visits to his father's friends. An extract from a brief summary of his life which he wrote will give the best idea of this period:

1750.	March.	Attacked with violent malady: owed my deliverance to Dr. Ward.
	August.	Went to Bath for the first time.
	December.	My father took me from Bath and brought me up to London.
1751.	Febr.	Was put under the care of Mr. Philips.[2]
	March.	Was removed from thence and again sent to Bath.
	August.	Sent to Winchester under the care of Dr. Langrish.
	Dec. 24th.	Was settled at Putney in a private house.
1752.	Febr.	Was taken from Putney and carried about with my father.
	April 3rd.	Was matriculated at Oxford.[3]

Gibbon wrote off the four years 1748–52 as lost. But there was a ray of light in the darkness. He was nearing the end of his childish ailments. For a brief period he was put with a clergyman at Bath and read with pleasure some Latin poetry with him. In a further improvement of health he was sent to Philip Francis at Esher. Francis was a scholar and, like many other parsons of the day,

[1] *Gibbon's Journal*, pp. xliii-xlv.

[2] A slip for Philip Francis.

[3] Add. MSS. 37772. The whole is printed in *Gibbon's Journal*, pp. xlvi-xlvii.

had tried to be a dramatist. His translation of Horace enjoyed a long lease of favour. Since it was understood that he was not to have more than two or three pupils, the prospect seemed good. But Francis was too often up in town leaving the boys 'in the custody of a Dutch Usher of low manners and contemptible learning'. Mr Gibbon descended and took away his son in indignation. All the varieties of education had now been tried save one. The perplexed father adopted it and entered his son as a gentleman commoner at Magdalen College, Oxford.[1] In April 1752 Gibbon arrived there 'with a stock of erudition which might have puzzled a doctor and a degree of ignorance of which a schoolboy would have been ashamed'.[2]

Did Gibbon tend to depreciate the extent of his scholarship at this time, or were the standards so much higher in his day? He was under fifteen. Yet in spite of his broken schooling he had read some Horace and Virgil with pleasure, and he could sit down by himself to puzzle out the crabbed Latin of Pococke's *Abulpharagius* and guess at the French of d'Herbelot's *Bibliothèque Orientale*.[3] He might have done better, he acknowledges. He had succumbed to the heresy that

[1] It is understandable that Emmanuel was not chosen, but why Magdalen? Dr. Wooddesdon had been there and his advice has been suggested. It does not seem very likely. Mr Gibbon leased some Magdalen land at Buriton. This connexion with the college may be the explanation.

[2] *Murray*, p. 122.

[3] According to D. P.'s (? Daniel Parker) recollections, *Gent. Mag.*, 1794, Gibbon bought d'Herbelot at Oxford. It seems possible that Gibbon tends to postdate the reading of certain books. He could not have been very ignorant of Latin when he consulted Scaliger, and he complains that Terence was too easy an author for Dr. Waldegrave to read with him. Although there can be no doubt that he began *The Age of Sesostris* in his first and only long vacation (Memoir F, *Murray*, p. 79), in Memoirs B and C (*Murray*, pp. 122 and 224) he might be understood to say he began this before he went to Oxford. No doubt it is true that his childish rest was disturbed by chronological problems; it is worth noting, however, that on 21st October 1762 he records thinking about Roman and Greek calendars in bed (*Journal*, p. 166). The general truth of Gibbon's account of his early reading cannot be doubted, but there is some evidence of sacrificing to epigrammatic effect.

nothing was to be gained by learning languages when there were serviceable translations, and his aunt, knowing only English, had not opposed him. But it is improbable that he has exaggerated his achievements on the other side. Before he was sixteen [1] he had not only surveyed the ancient world and mastered all the *English* authorities for Oriental history which he was later to employ, but he had ranged eagerly across the globe, sometimes in the company of Jesuit missionaries, from China to Peru.

Gibbon was always impressed by the part which accidents play in history. It was to an accident, the discovery of Eachard's *History of the Later Roman Empire* when visiting Mr Hoare's house at Stourhead in 1751, that he ascribes his introduction to those ages and lands which he was to make his own. But one accident is as good and as inevitable as another when a powerful impulse is seeking an outlet. If not Eachard then some other book. By one channel or another the swelling stream must find its way to the tracts it is destined to flood and fertilise.

Pious admirers have lamented that this or that influence did not bear on Gibbon's life. If only William Law had been in charge of the son instead of the father. If the Fellows of Magdalen had held Confirmation classes. If Gibbon had married the devout Mlle Curchod. Such speculations are futile. Whether it was reason or instinct Gibbon himself disclaimed to know, but we must recognise with him that from the start he was guided inexorably to what he rightly called his proper food. So much is this so that the chances of his life appear to be the essential expression of an ordered destiny. Those indeed who believe in Providence might have some odd reflexions in contemplating his career. Had these chances been different the external order of things might

[1] 'Sixteenth year' includes Oxford. See previous note.

have been altered, perhaps disastrously. Poverty or marriage might have sucked him down into daily affairs; but it is impossible to believe that the inner Gibbon would have been very different.

A year before the accident at Stourhead a letter, the earliest surviving piece from his hand, reveals the authentic Gibbon, a child still but with some of the man's characteristic predilections. The bent towards history is obvious.

'KINGS WESTON
'December 31st, 1750

'MADAM,

'Being arrived at Mr. Southwell's house at Kings Weston, I could not forbear writing to you to inform you that I like the Place Prodigously. I Ride out very often and Sometimes Go in Mr. Southwell's Coach which Last I infinitely prefer to the former. Kings Weston is a Most Grand House and Mr. Southwell has a Great Many Books. Yesterday I went to a Chappel (it being Sunday) and after Church upon our Return home we veiwed the Remains of an ancient Camp which pleased me vastly. Mr. Mrs. and Master Southwell all Desire their Compliments to you together with Whom I also Join myself, and your Enjoyment of many happy New Years is the Sincere wish of

'Madam,

'Your Most Dutiful Nephew,

'EDWARD GIBBON

'P.S.—Master Southwell will come to Westminster the 17th of Next Month.' [1]

Reading—free, desultory reading had been the consolation of his ailing years. It now became a master passion. His imagination had been led captive from one enchanted castle to another along the road to the Empire and the East. From D'Aulnoy [2] and the *Arabian*

[1] Add. MSS. 34883.

[2] Do children still read D'Aulnoy? Forty years ago there was a capital English edition.

Nights to Pope's *Homer* was a beginning whose impression was never effaced; the spell weakened with Dryden's *Virgil* but recovered at the gate of Sandys' *Ovid*. Then the path broadened out and seemed lost in the profusion of poetry, romances, history and travel revealed in the old house by Putney Bridge. At last came that morning in Wiltshire when he crossed the Danube with the Goths into the heart of the Roman Empire. He never came out of it again.

The demand for books now became incessant. He bought, he borrowed, he ferreted. At home or on visits the astonishing boy was found in the midst of forgotten folios of the last century, on which he was ready and anxious to lecture the perplexed ladies and gentlemen. One begins to be almost sorry for the unconsoled widower who had to 'carry about' such a problem round the country houses of England. Gibbon can seldom have met anyone capable of helping or following him in his progress. He never was to meet many travellers on that long road. From the beginning must have grown up that self-sufficiency which is so often evident in the rather hectoring notes to *The Decline and Fall*.

The mere names of his authors, devoured like so many novels, are terrific—and he knows it, marshalling them still with pride after forty years. But think of the heavy leather tomes, the columns of close print and the almost complete absence of the modern aids to quick reference. Let anyone take up Scaliger's *De Emendatione Temporum* to solve a chronological problem and remember the untaught Gibbon consulting it. For with puberty came mind; so Gibbon experienced and believed. And mind meant the pressing need for solidity and harmony; it brought out the creative and critical instinct of a man. He studied geography and maps and acquired a satisfying picture of the ancient world. Then dates had to be settled. He entered into the most complicated investigations. Strauchius and Usher, whose dates we used to marvel at in our Authorised Versions, Prideaux and Petavius, Scaliger, Marsham, Newton, were summoned to the debate. The boy presided and presumed to be critically weighing these venerable authorities against one another; he was at times unable to sleep because the chronology of the Hebrew Old Testament disagreed with that given in the Greek translation.

What a mixture of anticipations must have been his as he rolled over Magdalen bridge for the first time. A child not quite fifteen was now an Oxford man. He had three spacious rooms to himself in the stately pile of New Buildings, money such as a schoolboy scarcely dreams of, the fine silk gown and velvet cap which brought obsequiousness even from the highest, with no duties and many privileges, and his own key to the college library. Oxford had long had a name for Oriental learning: his old friends Pococke and Prideaux for instance. There were libraries here; there should be scholars. What could they not do for him? Latin, Greek, even Arabic should be his for the asking.

Chapter 4

OXFORD

1752–1753

HE ALWAYS wore black, it is recorded, and often came into Hall late. As a gentleman commoner he was allowed to join the Fellows as the fiery Oxford port wine went the round. Boylike he expected that their conversation would turn on the subjects of their profession, on Cicero for instance, and Chrysostom. But he was as disappointed as Verdant Green on a livelier occasion. The dons were absorbed in stale gossip and scandal, enlivened only by the interest of a local election.

The stagnation of the college was complete. The Fellows held their places unmolested by any duties or criticism until their turn came to go down, if they chose, to a country living. The Demies or Scholars, who owed their gowns often enough to the lucky chance of being born in a certain county rather than to their wits, were waiting, if they could endure it, to succeed to Fellowships and were often allowed to retain their Demyships beyond their statutory term. A great number of them were graduates. Of the handful of gentleman commoners nothing was expected but that they should display their gentlemanliness according to the mode of their time. For them certainly there was no discipline, and for neither class any instruction or incentives. There were no ordinary commoners. The medieval exercises for a degree had ceased to be of use, and only the empty form of them survived. No one had thought of introducing anything else. The tale was much the same throughout the University, but 'at Magdalen some of the conditions which favoured the slothfulness of the time were even more powerful than in other societies'.[1]

In such conditions Gibbon, appearing but fitfully, became at once a legend rather than a figure. He was seen in Parker's bookshop buying not the latest play but d'Herbelot's *Bibliothèque Orientale*. He was known to be full of Oriental learning, perhaps even a Mahommedan. Everyone could see the humour of that. A Fellow certainly did tell the laughing young gentlemen that if their heads were scooped—a coarse joke that, thought Dr. Routh later—there were enough brains in little Mr Gibbon's big head to fill them all. Had he been older and more robust no doubt they would have ragged him. They let him alone. Everyone let him alone. He was nobody's business in this rich corporation endowed for learning and the edification of youth.

That is not absolutely true. He was assigned to a tutor according to such system as there was, to whom was due twenty guineas for his mental and moral instruction. Dr. Waldegrave did betray a faint interest. He even took his pupil for walks on Headington Hill. He dissuaded him, not unwisely, from beginning Arabic as yet. But of the life that was seething in that head he seems to have been quite incurious. 'Had I in the least suspected your design of leaving us', he wrote with cool urbanity when Gibbon had gone, 'I should immediately have put you upon reading Mr. Chillingworth's *Religion of Protestants*.' In the meantime he put his pupil upon reading Terence's plays. But his exposition was so dull and the Latin so easy that Gibbon ventured on an experiment. He tried cutting a lecture and offering an excuse. It succeeded. He cut again and finally al-

[1] H. A. Wilson, *Magdalen College*, p. 222.

together. Nothing happened, all was smiles and courtesy still for a gentleman commoner.

After a vacation Waldegrave had slipped away in silence to a Sussex rectory. His pupil was transferred—he had no choice in the matter—to Dr. Winchester, whom he could not respect at all. In one memoir he hints against his moral character; in another he says that his reputation in the college was that of a broker and salesman. The Doctor was eager to take his fees but did nothing in return. By this time Gibbon had got beyond cutting a lecture. He had discovered that he could absent himself from the college for a night, for several nights, and return again unquestioned as though it were to some hired lodgings. His excursions were quite innocent. He who had seen little of the world but sickrooms and schoolrooms was seized with a zest for travelling. Sometimes alone, sometimes in company, he made visits to London, to Bath, to Buckingham, to Nuneham Courtenay and to Lord Cobham's place at Stowe. Nothing was said.[1]

College life is a mixture of solitude and inconsiderate interruption. At the best it requires some strength of character to make the most of the former boon. In the absence of direction from above and stimulating companionship Gibbon found the conditions fatal to his studies. He became idle and aimless. The time was completely lost. Only in vacation did he find his zest for study returning, but it was still 'the same blind and boyish taste for the pursuit of exotic history'. Inspired by Voltaire's *Siècle de Louis XIV* he determined to write a book. He dived into Egyptian history, and began an essay on the Age of Sesostris. The long summer days passed unmolested while he laboured once more

[1] His first absence was in his first term, a visit to Lord Nuneham, 1st June 1752. In the following year they became frequent. There was no secrecy apparently; he met his father in London on one occasion. For his record of these movements, see *Gibbon's Journal*, p. xlvii.

with vigour and ingenuity on chronological problems. Several sheets were written. He was eager for publicity and applause, but his first symptoms of taste appeared when he perceived his own weaknesses, and the work was abandoned. The next adventure of his mind was to bring him more than enough publicity.

Gibbon asserts that he was too young to sign the Thirty-Nine Articles on matriculation, and although the Vice-Chancellor told him to return when he was fifteen, the matter was forgotten. But his signature to the Articles on 4th April is in the University Archives. Anyone over twelve could sign. Perhaps there is a confusion with the Oath of Supremacy, which could not be taken under sixteen. Gibbon in any case was as good as lost by then. This inaccuracy impairs his attack. Yet it is plain that not only in outward forms, so important to the young, was there neglect. In the very citadel of the Church of England no one troubled to see if the young soldiers possessed the most ordinary equipment. Uninstructed, unconfirmed and unchallenged, Gibbon groped his way alone to the communion table. What did it matter, what difference did it make whether you catechised the gentlemen commoners between their hunting and their nightly toasts? But it was inevitable that a boy of Gibbon's intelligence must cry for satisfaction on these great questions. If no one was to do anything, he must help himself. He sought for enlightenment from books, and was led by the clamour of the day to the most provoking mind in the theological arena.

Dr. Conyers Middleton, D.D., a fellow of Trinity College, Cambridge, and a beneficed clergyman, is assessed by Leslie Stephen as 'this most insidious of all assailants of Christianity'.[1] He was a lively, pugnacious man, a real danger to tranquillity. He could think and he wrote admirably. As a young man he had dared to

[1] *English Thought in the Eighteenth Century*, i. p. 270.

abuse Dr. Bentley, the masterful Master of Trinity. By sallies of this kind he spoiled his chances of the high preferment which his talents deserved. He travelled and recorded in *A Letter from Rome* his observation of pagan survivals in the Catholic rites. It was all in the cause of Protestantism he said.

Religious controversialists are generally short-sighted men with longer weapons than they imagine. When they take a smashing blow at an adversary they are apt to be carried full circle and catch a valuable ally in a vital part. It was all a question of miracles once more, that sad embarrassment of religious aspiration.

The problem was an old one for Protestants. They agreed that God had withdrawn the power of working miracles. But when was that? In the fourth century, or the third, or the second? The English Divines had shirked the question of determining the exact date of the cessation of miracles, but it was generally agreed that miracles had continued for some three centuries. They accepted this because they wished to rely not only on the Bible but on the tradition of the primitive church of which the miracles were an inseparable part. Middleton, stimulated by his visit to Rome and not improved in temper by his lack of preferment, attacked this position. He showed that the purity of the primitive church's doctrine was imaginary. Most of the practices repudiated by the reformed churches had grown up during those early centuries, and therefore, if miracles were God's method of signalising his approval of pure doctrine it was impossible to accept these miracles.

About four years before Gibbon went up to Oxford, Middleton published a book whose full title is suggestive. It was *A Free Enquiry into the Miraculous Powers which are supposed to have subsisted in the Christian Church from the Earliest Ages through Successive Centuries*. The line of attack was mainly to discredit the literary evidence. He showed some of the Fathers to have been of poor intellectual powers and of doubtful honesty. Miracles were propagated by impostors or their easy dupes. This was hard on the Fathers. To those who do not believe in these miracles to-day Middleton may appear lacking in psychological and historical insight. But the great advance which he made was in reducing a theological question to a matter of historical criticism. It was an attack on the doctrine of inspiration, a demonstration that Christian testimony must be treated like any other evidence and that history was continuous.

It is true that he still allowed the immunity of the Bible, or at least the New Testament, from such methods. No one doubted the truth and excellence of God's revealed word nor the reality, therefore, of the miracles by which men were to be impressed. But this was an artificial position which could not stand long. Middleton's sincerity is not the question here. Gibbon wrote of him twelve years later, 'he saw where his principles led; but he did not think proper to draw the consequences'. Middleton was in fact a true forerunner of Gibbon. His book marks the end of a chapter of controversy, simply because his adversaries were not prepared to follow him on to the new ground of historical criticism. It is not surprising, therefore, that the young undergraduate was bewildered.

He read the book, and the shock carried him exactly into the position that Middleton had foreseen and was trying to overthrow.[1] Gibbon had an implicit belief in the continuance of miraculous powers. Middleton could not destroy that. He had, on the other hand, obligingly revealed to him the full tale of the doctrines and practices of those times which must be accepted with the miracles. The logic of it was simple and inexorable. All thanks to Dr. Middleton.

[1] Middleton, *Introductory Discourse* (1755), p. xlv.

The rest of the journey was soon accomplished and in excellent company. By one of those chances which so often turn up at such a juncture, Gibbon had fallen in with a young man, not a member of his college or of the University apparently, who had already gone the same way.[1] This youth lent him some Popish books and the conversion was completed by reading in English two famous books of Bossuet—*L'Exposition de la Doctrine de l'Église Catholique sur les matières de controverse* and *Histoire des Variations des Églises Protestantes.*

In the *Exposition* Bossuet had stated his case with such moderation as to draw upon himself the suspicions if not the censure of his own side. His *Histoire des Variations* was a masterly dissection of the innumerable phases of Protestant thought. Where Locke and his followers had seen in the inability of human minds to agree upon a single conclusion a fundamental plea for toleration, Bossuet surveying the same phenomena called for a recognition of the one authority, namely, the Church, with whom the only truth had been deposited throughout the ages. He makes his points with the suavity and seeming candour of one who was accustomed to win the ear of the most cultivated audiences in Europe. There was all the difference between this highly placed advocate suavely addressing 'Messieurs de la Religion Prétendue Réformée' and the slashing methods characteristic then of Anglican controversy. The boy was easily won, and if he was lost later, he had learnt something of permanent value from the Frenchman's serene art.[2]

His next steps are well known. He went to a Roman Catholic bookseller, John Lewis of Russell Street, Covent

[1] Gibbon left the name blank. Sheffield gives Mr Molesworth. The name is neither on the college books nor in Foster's *Alumni Oxon.*

[2] Sheffield relates that Gibbon only discussed his conversion with him once and then imputed it to the works of an Elizabethan Jesuit called Parsons, who had urged all the best arguments in favour of the Roman faith.

Garden, and by him was passed on to Father Bernard Baker, S.J., one of the chaplains to the Sardinian Ambassador, whose chapel was at Lincoln's Inn Fields.[1] The priest had nothing to do but accept the sincerity of the conversion, and on the 8th June 1753 at his feet Gibbon 'solemnly though privately abjured the errors of heresy'.[2]

This was high treason. Both Gibbon and the priest were liable to severe penalties. The humanity or indifference of the age might give them confidence. But the conversion or seduction of a young man of property was no small matter. It made some stir when the news came out, and the bookseller was brought before the Privy Council for interrogation. Before that, on his new director's advice, Gibbon had written a letter to his father announcing his conversion. He described it in later years as 'written with all the pomp, the dignity, and self-satisfaction of a martyr'.

His father, he says, was neither a bigot nor a philosopher, but he was justifiably alarmed and outraged. He had sent his son with every generous advantage to play the gentleman at Oxford, and his son had rewarded him by taking a step which would cut him off from every office and privilege which an English gentleman might look to.

It was impossible to keep the secret and consequently the gates of Magdalen were shut against the pupil's return. There was no formal expulsion, and no disgrace.[3] But something would have to be done.

Mr Gibbon acted with his usual precipitation and

[1] For John Lewis and Father Baker, see article by Edward Hutton, 'Gibbon's Conversion', *Nineteenth Century and After*, March 1932.

[2] He had begun to consider this step in March apparently. *Murray*, p. 296. It was in this month that he made his excursion in Bucks. On 18th April he went to London alone and stayed there till 30th. From May 10 to 18 he was on a visit to Bath. After his reception into the Roman Church it does not appear that he ever returned to Oxford. *Gibbon's Journal*, p. xlvii; Add. MSS. 37772.

[3] His caution money was returned to him in 1755.

originality. Pending something more final, William Law's old pupil deposited his son with a leading free-thinker. Mr David Mallet is unforgettably the beggarly Scotchman of Johnson's taunt, to whom Bolingbroke left half a crown to discharge the blunderbuss against religion and morality which he had not dared to fire himself. He was now living at Putney, engaged on priming this weapon. A friendship of some intimacy had sprung up with the Gibbons. Some clumsily playful verses are quoted in the Autobiography, in which Mallet invites an inconsolable widower to throw off his melancholy for once and join in their festivities. How far his deistical opinions were making way with Mr Gibbon we do not know. But two years after Gibbon's departure for Lausanne there was a curious explosion which throws some light on the scene. Hester Gibbon came on a visit to Putney—a rare and formidable event we may suppose—and expressed her disapproval of the Mallets to her niece Catherine Elliston. Catherine not daring to answer her aunt to her face, stood up for her friends in a spirited letter. The aunt concocted a stirring ungrammatical reply: 'If Miss Elliston had not lost all sense of duty, both to God and man, she would not treat in such a saucy and contemptible manner her who is the nearest female relative she has . . . and for no other reason than for acting as suitable as I could to these relations I bear to her. . . .' Law restrained her from letting go this tirade and substituted a letter of his own dictation which deplored the fact that the Gibbons were 'shut among infidels, rejoicing in their friendship, and thankful for having a seat where dead Bolingbroke yet speaketh . . . both you and your unhappy uncle sooner or later must find that falseness, baseness and hypocrisy make the whole heart and spirit of every blasphemer of Jesus Christ'.[1]

[1] Overton's *William Law*, pp. 355-6.

That was going rather far certainly, and one wonders what complications would have ensued if Aunt Hester had intervened two years earlier. As it was, the young convert was sufficiently scandalised by Mallet's philosophy, while from his father he got nothing but threats of banishment and disinheritance.[1]

But he had only a few days of this. With headlong speed his father made other arrangements. Lord Chesterfield had made a residence in Switzerland fashionable for young men. Philip Stanhope had been sent there in 1746 and with him had been Edward Eliot of Port Eliot, Cornwall, a wealthy young landowner. He was a friend of the Gibbons and a few years later was to marry Catherine Elliston with sixty thousand pounds. On this young man's advice Lausanne was determined on for the convert. Without waiting to correspond with anyone there, Mr Gibbon despatched his son on the 19th June in the charge of M. Frey of Bâle, a professional bear-leader.

As they rolled across France Gibbon's spirits rose. Here was real travelling. M. Frey was an agreeable companion, a man of the world and well read. At every stage new interests distracted the young man's mind, as they passed through St. Quentin, Rheims, Langres and Besançon. His father's angry threats grew faint in his ears. One could not really believe in them. On 30th June they drove into Lausanne.[2] Without loss of time M. Frey installed his charge with M. Daniel Pavillard, a Calvinist minister, and left for Geneva.[3]

[1] Mr Gibbon could banish but not disinherit.

[2] The journey cost £40 7s.; the Dover–Calais crossing £1 6s. Frey drew £42 from Mme Morel at Calais. *Magd. Coll. Papers.*

[3] Pavillard. He always signs his name Pavilliard in extant letters, but that seems to have been a concession to the English.

Chapter 5

No. 16 RUE CITÉ-DERRIÈRE

1753–1758

DISILLUSIONMENT was sudden and complete. It looked now as if Gibbon was to achieve a martyr's crown, though not a very spectacular one. The gentleman commoner was become a schoolboy once more: worse than a schoolboy, in fact. His contemporaries at Westminster might be roughing it; but they were gloriously free in comparison. Gibbon was neither free nor comfortable. His movements were restricted. He had no money beyond what Pavillard doled out to him. He was penned up in a gloomy house in a narrow street near the Cathedral, separated by a deep valley from the Bourg quarter, which was the centre of native and foreign social life.[1] He was cut off from all intelligent intercourse by his ignorance of French. Pavillard himself he found kindly and tactful, but of his wife, on whom he was dependent for comfort, he could only say in later years 'in sober truth she was ugly, dirty, proud, ill-

[1] No. 16 rue Cité-derrière. The house was standing in 1935, though marked for destruction. Its amenities have not been improved by its being used for years as a military prison, and the interior has been altered considerably. On the first floor is a long narrow room looking on to the street. It is the only room in the house with a fireplace, and since Pavillard tells Mr Gibbon that he has given his son a room with an open fire, we may identify this as his room. In the following year Pavillard transferred to a house now pulled down, which stood near L'Escalier des Grandes Roches, on what is now the wide roadway at the Cité end of the Pont Bessières.

tempered and covetous'.[1] Everything was wrong. His books had been stopped in Paris and he had no clothes suitable for the hot weather. He had nothing left to console him but his new-found religion and the consciousness of having acted from pure and unworldly motives. Even here, to his lasting amazement, he was abandoned. The Catholic clergy were supposed to have spread a network of vigilant communication across Europe. But no one ever followed up the young convert or even wrote to him.

It may be thought that Gibbon has exaggerated his plight in his Memoirs. A letter written to his father exactly a month after his arrival is perfectly cool and detached and betrays no depression of spirits. The journey had been pretty tiresome, but during a month with Mr Pavillard he had been treated with the greatest civility imaginable. Everyone did his best to make the town agreeable to strangers. Among these were several Englishmen, including his school friend Lord Huntingtower, and he had been introduced to the Earl of Blessington and his family. He had also followed up an introduction given to him by his father to Mme de Brissoné, whom he found 'an extremely agreeable woman'. He complains about nothing and asks for nothing. He begs his sincere compliments to his cousin Miss Elliston, and ends 'I am, dear sir, with the greatest respect and sincerity your most obedient and most dutiful son'.

Gibbon was evidently not quite so lonely as he subsequently made out. But in other respects this letter only masks the real position, which can be discerned from Pavillard's letters and accounts.[2] The worst aspects of it

[1] Gibbon's friend Deyverdun bears him out independently in his diary, 14th July 1754, quoted by *Meredith Read*, ii. p. 303. He calls her Carbonella, and gives her as one of the reasons for not seeing Pavillard more often.

[2] The letters are in Add. MSS. 34887. Some of the accounts are there too, and some in the *Magd. Coll. Papers*. The letters were printed, with omissions, as footnotes by Lord Sheffield.

must be attributed to Gibbon's father, who having discovered that generosity did not pay, swung over to the other extreme. If Gibbon found himself half-starved and frozen, and revolted by Madame Pavillard's little meannesses, the unchanged table linen, the too familiar joints, it was because his father was not paying more than four pounds a month for him,[1] and Madame Pavillard was entitled to make a profit if she could. To begin with Gibbon had asked for, and obtained, about two guineas a month for pocket money, and had assured Pavillard that his father would give him as much or more. But it was too much, and after letters had come from home he was cut down to a guinea a month for September and October to even up. Naturally in such a state he was not allowed a personal servant, a deprivation which hit him particularly hard, for he was always rather clumsy and helpless. But more inhuman perhaps, and certainly more petty, is the fact that his father objected to the summer coat which Pavillard had had made. The minister has to plead that it was of camelot de Bruxelles, a cheap material, that Mr Frey had advised it, and anyhow it was made now.

Pavillard comes out of a difficult task remarkably well. He deserved the respect and affection which he earned from Gibbon. He had frequently to act first and make the best of contradictory instructions afterwards. He was constantly on the defensive. Even four years later we find him explaining that he has had six handkerchiefs made because Gibbon had lost some. He stood up for Gibbon against his father's desire that the boy should not be allowed to go out much, arguing very sensibly that if he was compelled to brood by himself without any diversions, he would become still more attached to

[1] This, in fairness it must be said, is what Pavillard himself asked. But it is clear that Mr Gibbon expected all expenses to be at the minimum. This did not include heating: 60 livres or francs a month. Livre=about 1s. 3½d.

his views, and would be less likely to listen to Pavillard's reasoning. In this connexion too he probably scared Mr Gibbon shrewdly by telling him, as an example of what could be brought about by solitude, that his son had declared for the Pretender, and showed how artfully he had met his views without appearing to be too combative.

Here, at last, was a man who was prepared to take pains to understand a pupil and could discern unusual qualities in the 'thin little figure with a large head disputing and urging with the greatest ability, all the best arguments that had ever been used in favour of Popery'. Gibbon responded by earning the epithets, *doux*, *tranquille et sérieux*. He was not slow to recognise that at last he had opportunities such as he had long hoped for and never found. Pavillard was not a man of outstanding gifts, but he was well enough equipped for teaching and had had plenty of experience. Above all he was not likely to fall into Mallet's error of scandalising a young mind by an unceremonious introduction of unpalatable ideas.

Mr Gibbon was quite possibly anxious to get early news of his son's second conversion. Pavillard was not going to be hurried. He allowed his pupil to settle down and excused himself, rightly enough, for not opening the debate on account of their common shortcomings in languages. Later he left two controversial books lying about, and saw Gibbon take them away to read in his own room. Meanwhile he propounded a plan for general reading in the mornings, French and Latin, modern history and geography. After 'some youthful sallies' Gibbon surrendered with pleasure to the methodical programme, and in a short time was pursuing the road on his own. Equipped by a study of logic he was able to follow, and dispute step by step, Pavillard's exposition of his errors. In after years he did not grudge his tutor his share in the matter, but claimed that his conversion was chiefly effected by his private reflections, and he remembered his 'solitary transport' on discovering an argument against the doctrine of transubstantiation. The text of scripture which seemed to inculcate the real presence was attested only by a single sense—our sight; while the real presence itself is disproved by three of our senses—the sight, the touch and the taste. Gibbon calls this a philosophical argument. He had perhaps forgotten that Bossuet had already met it so far as disputants can meet across an unbridgeable gulf.[1] In truth it was not philosophy but weariness of what was seen to be nonsense. From this point indeed 'the various articles of the Romish creed disappeared like a dream'.

It is natural that Pavillard should represent the process as more protracted. Writing to Mr Gibbon in June 1754, he says that he has been hoping week by week to announce his pupil's complete renunciation of his false ideas. But the ground had been fought over step by step. He had judged it wise not to push Gibbon into a corner and extort an avowal. Pavillard had thought that when the principal tenets of Romanism were disposed of, the rest would follow. In this he was mistaken. Every article had to be taken on its own merits. Finally it could be affirmed that Gibbon was no longer a member of the Church of Rome although he still clung to some remnants of his beliefs. He had shown steadfastness in his tenets, but was open to reason and never captious. He had surprised Pavillard by an unexpected resumption of fasting on Fridays some time after he had admitted that the Roman Church was not infallible. It was a last gesture of adherence to the faith he had chosen for himself.

[1] Quoique les choses paroissent toujours les mêmes à nos sens, notre âme en juge autrement qu'elle ne feroit si une autorité supérieure n'étoit pas intervenue. Bossuet, *Exposition. Œuvres* (1816), xviii. 126.

At last, in December 1754, he was judged worthy to be readmitted into a Protestant congregation. Unlike the Oxford dons, La Vénérable Compagnie Pastorale de Lausanne knew the value of making the occasion impressive.

Gibbon appeared before the Company on 22nd December, and made an acknowledgment of his errors, and to testify his gratitude to Heaven asked to be readmitted to communion in the Protestant Church. He then withdrew, and Pavillard vouched for the reality of his conversion and also the purity of his feelings and his unexceptionable morals. The meeting thereupon charged Monsieur le grand Ministre Polier de Bottens to examine Gibbon. On 10th February 1755, the Company met again when M. Polier de Bottens reported that he had seen M. Gibbon and had been 'très édifié et satisfait'. Pavillard reported at the same time that after M. de Bottens' examination he had admitted M. Gibbon to communion on Christmas Day.[1] 'It was here', says Gibbon, 'that I suspended my religious inquiries, acquiescing with implicit belief in the tenets and mysteries which are adopted by the general consent of Catholics and Protestants.'

There is no reason to suppose that these words are not to be taken literally. Gibbon has suffered from his friends as well as from his detractors, each side wishing to depict him as a child of light on the one hand free from any superstitious blots, or an imp of darkness with no redeeming piety on the other, according to their respective prejudices. But to assume that Gibbon was a complete sceptic from the time of his reconversion is to falsify both biography and history.

Those who abandoned the Biblical cosmogony in the

[1] H. Vuilleumier, *Histoire de l'Église Réformée du Pays de Vaud*, iv. 364-5, and Actes de la Vén. Comp. pastorale, 22 déc. 1754, 10 fév. 1755. Polier de Bottens was Mme de Montolieu's father. He was a friend of Voltaire.

middle of the eighteenth century were in very different plight from those who cannot accept it at the present day. Not merely the weight of tradition but the insecure status of natural science created a presumption in favour of the inspired text. In the absence of obvious alternatives it had to be abandoned with caution.

These adventures had not touched the central and common core of revealed religion. They had turned on questions of historical and theological interpretation lying almost entirely outside the Bible. Gibbon believed in the bulk of traditional religion implicitly because he had not yet examined it critically. 'I was still the slave of education and prejudice', he says in reference to his correspondence with Allamand, 'he had some measures to keep; and I much suspect that he never showed me the true colours of his secret scepticism.' [1]

From theological speculation he turned to survey in Giannone's *Civil History of Naples* the baleful consequences of priestly power. Giannone is coupled with Pascal in one of the memoirs as having first accustomed Gibbon 'to the use of irony and criticism on subjects of ecclesiastical gravity'.[2] A third book read at this time, a life of the Emperor Julian, was not the least influential. Gibbon found a new field of history and took his stand by the last of the pagan emperors looking back wistfully into the disappearing world of the ancients.

Meanwhile it was with unfeigned, if not very profound, joy that he wrote to his aunt to announce his recovery from the Popish malady. 'I am now good Protestant', he writes in an English that was already full of foreign idiom, 'and am extremely glad of it.' But is

[1] *Murray*, p. 146. Henri Vuilleumier, the historian of the Reformed Church in the Pays de Vaud, indignantly rebuts Gibbon's insinuation of Allamand's scepticism. But Allamand was at least, like a number of Swiss clergy, in correspondence with Voltaire. There was at any rate a pleasing absence of theological zeal in the Pays de Vaud at this time.

[2] *Murray*, p. 235.

there a first flicker of irony when he goes on to say that after all the storm and upheaval and this long and momentous debate, of which, apparently, he had kept her informed, his last difficulty was whether a member of the Church of England should join in communion with Presbyterians. He could scarcely resolve to do so. But he did and all was well, and M. Pavillard, good man, appeared extremely glad of it. Gibbon assured his aunt that he felt 'a joy extremely pure, and the more so, as I know it to be not only innocent but laudable'. It would seem that the young proselyte had only to claim his temporal reward, more money and liberty, if not deliverance from his dependent state. But this remarkable letter goes on to relate how he had put the fruits of his conversion in jeopardy by his incautious behaviour.

In the first flush of his elation, and indulged perhaps by Pavillard in the increased liberty which his father was expected to sanction, Gibbon went out one evening to visit an Englishman. Mr Gee was conducting a faro party in his room. Gibbon would have gone away but was prevailed upon at least to take a chair by the fire. The inevitable happened. One of the players left, and the youth was asked to take his place. He refused. They told him he could play as low as he liked. Gibbon tried his luck and lost half a guinea. This touched him up and he warmed to the work. They all warmed to it and by 'about three o'clock the next morning I found I had lost only forty guineas'. Again a flicker, a very rueful flicker, of irony. He had lost twenty months' pocket money. He could never pay it. He dare not tell anyone. Unhinged by fear he chose the worst course. He would show them he was a man and demand his revenge. He rose from the table at last—he does not say at what hour—in debt for 1760 francs or 110 guineas.

In that black January dawn he was a prey to a violence of feeling he had never known. A debt of 110 guineas.

What were the differences of Papist and Protestant to this? The money must be found, it would have to be borrowed, and London would be the only place where he could command credit for such a sum. His father's anger would be kindled all over again. He would risk that rather than default over a debt of honour.

He saw Gee again. That scamp now sold him a horse, a watch and other things which were to be paid for with the rest of the debt in England. Gibbon escaped from Pavillard's house and set off in the middle of the Swiss winter. He rode as far as Geneva. Imagine him there vainly trying to sell the horse. A day or two was thus lost and Pavillard found him there and, 'half entreaties, half force', carried him back to Lausanne. Time was running on. He had till 15th March to find the money. He turned to his aunt as a last resource.

> 'Tell me not you are poor,' he wrote in his frenzy, 'that you have not enough for yourself. I do not address myself to you as the richest but as the kindest of my relations; nor do I ask it you as a gift, but as a loan. If you could not furnish me the whole sum let me have at least a part of it. I know you have thoughts of doing something for me by your will; I beg you only to anticipate it.'

He begged for a speedy reply. He was too agitated to say more.

Pavillard had already written a much less alarming letter which Gibbon had translated.[1] In it, after announcing that his pupil had communicated Christmas Day last with devotion, and after dilating upon his own tactics, he says that Gibbon's behaviour has been very regular and there have been no slips 'except that of gaming twice and losing much more than I desired'. Pavillard appeals to Miss Porten to reinstate her nephew in favour, and as his father has allowed him but the bare

[1] Add. MSS. 34887. It is probably in Gibbon's hand—a boyish best-behaviour fist. It is certainly not Pavillard's.

necessities he asks her for 'some tokens of satisfaction', assuring her that they will be employed well and under his direction since Gibbon has promised never to play any more games of chance. A conflicting and agitating couple of letters for an aunt to receive. She showed them to her brother-in-law.

What Mr Gibbon did we do not know since there is silence on the subject until the following September. In a letter to his father of 1st March, Gibbon pleads rather pathetically for a restoration to favour and for lessons in riding, fencing and dancing (some of which he had already had) but makes no mention of the escapade, no doubt because he had not yet had his aunt's answer to his appeal. In his letter to his aunt of 20th September, he gives the sequel to the tale and a rather different aspect of it.

Gee, about whose subsequent discreditable career in France Gibbon appears remarkably well informed, had been compelled to take back the mare and the watch, and Gibbon's debt to him was fixed at fifty guineas. In addition he had had to buy Gee another watch for twenty guineas, for which he was paying the watchmaker two guineas a month by means of cutting down other expenses.[1] A great part of his losses had not been to Gee but to someone of Lausanne who had heard reason easily enough. Does that mean that he had excused the boy the debt, as he well might, though such

[1] The bill for this watch is preserved, *Magd. Coll. Papers*. It is dated 20th May 1755, but was not finally settled till 16th July 1758, after Gibbon had left Lausanne. The watch cost 320 francs and the bill agrees for a monthly payment of 12 francs; that is, rather less than £1. In fact, payments of varying amounts were made from time to time. From 1755 onwards Gibbon appears to have been receiving 24 francs a month. This was paid in two instalments and he frequently received small advances. 24 francs of the bill were paid off in July 1755, and it appears that this was found by Gibbon's only receiving 12 francs each for April and May. 72 francs were paid off in March 1756, and again in October, but it is not very clear that deductions had been made from his pocket money. 107-8 were paid in October 1757, and the balance, 44, in July 1758.

a course was hardly consistent with Gibbon's pride. And how was the fifty guineas paid to Gee? If Mr Gibbon supplied the money there is no mention of the fact.

It does not appear, as one might expect after this crisis, that Gibbon enjoyed any greater liberty or luxury. But he seems to have rubbed along not unhappily. His father was known to be impulsive but careless. Moreover he was at a great distance and had to accept the *fait accompli* as in the matter of dancing, fencing and riding.[1] Pavillard continued to order or at least pay for his clothes; his shirts and handkerchiefs, his muffs and muff-strings are all entered. We find too his medicine bills, the hire of carriages to go to the comedy at Mon Repos, his billiard parties, his gratuities to servants and occasional charities to indigent Irishmen in the place. And when at last in 1757 a servant was allowed, they debited the bell with which Gibbon was to summon him.

He learned to walk a minuet but could not master the intricacies of a country-dance. He had no ear for music. He had drawing lessons but makes no comment on his progress. He was slow and clumsy with the foil and once fought a boyish quarrel with some loss of blood. Of his riding he says that he finally withdrew 'without an hope of being ever promoted to the use of stirrups or spurs'. He was at any rate charged for them as well as for switches. How did he get Mr Gee's mare to Geneva?[2]

But if he spent less money than the other Englishmen

[1] The *manège* bills are also preserved. Gibbon began lessons in August 1753, two days before Pavillard wrote to Mr Gibbon asking for his permission. He had lessons for nine months altogether, not five as he says; *Murray*, p. 236. These bills were not sent in until 1757 and were settled by Pavillard, January 1758.

[2] Gibbon was constantly on horseback in the Militia. Thereafter he seldom rode. A malicious gossip of later years relates that he was gratified by a description of himself as riding at Lausanne, although he was long past such exercise. B. de Lalonde, *Le Léman ou voyage pittoresque*, etc., i. pp. 277 *sqq*.

in the place, he claimed to be the one most generally liked. As his letters show, he had mastered French and allows its idiom to invade his English. Within a year of his arrival he had made friends with Georges Deyverdun. Deyverdun was a few years older than Gibbon. He lived with his widowed aunt, Madame de Bochat, in an old house called La Grotte, which stood on the crest of the ridge which falls away down to Ouchy, commanding a view of the lake and the 'stupendous mountains of the Savoy'. Here Deyverdun was occupied in arranging his uncle's papers, a historian of some distinction. He was fairly intimate with Pavillard, and would have been at his house oftener but for the minister's many engagements and Deyverdun's dislike of Mme Pavillard already mentioned. Gibbon's friendship with Deyverdun grew steadily and in 1756 we find him lending him sixteen francs, an act which perhaps argues a greater intimacy for those days than it would now.

Ten to twelve hours' reading a day was another and even greater source of satisfaction. The burden of religious controversy was removed; Latin as well as French had been mastered, and Gibbon was reading deeply and with increasing method in both languages, making 'very large collections' as he went. He had begun Greek, and it is to this year in his Journal that he assigns the study of de Crousaz's logic, which formed his mind to a habit of thinking and reasoning he had no idea of before.[1] Altogether his condition was improving and his spirits were further raised by a 'vastly kind letter' received from his father at the beginning of September.[2]

In this all his past faults were forgiven and were never to be mentioned again, provided Gibbon behaved him-

[1] *Gibbon's Journal*, p. 5.

[2] The letter was dated 18th August and was about a fortnight on the way.

self. He was to be allowed to make the tour of Switzerland (which he lost no time in doing solemnly in a coach accompanied by Pavillard), and when his studies were completed he was to travel in France and Italy. A charming prospect. But amid this outburst of returning favour there was not a word of a most agitating event of which a tantalising inkling arrived three days later in a letter from a Hampshire neighbour.

Mr Gibbon had married again. But when? where? whom? Mr Hugonin did not say. Later, no doubt from his aunt, news came that the new wife was Miss Dorothea Patton, the lady who had had Dr. Ward called in when he was so ill during his Westminster days. They were married on 8th May. It was most disturbing news. There might be children 'of the second bed' and in that case he might be left with only £200 a year. That was his impression of his grandfather's will. He had written for a copy of it out of Doctors' Commons. But '*Could not do it YOURSELF?*' he wrote emphatically and disjointedly to Dear Kitty.[1]

Unsettled by this news he passed on to criticise his father's plans for himself. He was not anxious to go at once on his grand tour. 'I never liked young travellers,' (he was himself at once so young and so old); 'they go too raw to make any great remarks, and they lose a time which is (in my opinion) the most precious part of a man's life.' He would prefer to spend another winter in Lausanne, return to England and finish his studies either at Cambridge or at a university in Holland. He urged his aunt to get his scheme put before his father '*by Metcalf or somebody else who has a certain credit over him*'.

This letter and perhaps others from him were shown by Miss Porten to his father, and eventually drew from him an unfeeling reply which deserves to be printed.

1 'Could you not do it?' *Prothero* i. p. 8. The 'you' is omitted in the original, Add. MSS. 34883.

'Sir,

'I received your letter with your Journal and I have since paid a bill for the Expences of your Tour amounting to 35 louis. I have never grudged you any reasonable expences, notwithstanding the many unjust and undutiful things you have said of me to the contrary. The news that you heard of my being married again is very true, it is to a Lady that saved your life at Westminster by recommending Dr. Ward when you was given over by the regular Physicians; but if you behave as you ought to do, it shall not make any difference to you.

'I am very sorry to hear of the many complaints you make to your Aunt, of the place where you are, and make none, but you may as well make yourself easy for I am determined you shall stay abroad at least two years longer. I desire to know what proficiency you make in your studies as well as your exercises, and if you have begun Algebra which I so much recommended to you.

Are you thoroughly sensible of the Errors of the Romish Church which you rashly embraced and destroyed all my plan of Education I had laid for you at Oxford; your scheme of coming over and going to Cambridge I can by no means approve of now, and if you would but give yourself leave to think about it, you will easily see the impropriety of it. I think upon all accounts you are [much] [1] better where you are but if you behave as you ought to do, let you be where you will, you may be assured not only of my Affection, but my doing everything for you, that you yourself can desire.

'E. G.

'Beriton, 24 Decr 1755.' [2]

Gibbon evidently believed in the power of a soft answer, and composed a masterpiece of tactful conciliation.[3] Not the least effective stroke was choosing to write in French, thus gaining an initial superiority of which his father could not complain, and enabling him-

[1] Paper destroyed here.

[2] A kind-hearted reader may exclaim, 'Fancy writing a letter like that to his son on Christmas Eve!' But Gibbon's correspondence alone shows that little attention and no sentiment attached to Christmas in his day and society.

[3] It is letter No. 5 in *Prothero* i. p. 9. It is incorrectly dated there as '10 juin'. The MS. has '10 janv.' Add. MSS. 34886.

self, I think, to convey a sense of reproof with less risk of offence than English might have entailed.

'Mon très cher Père', he begins imperturbably, 'je reçus hier votre lettre avec beaucoup de plaisir, mais qui ne fut pas tout-à-fait sans mélange d'Inquiétude.' He was afraid he had given new offence. A lively and sincere affection was apt to take alarm over trifles, and so he could not but be struck on opening the letter to find the usual 'Dear Edward changé en un froid Monsieur'.[1] Having thus gently put his father in the wrong he insists on seeing in the unkind letter nothing but evidences of paternal solicitude, and assures him that he will always be worthy of it. He assures him that he is prepared to love his stepmother in advance. The rest of the letter is devoted to an account of his progress. But he ends with an effective stroke. His father had recommended Locke to him. Very well. Locke held definite opinions about the inadvisability of travelling too young. Gibbon was determined not to go to Italy before he was prepared.

He did not write again apparently until October. This is a remarkable letter foreshadowing the grand Gibbon in several ways:

'Monsieur mon très cher Père,

'Comme un tems assez considérable s'est écoulé depuis ma dernière lettre, je ne puis pas me dispenser plus longtems de vous réitérer les assurances de mon respect et de mon affection, et de demander toujours la continuation de votre Tendresse.

'Ma santé va toujours bien et il me paroit que l'air de ce pays convient assez bien à mon temperament qui semble s'être sensiblement fortifié depuis que j'ai quitté ma Patrie. Mes études vont leur petit train. La dernière fois que je vous écrivis, j'avois (à ce que je crois) commencé Tacite. Je l'ai achevé heureusement sans même qu'il m'ait donné à beaucoup près autant de peine que je m'attendois à y trouver. Dès là j'ai lu Suetone, Quinte-

[1] I believe there is no letter extant in which he is either addressed or referred to as Edward. It is always Gibbon or Mr Gibbon or the Gibbon.

Curce, Justin et Flore qui a fait la clôture de ma Classe d'historiens. J'ai depuis commencé celle des Poëtes par Plaute le plus ancien de Tous à moins que je n'eusse voulu entreprendre le peu qu'il nous reste de Livius Andronicus de Naevius et d'Ennius [car] ce qui n'auroit pas répondu à mon but, car ne voulant voir que le beau Siècle des Lettres et de la langue des Romains, leur enfance aussi bien que leur Vieillesse auroient été pour moi des hors d'Œuvres, peut être même pernicieux. J'ai eu grand soin d'accompagner ces lectures par celle d'un grand nombre d'articles du Lexicon des Antiquités Romaines du célèbre Pitiscus, et je me suis même hazardé à faire de tems en tems quelques remarques de Critique lesquelles ont quelquefois eu le bonheur de plaire aux personnes à qui je les ai montré. J'ai taché autant que j'ai pu de saisir le caractère distinctif de mes auteurs différens. Cependant je suis bien sensible que ce n'est pas l'affaire d'une première lecture. Ce sera beaucoup si j'ai pu atraper celui de leur Siècle et de leur pays; car chaque pays et chaque siècle en ont certainement un, et celui de tout Ecrivain qui y vit ne peut éviter de s'y plier jusqu'à un certain point. Pour mon Grec je vous dirai qu'après avoir lu assez facilement les deux premiers livres de Xenophon, j'ai attaqué le redoutable Homère et j'en suis actuellement au Second livre.

'Quelles nouvelles vous mander, Mon cher Père, depuis un Pays qui a l'avantage inestimable qu'on ne parle jamais de lui dans le monde. On y est cependant fort Anglois, c'est à dire fort Prussien, car à present ces deux terres paroissent assez synonimes. En voici une cependant.' . . .'

Here he begins a report by someone from Spain about the Spanish warships in the Mediterranean. The end is lost, a quarter of the page having been torn off. He also repeats his request in this fragment for an allowance of £200 a year and permission to have a valet.

'Tout ce que je ferai ici c'est de vous rappeller la requête même qui vous sera peut-être sortie de la memoire.

'Après avoir, mon très cher père, dit quelques mots de ma Situation et des mes Études il ne faut pas que je vous importune plus longtemps. Permettez donc qu'après avoir assuré votre chère Épouse des sentiments de respect et d'affection qu'elle a droit de demander de moi je me dise avec un dévouement entier et une tendresse à toute Épreuve,

'Mon très cher Père,

'Votre très humble et très obéissant

'Serviteur et Fils,

'E. GIBBON

'P.S.—Pourrois-je vous rappeller ma Bibliothèque Orientale et les Cartes de l'Amérique. Les Voituriers Suisses doivent être actuellement à Londres.'

There is an endorsement by Pavillard, but most of it has been torn off. It is dated by him 'Lausanne, ce 30me 8bre 1756'.[1]

Gibbon continued to woo his father with unflagging diplomacy and urbanity for the next two years. There were no more outbursts of wrath, only disheartening silences. Amid his protestations of filial devotion he kept on with his request to be allowed to come home. But in vain. His father had said he was to remain two years longer and kept to his word.

This remaining period was far from unhappy. His satisfaction was centred in the progress of his studies. In this respect he was now entirely independent of tuition with the exception of his attendance on the mathematician, Professor de Traytorrens.[2] By the time he was twenty he had mastered classical Latin literature, was writing critical dissertations and had entered into correspondence with learned professors. To Greek he was not paying so much attention, yet he had read a considerable amount, including St. John's Gospel and portions of Xenophon, Herodotus and the *Iliad*. In

[1] Add. MSS. 34883, f. 10.

[2] He began studying under Traytorrens in January 1757 (*Journal*, pp. 5-6). In December 1756 he had been enrolled in the Academy. His autograph is in the *Album Academiae Lausanniensis*, i. f. 240: 'Edwardus Gibbon Anglus Kalendis Decembris (*sic*) 1756'. Among other names of about the same time are Edward Moore, Earl of Drogheda, le Chevalier Davers, Savile Finch, Roger Mostyn, Crofton Vandeleur and Alex. Cramaché, the two last with Lord Drogheda being described as Irish. *Archives Cantonales de Lausanne.*

this language he was still far behind what a Sixth Form boy at Westminster might have accomplished, and in Latin he was far from having attained the minutiae of scholarship. On the other hand no boy and very few undergraduates would have read so widely or with such mastery of the subject.

Gibbon's scholarship, as he himself was well aware, always remained somewhat rough-and-ready, massive rather than delicate. It is easy to find him sadly at sea with a Greek text, or advancing some ludicrous etymology. In part he suffered from his personal experience, in part he is representative of his age. Philology was still tentative and rash, full of easy guessing. It may have been the age of Porson, but Porson was not of his age. Gibbon's blunders in etymology are no worse than the portentous Dr. Parr's. And Dr. Parr was accustomed to boom out that Porson was the first Greek scholar in England and Dr. Burney the third; he would leave it to his listeners to say who was the second.[1]

Gibbon was far from being a recluse. His chief link with the outside world was his friendship with Georges Deyverdun. They had worked together, though Deyverdun, an easy-going dilettante, had been unable to sustain the English boy's pace. But over their Virgil and Cicero had sprung up an intimacy which Gibbon at any rate hoped would prove lifelong. 'Every idea, every sentiment, was poured into each other's bosom; and our schemes of ambition or retirement always terminated in the prospect of our final and inseparable union.'[2]

Deyverdun belonged to the aristocratic Bourg section

[1] People who make wild shots are often shrewd critics of similar flights in other people. So Gibbon: cf. his etymological notes in *The Decline and Fall*, c. lv. n. 25; lvi. nn. 55, 77; and lvii. n. 20. Parr somewhere explains a superlative like *κάλλιστος* thus: *κάλλος* + *ἵστημι*, *i.e.* beautiful to the point of coming to a stand, unable to achieve more!

[2] *Murray*, p. 238.

of Lausanne society, and through him and other sources Gibbon's general acquaintance was increasing. His billiard parties now figure in the accounts.[1] A valet had become a necessity, and Pavillard acquiescing engaged François for him and in the usual way justified the event later to Mr Gibbon, reminding him that his son was now a young man and should have more liberty. The reports are invariably of the good use Gibbon made of his time and money. There were no more Gee episodes. It was, however, the appearance of the most famous and agitating man in Europe in the quiet coteries of Lausanne that offered Gibbon his best opportunities of mixing in general society and of making acquaintances, some of which were lifelong.

The social scene upon which Voltaire and Gibbon were now entering from opposite sides was set in a still atmosphere of dependency and arrested development. The Pays de Vaud formed part of the Canton of Berne, and the bourgeois government of Berne had crystallised into a closed oligarchy which governed with extreme jealousy. Effective power in fact by this time was concentrated in the hands of about ninety Bernese families. Collectively they called themselves *Le Prince*; more commonly they were known as Their Excellencies. Outside their privileged circle these families viewed with equal indifference the feudal aristocracy and the common people. Neither class could aspire to any part in affairs beyond municipal administration.

The rule of the Bernese was not severe. The taxes were light. Provided no attempt was made to subvert their supremacy they had no inclination to interfere. Their subjects acquiesced in an arrangement that was not uncomfortable. Major Davel's rising in 1723 had failed through the apathy of the Lausannois who had concurred in the execution of a man destined to be

[1] They cost from 10 to 20 francs, *i.e.* 15 to 30 shillings a time.

revered as a national hero. From that date to 1791 Lausanne may be said to have had no history. In the fifties everyone was anxious to forget that such a thing had happened. The Bailli or governor from Berne who resided in the ancient castle of the bishops a little above the Cathedral, mixed without embarrassment in the society of the town and there was, to a foreigner at least, a pleasant appearance of contentment and tolerance.

A young man, however, might feel differently, and in *Lettre d'un Suédois* Gibbon composed a document which Their Excellencies would have scarcely forgiven, which the writer himself must have viewed with some uneasiness some thirty-six years later, and which subsequent historians of the Pays de Vaud have hailed as a first raising of the banner of liberty in their midst. There is no reason, however, to suppose that Gibbon waved this banner anywhere except in the privacy of his own rooms and perhaps in the presence of such a discreet friend as Deyverdun. Yet the unfinished essay, with its prudent pretence of coming from the hand of a Swedish traveller, is a searching criticism of the evils which the Bernese supremacy caused in spite of its apparent mildness, and the writer intended, apparently, to discuss how the yoke was to be removed.[1] Gibbon's argument is the reverse of what he was to say in his last years. Then, he said that 'while the aristocracy of Berne protects the happiness, it is superfluous to enquire whether it is founded in the rights of man'. The first

[1] There can be little doubt that Sheffield was right in assigning this *Lettre* to Gibbon's first residence in Lausanne. Vuilleumier, *Histoire de l'Église Réformée du Pays de Vaud*, iii. 735, has some interesting remarks about it; he evidently thinks with some other Swiss scholars that the letter was written in Gibbon's second or even third residence. That seems very improbable. Its appearance in 1796 made some impression among Vaudois patriots. Most of it is reprinted in Henri Monod's *Mémoires*, 1805, i. 45-48. See also *Edward Gibbon und die Schweiz*, by C. Schirmer, Festschrift zum 14 Neuphilologentage in Zürich, 1910, p. 100.

stroke of a rebel drum would be the signal of his departure. His earlier theme, and it is one that is implicit throughout *all* his writings, was that such happiness was specious without the firm foundation of political freedom, and he makes great play of the fact that in spite of two hundred years of peace, a blessing not easily to be despised, the subjects of Berne had not made the progress in arts and science equal to that of the surrounding nations who had been in a much more backward position. Gibbon certainly had the facts on his side when he drew attention to the somnolent state of the three well marked divisions of Lausanne society.

The Cité, the Palud and the Bourg were the districts of Lausanne which at that time denoted classes rigidly defined in theory, though there must always have been individuals and families with a footing in more than one circle.

In the Cité—the central hill on which stood the Cathedral, the buildings of the Académie and the old Bishops' castle—were the homes of the ministers, professors and others. One of the complaints made in the *Lettre d'un Suédois* is that the Académie had not been developed into a university owing to the jealousy of Berne. Its life had not been without distinction and it had had among its professors such men as de Crousaz, familiar to English readers through his writings on Pope, or Allamand, whose qualities Gibbon himself praises warmly. Less narrow and austere than the Genevan clergy, the Lausanne ministers were scholarly and tolerant men, but devoid of ideas or incentives. By the time he was eighteen Gibbon was anxious to find a more stimulating atmosphere.

Below the Cathedral—one descends still by the ancient covered stairways—lies the Palud with the picturesque Town Hall of the seventeenth century as its centre.

This was the quarter of business and banking. Its richer members had connexions in the Bourg above them. Here again, however, there was stagnation and little scope for enterprise. After the revocation of the Edict of Nantes numbers of valuable French craftsmen had sought refuge here. But the government had failed to encourage them to stay and the best had gone on to other countries.

It was in the fashionable quarter of the Bourg that the chill hand of a despotic government was most felt. The rue de Bourg runs along the crest of a ridge that lies like a wall parallel to the lake. At its eastern end the street begins to climb inland on the way to Berne. Towards the west it comes out by the church of St. François, and beyond lies the rue Grand Chêne mounting to the wooded promenade of Montbenon. The street has long since exchanged its noble residents for fashionable shops, and but few of the old well-proportioned houses remain which once stretched its whole length. On the lakeward side they backed on to gardens which ran down across what is now the avenue Benjamin Constant. Below again rustic lanes led to Ouchy, passing country houses and the *chaumières* where some of the fashionable ladies occasionally sought the simple life, a faint reflection of Parisian whims. But gardens and lodges were subsidiary and we are told that the best rooms of these houses looked out on the rue du Bourg, interest concentrated on the passing of neighbours, the morning interchange of notes fixing the mild festivities of the day, and on the coming and going of important foreigners at the Lyon d'Or opposite.

Some of these families lived here only in the winter. Others had sold their estates in the country, often to French arrivals who had made money in the speculative era of John Law, and had come to live the social round year in year out in the town.

If the men had no estates to look after they had nothing. There was no public career for them, and what scope there was for the learned professions lay in the hands of the Cité. Nor was there much prospect abroad. Some young men like Deyverdun became tutors to German princes or dukes. More entered the service of Holland or France. But these outlets were strictly controlled from Berne, and according to the *Lettre d'un Suédois* we learn that the service of France was ruinous to a young man and barely paid the seniors. The most enterprising found their way to India. Such an idle society might be expected to be vicious. In fact it was not so. Only rather insipid and sterile. Great interest was evinced in art and letters but little was produced. Literary coteries were formed. Verses were read and innocently intriguing problems of psychology were discussed. Could there be real friendship between a man and a woman for instance? For the rest, there were picnics in the summer and strolls on Montbenon, parties afternoon and evening in the winter. Cards and coffee, coffee and cards, and an occasional romp at Blindman's Buff. Thirty or forty people would meet in the afternoon and play till six o'clock, they would then pass on to another house for supper about seven, and spend the evening with cards once more and dancing. 'Nos pères en étaient reduits à s'amuser comme des enfants.' [1]

From his confinement in the Cité, Gibbon made his entry into this happy circle of families gladly enough. He never lost his zest for its amusements. By the end of his first stay in Lausanne he was known and liked and could go to parties any evening he chose. This was his privilege as a foreigner of position, for his hosts and other acquaintances in the Cité would have but an uncertain footing in the Bourg. Gibbon availed himself of it more than most young Englishmen, who would find

[1] See C. Burnier, *La Vie vaudoise et la Révolution*, 1902.

the language still a barrier, or whose notion of pleasure was more boisterous.

Into this perpetual Christmas party came the most famous man in Europe. Gibbon says that Voltaire refined the manners of Lausanne in a visible degree. Swiss historians have said that he exercised no permanent influence. Nor had Voltaire come to improve or to ruffle the placid waters. Foremost among those who had invited Voltaire to the shores of Lake Leman was Gibbon's catechiser, Polier de Bottens, 'un prêtre hérétique de mes amis, savant et philosophe', a contributor to the *Encyclopédie*. Voltaire delighted in the free and detached atmosphere of the place, where they could pity those who were cutting one another's throats in Europe for the sake of a few acres of ice in Canada.

'C'est une belle chose que la tranquillité! Oui, mais l'ennui est de sa connaissance et de sa famille.' The most innocent remedy was a theatre, one which was bound to appear wherever Voltaire was, and Voltaire's chief reputation during most of his life was as a dramatist. He had but to suggest, to find eagerness and talent as well. A theatre was fitted up, a cast formed, and a select audience was at hand to fill the two hundred seats.[1]

The coaches ambled down the steep streets. The guests assembled. The candles twinkled and the fiddles preluded. M. de Guybon sat among the élite of Lausanne, 'un parterre très bien choisi', and M. de Voltaire on the stage appeared as old Lusignan in *Zaïre* and declaimed with 'the pomp and cadence of the old stage'. Be that as it may, the bonhomme Lusignan, according to himself, drew tears from all the Swiss eyes. There was nothing like a Swiss audience apparently; they were always ready to weep. The acting was as good and better than that of Paris. Mme Denis had not such fine eyes

[1] This was at Mon Repos, a country house at the eastern end of the town belonging to a Frenchman, de Gentils.

as la Caussin, but she played Zaïre better. Voltaire's letters breathe the very spirit of amateur theatricals.

'The parts of the young and fair were distorted by his fat and ugly niece', was Gibbon's recollection in after-years.[1] But that was after he had had experience of 'our admirable Pritchard' and many others. Now he was enjoying himself and was a conspicuous follower of the company. One would like to know if Voltaire drew tears from him too. In any case these performances—the first probably that he had seen—exercised a great influence on his taste. His preference was always for the French theatre. *Zaïre* remained a particular favourite to the end of his life and had some curious associations for him.

After the play the supper. Dainties such as 'gelinottes et coqs de bruyère et truites de vingt livres'. For Voltaire was rich and liked to do his guests well and was tempted himself to brave indigestion on these occasions. The young Englishman was sometimes asked to join the actors at these feasts. He had been presented at some time to the great man, who received him with appropriate civility.[2] That was all. What more could Voltaire do? All Lausanne had flocked to Monrion on his arrival, and there were always so many young Englishmen and young Scotchmen too, even more persistent, who were bent on seeing him, well or ill, alive or even dead. But the notice of one's host in these merry evenings did not matter a great deal perhaps. In this

[1] *Murray*, p. 149. Gibbon might have spared his sneer at Voltaire for being reluctant to play the *Iphigénie* of Racine. The play was, in fact, a new one called *Iphigénie dans Tauride*. Voltaire did not think much of it but put it on out of good nature. See his letters for 1758 *passim*.

[2] This was probably in December 1755, when Voltaire first resided at Monrion. Gibbon claims to have been the means of divulging Voltaire's poem on Lake Leman, to Voltaire's annoyance. Voltaire refers to the unauthorised publication of this poem in June 1755. He does not appear to be annoyed about it. See his letters to Polier de Bottens, 4th June, and to Clavel de Brenles, 6th June 1755.

gay entry into general society, with heightened emotions produced by the plays, and amid the chatter of the delighted and delightful actresses, it would not be surprising if the young man fell in love. He did; but not with one of the ladies of the Bourg.

Chapter 6

SUZANNE CURCHOD

1757–1759

THE story of Gibbon's love has been told many times; by himself in unforgettable phrases which have been turned against him, by others who have seldom been impartial, some straining to fit the tale to their previous conceptions of his character, others falling into the equal error of attacking the girl. Brilliant wits have been exercised on the theme before half the evidence came to light. The story has never been told by the aid of all the available documents.[1]

All the world knows that Suzanne Curchod was fair and blue-eyed, that she was vivacious, clever and even learned. She was the only child of a country minister, who had taught her what he would have taught a son. She could write letters in Latin which her admirers acclaimed as Ciceronian. She knew a little Greek and perhaps some English. But she was no blue-stocking. She could play the clavecin and the tympanon and she could draw. And everyone agreed that she was as good as she was charming and accomplished.

Her home, Crassy, lies about twelve miles from Geneva

[1] Quotations in English from the correspondence between Gibbon and Mlle Curchod are translated from the original French. The series of twelve letters exchanged in 1757–9 will be found in *Gibbon's Journal*, Appendix I.

Other useful authorities are P. Kohler's *Madame de Staël et la Suisse*, pp. 6 *sqq.*; d'Haussonville's *Le Salon de Madame Necker*, imperfectly documented, however, and strongly against Gibbon; also *Meredith Read*, and J. M. Robertson's *Gibbon*, and *Gibbon's Journal*, pp. lxiv, *sqq.*

but just inside the Pays de Vaud, not, as Gibbon says, 'in the mountains' but on the sunny and fertile slopes which rise from the lake behind Rolle. She had been baptized there on 2nd June 1737, and had known no other home. Her father belonged to the country, but her mother was the daughter of a French refugee. She had some interest in property at Montélimar, and her maiden name, Albert de Nasse, indicates a claim to nobility, over which nevertheless some doubt has been cast. She is said, however, to have preferred to throw in her lot with the obscure man she loved rather than aim at a higher position to which her qualities would have entitled her. She passed some pride of family on to her daughter, who at different times of her life signed herself de Nasse or de Nasse-Necker, and is also said to have tried to establish the nobility of her father's family.

Such a prodigy could not be kept hid or confined to a country village. It was Curchod's practice to obtain assistance and variety in his work by inviting theological students from Lausanne or Geneva, a duty which the young men accepted the more willingly when the fame of the pretty daughter spread. Still more delightful was it when the daughter was entrusted with arranging the visits. Letters had to be exchanged, and thanks for the loan of the minister's horse were mingled with gallant compliments. Some verses even strayed into the magazines. Mlle Curchod had had a taste of coquetry before she came to Lausanne.

Solid facts are wanting for her coming there. We do not know whether she made occasional visits or prolonged stays or with whom she was living. Nor do we know when it was. Perhaps in 1756; more probably, I think, in 1757, when Gibbon saw her for the first time. It seems unlikely that she can have been there long without being noticed. For she was soon seen everywhere with admirers, and people said 'Voilà la belle

Curchod' as she passed with her escort. A professor singled her out as an example to all, and students pressed for the honour of dancing with her. She belonged of course to the Cité, and it is unlikely that she appeared among the young people of the Bourg at Voltaire's theatre.[1] But in her own realm she reigned supreme. She either founded or ruled a society called L'Académie des Eaux or de la Poudrière which met in the valley of the Flon—a sadly tarnished quarter now, but then a pretty sylvan scene which came up to the walls of the Cité beneath the windows of the Bailli's castle. The members called each other by high-flown names and debated with wit and sentiment, and Mlle Curchod, it is said, would be set on a throne of turf with her Celadons and Sylvandres around. Prominent among these was Deyverdun, who though belonging to the Bourg was a frequenter of the Cité, and through him, perhaps, Gibbon was brought on the scene. He fell an immediate and complete victim.

Some play has been made with the fact that the references to Suzanne in his Journal are scanty and terse and do not stand out from entries concerning M. de Traytorrens on conic sections or long dissertations on Virgil. This Journal, however, was not begun till 1761, and when Gibbon made these retrospective records his feelings, whatever they were, were very different from his state of mind in the summer of 1757. Even so, his first entry is eloquent in its brevity: 'June. I saw Mademoiselle Curchod. *Omnia vincit amor et nos cedamus amori.*' It was true. In August he was staying at Crassy. He was there again in October. He saw her at Rolle in November and spent six days at her home again in the

[1] Though not impossible, of course. But as an example of the rigidity with which these distinctions were maintained it may be remarked that a generation later Rosalie de Constant, an aunt of Benjamin, referred to Mme de Staël as 'cette parvenue'.

same month. In the following year he paid a last visit there at the beginning of March. He left for England on 11th April. This was not bad for one whose movements and expenses had been so carefully controlled for four years. And all the while never a word home either from Gibbon or Pavillard. Only from Gibbon a brief account of his visit to Geneva, a place omitted on his previous tour. A company of French actors were there, and it was natural to take the opportunity of passing through Crassy on the way. But he did not mention that.

Fuel which had not been spent on other affections was added to the consuming rapture of first love. Gibbon's attempts to placate and win his father cannot be considered as merely cupboard love. That would be against all common sense and experience. There is much to show that at all times of his life, in spite of many exasperations, Gibbon was genuinely fond of his father. But now his advances had been rejected, his letters were often unanswered; he had been made to suffer severely for an act which was not discreditable, however foolish.

At such a juncture this enchanting being appeared. Gibbon fell and began to weave an imaginary future with her. He forgot any calls of duty or ambition at home. His family did not seem to want him. He knew his own mind. He was committed for life to scholarship. He and she would lead a modest career in this land where, as Voltaire said, the refinement of Athens was linked with the frugality of Sparta, where there were no wars or politics or scrambling for places.[1] There was Deyverdun too; Gibbon's ties seemed to be all in the town which he had at first thought so ugly.[2] His infatuation is said to have gone beyond ordinary bounds.

[1] This is the impression from Gibbon's letters to S. C.

[2] Perhaps he thought it was ugly still. Voltaire said it was a 'très vilaine ville'. Gibbon always thought Lausanne was 'very plain'. See below, p. 309.

Julie de Bondeli, a Bernese lady in Suzanne Curchod's confidence, told a correspondent, four years later than this, that Gibbon had roamed the fields round Lausanne like a madman, compelling the peasants to agree at the sword's point that Mlle Curchod was the most beautiful person on earth. How should such a story arise? Fancy may play with the notion that there may have been some extravagant incident during one of those *pique-niques* up the ravine of the Flon. We can never know. It does not matter. The circulation of the story alone shows the impression that had gone abroad. Anyone might have believed it who saw Gibbon's first letter to Suzanne, written after a visit to Crassy.

The infatuated youth sits pen in hand eager to avail himself of the permission given to write. He gazes at the sky and bursts into loud laughter. One hundred and one hours eighteen minutes and thirty-three seconds of exile have already passed. As the chaise increased the distance between them he saw himself on his knees to her—. But he is not shocking her modesty by telling her all this. These are confidences between himself and his familiar spirit. We may smile at the lumbering progress of these old love affairs! It is a coach to a sports car. To conclude he has the honour to be 'avec une considération toute particulière', her very humble and very obedient servant.[1]

In her first letter Mlle Curchod shows herself cautious. She takes him up on his affectations and ignores the fervour. And who ever heard of a person

[1] Some of these letters are undated. The missing dates can be supplied with some certainty. Gibbon's first letter was written about 19th October 1757; S. C.'s reply is dated 24th October. Gibbon's next two letters were written about 1st December and in January 1758. Then come S. C.'s letter of 10th January and Gibbon's of 9th February, and an undated letter from S. C. which must also have been written in February. These are the seven surviving letters exchanged before Gibbon went home.

bursting into laughter over another's charms? After rallying him pretty thoroughly on his own ground of angels and familiars, she enjoins him earnestly not to come to Rolle. Her mother would not hear of it. Yet, as we have seen, visits were made and the following letters only show Gibbon deeper in the toils. His destruction had been completed by seeing her in her home, and the mutual devotion of herself and her parents. He had known so little of that, and there is an unmistakable seriousness in his words. Now, alone or in company, even in those studies for which he had earned the reputation of madness, he sees, hears and thinks of nothing but her. Since he has known her the world is changed. He reiterates his devotion. He may be boring. She may yawn over his letter if she will admit it would be better if many preachers were as convinced of what they say! An odd comparison to make to a parson's daughter.

Now he has become *Le fils du roi Moabdar* and she *Zimerline*. Still standing her ground, still keeping *Monsieur le savant, son chevalier cauteleux et tranquille*, in suspense, she wrote to him in January, concluding with an elaborately allegorical allusion to some illness, 'une maladie assez fâcheuse. Ma chère mère en a été fort chagrine, et ma santé ne me paroît pas encore bien affermie'.

Incredibly this pathetic confession drew no reply! Suzanne was not too impatient. She let a month nearly slip away and then wrote again. She drew some thunder and worse. The explanation was simple. Gibbon had been away for a month at Fribourg for La fête des trois Rois, and then at Berne.[1] She must have written pretty

[1] In his letter Gibbon says he was away from 4th January to 3rd February. In his Journal (p. 6), under 23rd January, he says he witnessed *Alzire* at Mon Repos. The date in the Journal, written in 1761, is not to be trusted. There is no reason to suppose he was deceiving her.

sharply, for Gibbon complained not only that he was treated as 'le plus lâche des hommes', but a more suspicious nature could infer that she was waiting for a declaration of indifference, would be annoyed if she did not get it! This is said at the risk of offending. 'Mais vous me demandez de la sincérité et je n'ai pas voulu quitter le ton de la nature pour celui de l'affectation.'

'How could you doubt', he continues, 'for an instant my love and fidelity? Have you not read the depths of my soul a hundred times? Have you not seen a passion as pure as it was living? Have you not realised that your image would hold for ever the first place in this heart which you are now despising, and that, in the midst of pleasure, honours and riches, without you I should enjoy nothing?

'While you were giving rein to your suspicions fortune was working for me, I dare not say for us. I found a letter waiting for me from my father. He allows me to return to England and I hasten there with the first breath of spring. It is true that by a fate which is only mine I see a storm rising in the midst of calm. My father's letter is so tender and affectionate. He appears so anxious to see me again. He dilates with such pride on the plans he has formed for me, that I see the birth of a crowd of obstacles to my happiness quite different in every way from those of inequality of fortune, which were the only ones in my mind before.

'The condition which the noblest principles led you to require and which the tenderest motive made me accept gladly, that of making my abode in this country, will scarcely be listened to by a father to whose affection and ambition it will be equally a blow. Yet I do not despair of overcoming it. Love will make me eloquent. He will be anxious for my happiness and if he is he will not dream of separating me from you. My philosophy, let us say rather, my temperament renders me indifferent to wealth. Honours are nothing for the man who is not ambitious. If I know myself, I have never felt the touch of this baleful passion. The love of study was my sole passion up to the time when you made me realise that the heart has its needs as well as the mind, and that they consist in mutual love. I have learnt to love, you did not forbid me to hope. What happier fate for me than to see the time come when I could tell you every moment how much I love you and hear you say sometimes that I was not loving in vain.'[1]

'I have a little space. I have tried to fill it with something a little less serious. Mais mon cœur est trop serré. Je ne puis que vous répéter que je suis et serai toujours avec une considération toute particulière,

'Mademoiselle

'Votre très humble et très obéissant serviteur

'E. Gibbon

'Lausanne, 9 février.'

What sort of a lover was he, not to have let her know he was going away to Fribourg? Not to write when he and his friends decided to go on to Berne? It is easy to pick over the bones of a dead correspondence endlessly. It may be no excuse to say that Gibbon was never a prompt or ready letter-writer or to remind an age that sends off postcards and telegrams at every turn, and very often little else, that in those days correspondence was expensive and slow, and a letter from a young man to his lady an occasion. More important is it to remember that the moderate and equable flow of eighteenth-century expressions does not necessarily connote coldness or shallowness of feeling. They were accustomed to digest and arrange their emotions before committing them to paper. We, on the contrary, expect the signs of spontaneity and unpremeditated confidences as guarantees of sincerity. There must be heat and noise and colour. Not too much logic, but sparks must be struck at all costs.

If Gibbon's is not the language of sincerity, what is? And yet and yet. But we know too much, and so perhaps we think that this little clash first sounded an alarm in an inner ear. And when that happens, let the lover protest as he may, yet ultimately he cannot lie.

[1] 'Que je n'aimais pas une ingrate.'

Did the inner ear catch a whisper that freedom, that first of blessings, was in danger, that the girl was over-possessive? 'Le plus lâche des hommes': was there not a warning in this reproach?

Suzanne Curchod saw nothing to suspect. Her answer was humble and wise. She would not pretend that she was not anxious to have his letter and the assurance of his fidelity. She would not have hesitated to let him give up the position that might be his for her sake, because she was confident that he would never regret the step. To abandon his duty to his father—'un père si tendre!'—was another matter, and he must know from her own example that she would never lend herself to such a course.

She gave him the route of escape and he took it, it may be said. But again we must not forget the different position that filial obligations held in the lives of young lovers in those days. And there was *amour-propre* too. If these obligations were disregarded—as they were of course on occasions—it was none the less felt that something monstrous had been done. All honour to Mlle Curchod and no discredit to Gibbon if both were prepared to put their duty in the forefront of their deliberations.

There is the pathos of ingenuousness however in their calculations upon their seniors' lives. Suzanne may not have known Mr Gibbon's actual age; Gibbon himself may not have known; but she speaks of him as an old man, even of bringing his white hairs in sorrow to the grave! Gibbon could never tell him at his age that he was going to live abroad. Increase the distance to compensate the speed of travelling, but what son of twenty nowadays is going to tell a father of fifty-one that so long as he lives he will not go to live so far away as India? With this idea of Mr Gibbon's age and imminent dissolution Mlle Curchod could even suggest later that Gibbon should meanwhile visit her in Switzerland every other year!

Complete sincerity and unworldliness on both sides is surely the impression to be taken from this story at this point. Not only is there no wavering apparent in Gibbon but it is untrue to say that Suzanne was not seriously interested in him at this time.[1]

In testimony of the liveliness if not the depth of her interest is the portrait of Gibbon which she drew probably in the earlier stage of their acquaintance. She praises his hair, his hands and fine bearing. She had never seen so intellectual or remarkable a countenance. So full and varied in its expression that one could hardly tire of watching and noting its changes. She records too, and it is significant, that he enforced all that he said with appropriate gestures. He knew what was due to women and his manners were easy without being familiar. A moderate dancer. His wit varied enormously.[2] The short sketch breaks off abruptly, as though, as d'Haussonville suggests, the artist could not trust herself on paper any further.

Meanwhile there are no more letters surviving. On 5th March Gibbon came back from a last visit to Crassy. We do not know at all what the young lovers planned in the old white house with the green shutters, what the parents said, or what hopes Mlle Curchod had of a favourable issue to this struggle between love and duty with this unknown father. Did Gibbon carry it off bravely, saying that love would make him eloquent once more?

The time was now slipping away. His thoughts were

[1] It is sometimes said, *e.g.* by Meredith Read and J. M. Robertson, that it was only after the publication of Gibbon's *Essai* with the notice it got and the promise of further distinction that Mlle Curchod became anxious to marry him. That seems to me quite untenable.

[2] The French text is quoted in *Gibbon's Journal*, p. lxvii, from d'Haussonville, *op. cit.* i. 36.

turned towards his country and family, and the means of reaching them. Although the Seven Years' War was in progress, Gibbon rejected the alternative circuitous route through Germany and determined to travel through France disguised as a Swiss officer in the Dutch service. The risk of detection was small; for his French was perfect. Yet it was an act of hardihood which, as he reflected in later years, might have had serious consequences.

Armed with a passport in the name of his friend Deyverdun and arrayed in his Dutch regimentals he set out in a hired coach with two other travellers and was accompanied as far as Toigne in Franche Comté, where they 'made a debauch of it'.[1] From thence by uneventful stages the travellers passed through France and Flanders. At Maestricht Gibbon dined with the officers of the Garrison and visited M. de Beaufort, an authority on Roman history. He landed at Harwich about four in the afternoon, having been out of England four years ten months and fifteen days, and lay at Colchester. Did the young lover once more reckon up as well the days, hours and minutes of his exile?

He had landed on the 4th May 1758. The next day 'I got to London about noon, went immediately to Mrs Porten's. Heard of my father in the evening and saw him and Mrs. Gibbon in Charles Street, St. James's Square.'

Three days later he came of age.[2] It was an occasion of more satisfaction to his father than to himself. Mr Gibbon's 'sickly finances' had increased his anxiety for his son's return. 'The priests and the altar had been prepared, and the victim was unconscious of the im-

[1] *Gibbon's Journal*, pp. 7-8.

[2] *Murray*, pp. 155-6. After the reform of the calendar Gibbon's birthday fell on 8th May, N.S. The loss of eleven days in 1752 had caused the young chronologist some surprise. *Murray*, p. 79.

pending stroke.' The young man—his submission could not be but 'blind and almost involuntary'—was induced to consent to the cutting off of the entail of his grandfather's will. Some legal fictions were performed and the immediate consequence was that the father was able to raise by a mortgage on the Putney estate a badly needed ten thousand pounds, while a life annuity of three hundred a year was settled on the son.

The elderly memoirist looked back on this transaction without rancour. Something better might have been done for him perhaps. Even in his exile he had been asking for £200 a year. But he had done the right thing in acquiescing. Three hundred pounds a year—the amount of the pension given to Dr. Johnson in 1762—was by no means equal 'to the style of a young Englishman of fashion in the most wealthy Metropolis of Europe'. But the young man had no taste for extravagant pleasures and his long exile had cut him off from acquaintances who would have led him into them. On the whole he was content. But three hundred a year would have been no sum to marry on in England. It would have meant the most modest of establishments in the Pays de Vaud. He could only expect a more liberal arrangement if his bride was approved, if not chosen, by the family.

Half a stranger in his own country, palpably a little stiff with his English, not quite knowing whether to laugh or cry over the provisions made by his father, still in the first apprehensions of making contact with his new mother—here was slippery ground for a young lover to open his intentions on.

He bided his time not unwisely. He had been received with every mark of affection by Mrs Gibbon as well as by his father. When he felt the time was ripe, he told his secret. But the unfamiliar atmosphere of domestic harmony in which he felt at last able to open his case must have been prejudicial to his resolution. Let his letter to Suzanne tell the story:

'I cannot begin. Yet I must. I take up my pen, I put it down, I take it up again. You realise by this beginning what I am going to say. Spare me the rest. Yes, I must give you up for-ever. The decree is passed, my heart groans over it, but before my duty, everything must be silent.

'Arrived in England, my inclinations and interest alike coun-selled me to win my father's affection and dispel the clouds which had separated me from it for some time. I can boast of having succeeded. All his behaviour, the most delicate atten-tions, the most solid kindnesses have convinced me of it. I seized the moment when he was assuring me that all his thoughts were bent on making me happy to ask his permission to offer myself to the woman with whom every country and every state would be equally agreeable, and without whom they would all be a burden. This was his answer: "Marry your *foreigner*, you are independent. But before you do so remember that you are a son and an Englishman." He then expatiated on the cruelty of leaving him and of sending him to the grave before his time, on the baseness of trampling on everything that I owed to my country. I went to my room, stayed there two hours; I will not attempt to describe my condition to you; I came out again to tell my father that for him I sacrificed all the happiness of my life.

'May you be happier than I can ever hope to be. That will always be my prayer, it will even be my consolation. To think that I can only contribute to it by my prayers. I tremble to learn your fate, yet do not leave me in ignorance. It will be a very cruel moment for me. Assure Monsieur and Madame Curchod of my respect, my esteem and my regrets. I shall always recall Mademoiselle Curchod as the most respectable and charming of women. May she not entirely forget a man who did not deserve the despair of which he is the prey.

'Good-bye; this letter must appear to you strange in every way, it is the image of my soul.

'I wrote to you twice on the journey, at a village in Lorraine, from Maestricht, and once from London; you have not received them; I do not know if I should hope that this one will reach you. I have the honour to be with feelings which are the torture of my life, and a regard which nothing can change,

'Mademoiselle

'Your very humble and very obedient servant,

'E. Gibbon

'Buriton, 24 *août* 1758.'[1]

Those who thought that Suzanne Curchod was not seriously attached to Gibbon at this time had not read her answer to this letter. The distress is real to the point of incoherence. Yet in her passion the writer seems to waver between accepting her lover's renunciation and a desperate hope of holding him:

> 'The feeling I had for you', she says, 'was so pure, it was a union of virtue and affection, but a very tender affection. You are the only man for whom I have shed tears, the only one whose loss has torn sobs from me and how many others appear uninteresting compared with the only one——'

She breaks off. A little scornfully she tells him, 'You sacrificed to duty with a firmness that might afford an example', forgetting that a few months before they had been mutually pointing the way to that altar. She would have been ready to follow him anywhere, and could he not have proposed to his father to leave her in Switzerland during her father's life, visiting her there every other year? 'That, it seems to me, would not have conflicted with your status as *a son and an Englishman*.' She closes this letter with a further reproach which others have not missed:

[1] d'Haussonville, *Le Salon de Madame Necker*, i. 58, who first printed this letter, gives the year 1762, and from that he and others built on the idea that Gibbon had kept Mlle Curchod in the belief that they were engaged for four years. But internal evidence and comparison with the rest of the correspondence show that this letter must have been written in 1758. Mlle Curchod was at any rate ready to face a long engagement, as her letter of 7th September 1758 shows.

What appears to be the letter written from Bayonne in Lorraine is in the Pierpont Morgan Library.

'In two hours you made up your mind, I reflected on this part of your letter. Ah! how my dear parents would like me to have made my decision as promptly.'

What decision? Apparently about another offer to which she had already made an obscure, perhaps purposely tantalising reference. If this and a hint about her health were designed to rouse her lover's jealousy and pity, need we refuse to believe in the genuineness of her feelings?

Time passed with no reply to this letter, and her feelings were beginning to cool when she heard from Mrs Gibbon that her letter had been intercepted, with the insinuation that Gibbon was in connivance. This idea, after a momentary entertainment, she indignantly rejects. Her future is not yet decided, and once more she ventures to repeat her proposal of the occasional visits. But if Mr Gibbon remained inflexible she would not ask the son to forsake his duty. For herself she has no reproaches on the score of duty. Only her heart could be dissatisfied. But her actions had been founded on virtue and feeling, and whatever the consequences hereafter she would never abandon these two guides.

The date of this last letter is uncertain, but Gibbon's reply was written on 23rd February 1759.[1] He indignantly repudiated any part in his stepmother's proceedings, and complained that he had been long in ignorance of Suzanne's state. 'These parents say that they only desire our happiness. They believe it themselves.' He reiterates his constancy. Absence has only convinced him of his attachment, and he compares the rich but loveless matches of London with the simplicity of Crassy, where he had passed the sweetest moments of his life. He recalls an incident at Crassy which has the

[1] A letter from Suzanne has probably been lost. Gibbon appears to quote a phrase, 'Vos sentiments ne s'éteindront qu'après les miens', which does not occur in the extant letters.

stamp of truth, and he must have been heartless indeed if in reminding her of it his own feelings were not genuine.

> '*Pénétré d'amour*,' he writes and underlines the words, '*je vous jurois un attachement à l'épreuve du temps*; you did not turn away your eyes and I thought I read in them your affection and my happiness. My emotion was noticed. They rallied me for it. My heart was too agitated to answer. I made some excuse and ran to my room.'

But once more 'il faut céder à la nécessité et le devoir en est un pour les âmes bien nées'. As soon as he had got her letter he had left for Buriton and pleaded once more with his father, painting her picture in the brightest colours and insisting that this was no passing fancy, a spark that the first object had kindled, '*mais une passion durable fondée sur la Connaissance et épurée par la Vertu*'. He suggested a plan which would have removed all the difficulties. All was in vain. Mr Gibbon with his knowledge of the world knew that lovers exaggerated. Besides the lady had no fortune, and his son must have a considerable establishment. 'Granted', continued he, so Gibbon reports him, in calm but determined tones,—

> 'Granted that Mademoiselle Curchod were all that you depict and her fortune were worthy of her,—she is a Foreigner. You have already only too much inclination for foreign ways. You no longer know the language of your own country. Mademoiselle Curchod would find little to please her in England. She would use her influence to get you away. That would be natural. But what a misfortune for me, what a crime for you. I cannot contemplate it without a shudder. Make up your mind and try to forget about it, for nothing will make me consent to this alliance.'
>
> '*There are moments, Mademoiselle, when this refusal makes me think that I owe him nothing more and that free from every obligation I can try to find my happiness cost what it may to him or me.* You would despise me if I did not add that these moments are

not very frequent or long. *To live in the expectation of his death would be another way: at least we should not lose hope.* But what a hope. That of a father's death. *Besides I fear nothing for myself, but everything gives me uneasiness on your account. If my Father survived me, what a plight would be yours!*

'You realise where these sad reflexions end. *Yet I keep on putting off the fatal moment.* To forget you, to forget at least the lover to know only the friend. To marry another woman. To invite you to follow my example. What ideas. They frighten me. I would rather not look at them. I fear you may not be able to make this effort. I fear that you may. Alas, shall I be able to myself?'

In the final letter of this period Suzanne rings down the curtain on this drama with quiet and dignified resignation. She had been offended by the postscript of Gibbon's last letter in which he had made an offer to discontinue their correspondence, although he himself had disclaimed any such desire and had furnished her with a safe address in the Strand. But she would like to have news.

'Quels sont vos progrès litteraires? seriez vous attiré par l'ambition? favorisé par la tendresse? Marié? ou prêt à l'être? Will the chains be of flowers or solid gold? No evasions in this respect for I wish to know all. If it is true that I am still in love, it is with an affectionate eager, tender lover whom I had before. A pure fantasy, which exists no more except in my memory. My memory is tenacious when my heart has engraved upon it: "Votre soumission est juste, elle mérite mon estime, et mes éloges." '

One more word she had to say on their romance, and then it was to disappear from their future correspondence. She admitted she had let him know that there was another suitor, she had even enjoyed tantalising him. For several reasons she had resisted the repeated offers of M. de——.[1] Perhaps now she would be more ready to listen to him. She also told him there were

[1] No doubt M. de Montplaisir. See below, pp. 139 and 146–7.

hopes of recovering her mother's property in France. That would render them fairly well off in Switzerland. She seemed anxious to let him know that she could be independent.

There the correspondence ends until Gibbon's return to Lausanne in 1763, with the exception of a letter sent to Mlle Curchod with a copy of Gibbon's first book.

What might strike a modern lover in these letters is the lack of intimacy displayed on both sides. The feeling is undoubted, but the approach sometimes makes one imagine that the letters were exchanged by sympathetic attorneys to the Court of Love rather than by the principals. Or if one compares these letters to flowers, withered long ago, which one handles with careful questioning, they seem to be not merely brittle and scentless but of some species which grows no longer among us.

It does not seem that Mlle Curchod ever doubted the sincerity and even fervour of Gibbon's attachment. We may think he yielded to circumstances too easily. But what else could he do? Perhaps he did himself an injustice in that fatal mention of the two hours. But two hours' thought with him were not the hours of ordinary people. And even then, as we see by his later letter, he did not give up the struggle. But he had a clear mind, and a clear mind is apt to lose the sympathy that comes to more distressful doubts and suspenses. Three hundred a year—his father—possibly outliving his son—his obligations at home not to be denied—Putney and mortgages, the new-found retreat of Buriton—his books—study, peace, freedom. The argument possibly ran loosely into the pleasant sensation of restoration to his family and rightful position artfully fostered by his father and stepmother.

It will not do either to apply the modern romantic and ethical notions. We are far here from the day when young couples settle in a three-roomed flat on the hire purchase system and their expectations. And even granting the rudiments of such notions, we must admit that neither by his position, nor his upbringing, nor his physique could he hope—to put it briefly—to get a job.

Great heat and great pressure are said to go to the making of crystals, and such was the process through which Gibbon passed before this tale of youthful ardour and helplessness crystallised into the immortal 'I sighed as a lover, I obeyed as a son'.

Chapter 7

BURITON AND BOND STREET

1758–1760

LOVE was fighting a losing battle in which the opposing forces of family affection, engrossing occupation and English comfort were insidiously gaining strength every day. It is easy to believe that Mr and Mrs Gibbon played their part with skill. They had every right. In spite of divergence of tastes Gibbon got on well with his father, and in his stepmother he found nothing of what a natural suspicion and the wisdom of literature had led him to expect. Virgil's line about the *iniusta noverca* was running in his head as he went to meet her. But his first reserve broke down before her kindly welcome and efforts to please him. He discovered that this was not merely a surface smoothness but that she was a woman of 'warm and exquisite sensibility'. He admired her good sense and good management. A woman can feed other brutes than her husband, and Gibbon was not slow to compare her household with Mme Pavillard's.[1]

Esteem rapidly grew into a very real affection. The need for craft or dissimulation went. Gibbon may have been too obviously diplomatic—though it is difficult to

[1] Dorothea Patton was about 40 when she married. Her father, David Patton, died at Colne Engain, Essex, in 1746. He had also lived at Long Melford, Suffolk; but there is reason to believe he was Scottish. Gibbon says she had a moderate property, but her inheritance seems to have been a debt which brought new worries to her husband (Brit. Mus. 11907, dd. 25 (2)). Her brother Will also made his home at Buriton till his death in 1772.

blame him—in the first messages which he sent her from Lausanne. But his sincerity is as undoubted as it is warm when three years later he writes for his own eyes alone, 'I can't express the pleasure I had at seeing her, I love her as a companion, a friend and a mother'.[1]

Thus the summer passed away happily at Buriton in the sunshine of family harmony. In six weeks from the beginning of July he was hard at work on his *Essai*, and on the 24th August, the day he wrote the fateful letter to Suzanne, he records—it is the only record for that day—that he gave it to a French prisoner at Petersfield to copy.

For the interests of sport and farming which engaged his father, Gibbon pretended to no inclination or aptitude. He was content that the farm should supply the kitchen. This indifference is strange when one considers how he studied and admired Buffon, and remembers the notes concerning both animal and vegetable nature which abound in *The Decline and Fall*. But he seldom rode and still more seldom shot. A short stroll soon satisfied him, and he turned to his books or meditations without regret after watching his father ride off on his hunter for a meet of the Duke of Richmond's hounds. If a hunting saddle ordered in July 1758 was meant for him, his father was to be sadly disappointed, and his neighbours, ready to welcome the heir of Buriton with a day's sport, may well have cast up their eyes at the squire's Frenchified son. To what perhaps testy note or message was the following reply written?—

'BERITON, *Nov.* 16, 1758

'SIR,

'As I am extremely well convinced of your politeness, and your readiness to grant your neighbours any reasonable liberty with regard to country sports, so I should be very sorry if either myself or my servants had taken any improper ones.

[1] *Gibbon's Journal*, p. 72.

'I am no sportsman, Sir, and was as much tempted this morning by the beauty of the day and the pleasure of the ride as by the hopes of any sport. I went out, and neither acquainted with the bounds of the manors nor your request to the neighbouring gentlemen, could only follow my groom where he led me. I quitted your manor the instant I received your message, without having killed anything in it. I assure you that you shall never have again the same subject of complaint. With regard to the liberty you are so good as to grant me for other sports, I return you my most humble thanks, but shall not make much use of it, as there are still in my father's manor more game than would satisfy so moderate a sportsman as myself.

'My father would be extremely angry if his servants had destroyed any of your game; but they all assure him they have killed no one hare upon your liberties. As to pheasants, they have only killed one this season, and that in Inwood copse.

'I am
'Sir,
'Your obedient humble servant

'E. GIBBON, Junior'[1]

For the business of a country gentleman he had no more liking. But in his father's company he attended various balls, assemblies and race meetings. It must have been with the eyes of a long-lost Roman rather than those of a prospective squire. The colour and noise of Stockbridge races, and how gay and colourful an eighteenth-century race meeting must have been, served only to turn his thoughts to Olympia and the Circus Maximus.

It was in the spring and summer of 1759 that most of these excursions took place. There were constant journeys to Winchester and Alton upon the Militia business, and on 12th June Gibbon received his commission of Captain, little thinking what inroads on his time were to be made. In the same autumn there was a county election. Gibbon and his father supported

[1] *Notes and Queries*, 1st Ser., ix. p. 511, 1854, contributed by E. G. F. S.

Simeon Stuart, respectively subscribing £25 and £100 for him. They constantly attended the meetings and went canvassing at Waltham, Portsmouth and Gosport.

In the fifteen months out of two years spent at Buriton before the Militia was embodied Gibbon was for the most part left to spend his time as he chose. He occupied a room on the first floor. The library was on the same floor. Here was a mixed collection of books, obsolete political and theological tracts, some valuable editions of the Classics and Fathers which had been chosen and left by Law,[1] with some occasional later additions. He was left to dispose or add to this collection as he liked, and from this modest beginning was built up a library which he called the best comfort of his life at home or abroad. With a twenty pound bank note he purchased with unforgettable elation the twenty volumes of the publications of the *Académie des Inscriptions*, a collection of reviews and discussions which ranged over ancient and modern history and travel and which Sainte-Beuve described with truth as 'la patrie intellectuelle de Gibbon.' This was a big sum to take out of his allowance. Perhaps he received it from his father, whom he relates to have supplemented his allowance by occasionally discharging his arrears with the bookseller. But Gibbon was never a reckless or ostentatious buyer of books. Every volume was scrutinised before it was purchased, just as in reading them he was accustomed first to review what he already knew or believed of the subject before committing himself to a perusal. In fact in all his labours Gibbon kept an account, and balanced the profits and losses of his mind with an exactitude which seems to have derived, with a difference, from his grandfather's counting-house. Books were primarily things to use. But Gibbon was by no means insensible to

[1] They must have been brought down from Putney. It does not appear, I think, that either Law or Gibbon's grandfather ever lived at Buriton.

their possible beauty. It was a sense that grew, possibly, with ripe mastery of knowledge. A note written in the last summer of his life records:

> 'as the eye is the organ of fancy I read Homer with more pleasure in the Glasgow folio. Through that fine medium the poet's sense appears more beautiful and transparent. Bishop Louth has said that he could discover only one error in that accurate edition— Yet how could a man of taste read Homer with such literal attention?'[1]

Nevertheless Gibbon's early studies of the classics had been extremely minute and literal. He acquired from the editors whom he used the zeal for emendation which is so fascinating and often so futile, and the learned correspondence which he had entered into at Lausanne with Professors Breitinger and Gesner was taken up with corrections of Livy and Justin, which he defended somewhat obstinately against their superior learning and experience.[2] So too at Buriton in the midst of the first distractions of the Militia meetings he was driven by a difficult passage in Livy through 'the dry and dark treatises of Greaves Arbuthnot, Hooper, Bernard, Eissenschmidt, Gronovius, La Barre, Freret, etc.' Unflaggingly he would make the most searching calculations upon the ancient weights and measures, currencies or calendars. It is unlikely that he would have been lost for ever in these elaborate pedantries. They were but foundations, very solid ones, for a superstructure which was as yet not conceived.

But in this summer of 1759 his imagination was kindled afresh by a new turn in his course of reading. On Mallet's advice he had sought to recover the purity of English idiom. Swift and Addison had been wisely

[1] *Misc. Wks.* v. p. 583.

[2] One of his suggestions, 'otio' for 'odio' in Livy, is now universally accepted. It has MS. authority. It was not a difficult one to make, but Gibbon deserves the credit of having been apparently the first to see it. Livy, xxx. 44.

and successfully prescribed. 'The favourite companions of my leisure were our English writers since the Revolution; they breathe the spirit of reason and liberty.' From them it was a natural and exhilarating step to the most conspicuous of the moderns. The historical writings of Robertson and Hume filled him with a novel delight and sowed the first ambition of following these writers, whose achievements nevertheless he despaired of equalling.

With such ferments in his mind he found the day all too short and could become impatient with the wasteful ways of country house life, the prolonged meals, the morning dalliance in Mrs Gibbon's dressing-room, his father's leisurely perusal and discussion of the newspapers, the calls of idle but important neighbours—they might appear at half-past eight for breakfast and spend the day[1]—above all, those nights of full moon when the handsome set of bays or greys were brought from the farm, and the Gibbon family rumbled off in the landau-and-six to dine with some Hampshire Huddleston Fuddleston. Yet these interruptions were salutary or he might have worn himself out with incessant study, another Casaubon, and one of these sacrifices to domestic routine, such are the mysteries of Providence, afforded if not the seed yet the favourable soil to a further development of his intellect.

The church of Buriton lies not many yards from the front of the manor house. The scene can be little changed since his day. The ground drops down from the house to a pond shaded with gracious trees; on the other side are the old rectory and the church, whose square tower is at least unchanged. Across this rural English scene Gibbon accompanied his father and stepmother Sunday by Sunday not once only but usually twice. He was confronted week by week with religion. In London

[1] *Gibbon's Journal*, p. 89.

or abroad he might have gone on in unquestioning indifference about a thing which he never encountered. Here there was no escape. The time had to be spent. It must be turned to profit. In the family pew he deposited copies of the Old and New Testament in Greek with which he followed the lessons, Gospels and Epistles, at first, seemingly, with the idea only of improving his Greek. But what he read was apt to set him thinking furiously for the rest of the service. Perhaps Mr Barton's sermons were dull—Gibbon appears at different times of his life as a keen amateur of sermons —possibly they added new problems. The service over, he was eager to get back to the house through the groups of tenantry and villagers standing to pay their respects to the 'Maijer and the Captin', and there to consult learned divines who only left him still worse confounded. 'Since my escape from Popery I had humbly acquiesced in the common creed of the Protestant Churches.' Now he made a regular trial of it, reading Grotius 'On the truth of the Christian Religion' and finding that it was not at all true. Supernatural religion collapsed on 'the brittle basis of human testimony', and the only conclusion was 'that the faith as well as the virtue of a Christian must be formed and fortified by the inspiration of Grace'.[1]

Once again it may be noted how tentative was Gibbon's advance. His destructive criticism worked intensively within a limited area. He was concerned with the historical value of certain narratives rather than with the supporting philosophical or theological framework. He could still write quite naturally in 1761 of 'our Creator' and His works, and at the end of the same paper, which is so instructive in showing how he held the balance between strict concentration and elasticity of method, occur these significant words, 'I shall con-

[1] *Murray*, pp. 249-50.

tinue to search for the truth, though hitherto I have found nothing but probability'.[1] Little service has been done to Gibbon by trying to show that at the end of his life he went back on the position that he had reached earlier, but equally injudicious and unhistorical is this notion that he emerged Minerva-like from the brow of contemporary orthodoxy, as brightly and completely agnostic as the latest adherent of the Rationalist Press Association.

The charm of this even comfortable existence was only enhanced by two winters spent in London. It would be natural for the young man to be eager for such an experience; it would be natural for his father to encourage him to enter society and so to acquire more ties with his native country. Such however was not the consequence. Mr Gibbon had lost his place in society and his son had not sufficient address and energy to make his own way, especially on the moderate allowance which he enjoyed.

He lodged at one time in New Bond Street over a draper's, where he had three rooms on the first floor for a guinea and a half a week, and 'a very handsome chair for twenty-seven shillings'. But money soon ran short and his father, not for the last time, proved unpunctual with his remittances. Gibbon wrote to his stepmother that he was really distressed for money: 'I have hardly a guinea left, and you know the unavoidable expences of London'. He had vainly tried to borrow of his aunt and his father's lawyer. Could she not risk sending a bank note by the Hastings Post? 'For upon my word I shall hardly know what to do in three or four days.' All the same he was just off to the theatre to see Garrick play Sir John Brute in *The Provoked Wife*. Playgoing was his greatest satisfaction at this time. He was thus much like his father in his inability to conceive of more than

[1] *Misc. Wks.* v. p. 209. *Extraits Raisonnés de mes Lectures,* written at Dover, 14th March 1761.

one mode of life in town. Each learned his lesson in turn and retreated finally, the one to Buriton, the other to Lausanne. It was the way of their age and class and no one could have suggested an alternative.

'While coaches were rattling through Bond Street, I have passed many a solitary evening in my lodging with my books.' But he could read them better at Buriton. It must have been disappointing. Few people like not being invited to the party, least of all this young man who four years later was to complain that the Duc de Nivernois treated him more as a man of letters than a man of fashion.[1]

The few letters that remain of this first winter reveal him still not quite at ease with his father or the world. He is still most anxious to please the former, apologises for not having written to Mrs Gibbon, assures his father that he only keeps such company as he would approve. His manner is rather forced and heavy. He retails gossip of society in which he had so little part. 'Sir George Elkin, a man of family and fortune, has married Miss Roach, a woman of the town. Everybody pities him.' A Ciceronian sententiousness comes in. 'My unfashionable politicks are that a war can hardly be a good one, and a peace hardly a bad one.'

It is rather of Mrs Porten at Westminster with her houseful of measles, and of supping with her off a Buriton leveret, and of Mme Celesia receiving him 'in a dirty white linnen gown, no rufles', that he wrote home, and his Memoirs sum up less graciously that he went to 'some dull family parties, to some old Tories of the Cocoa-tree and to some casual connections such as my taste and esteem would never have selected'. There was always a touch of provincialism about Gibbon, and he was often most at home among rather humdrum people.

In such circumstances he often sighed for Lausanne,

[1] *Gibbon's Journal*, p. 202.

EDWARD GIBBON

After a pen drawing by Lady Diana Beauclerk

and the one house in London which appealed to him was Lady Hervey's, in which was to be found the nearest approach to a Parisian salon, where 'there is no card-playing, but very good company and very good conversation'.

It was to David Mallet, his old Putney friend, or to his daughter Mme Celesia, that he owed his introduction here. Through Mme Celesia also he was to meet 'the great David Hume'. He never mentions whether he did, and probably their acquaintance must be assigned to a later date. Through Mallet also he became acquainted with Garrick, either now or a little later. In 1762 when Mallet's *Elvira* was to be produced, he took Gibbon to breakfast with Garrick and thence to a rehearsal in the green-room. Earlier in the same year, when Gibbon had a mind to be made a brigade-major, Mallet promised to get Mr Charles Howard to speak to Lord Effingham about it. It is Mallet again who greets Gibbon on his entrance at the Smyrna Coffee House. There was no end to the usefulness of this dapper insinuating deist.

In this way he passed the winter from the middle of December 1758 to the following February, and again from the 20th November to the end of April 1760. Of this second winter in town there are no details beyond a record in his Journal that he learnt Italian. He was away for a longer period and perhaps felt more at home. But we may believe he was equally glad when the time came to return to Buriton and the simple company which he had learned to value so much.

A young scholar desires to see himself in print. In 1757 Gibbon had sent a critical article to Professor Breitinger which, in spite of being written in French instead of Latin, would have been put into the *Museum Helveticum* had not that journal been meanwhile suspended. The next venture was begun in March 1758 immediately after the last visit to Crassy, and it is more probable that the stimulus of love lent the writer additional energy than that the commencement at such a date should point to an incomplete devotion.

Fifteen chapters—we should call them paragraphs—had been written before Gibbon left Switzerland, and it was in the quietude of Buriton that *L'Essai sur l'Étude de la Littérature* was continued in July and provisionally finished in February 1759.

It was shown to Dr. Maty of the British Museum, a Dutchman, who was probably more conversant with continental thought than anyone else in London. He criticised and encouraged. But the work was laid aside for two years. The Militia had intervened.

In the spring of 1761, however, Gibbon revised it for the press and added a considerable portion. This was in deference to his father. The war was apparently ending and the time was ripe for a publication which might help towards a diplomatic appointment such as Gibbon himself would have welcomed.

Maty and Mallet in London helped to see the Captain's work through the press. In return for a number of copies, most of which went to prominent people whom Mr Gibbon considered his friends, the profits or losses were left to the bookseller Becket. Maty, without telling Gibbon, contributed an introductory letter addressed to him. In it he unjustifiably went out of his way to sneer at Johnson, an old enemy. Warning the young author of his temerity in composing in French, he says, 'le vieux Caton frémit et dans son Club Antigallican vous dénonce, le punch à la main, un ennemi de la patrie'. Maty's prophecy was to be fulfilled, though on different grounds.

The book excited some interest among Lady Hervey's circle and Mallet sent him a letter containing the Comte de Caylus's appreciation, and later in the year it was thought worth while to have an English version made. It was very badly done.

In this little work Gibbon made an outlet for himself something like that which undergraduates now find in the prize essay. It would be unfair to compare Gibbon's effort with such competent performances, which have had all the advantages of systematic training and direction. His own criticism of his work remains just. A lack of arrangement and the introduction of irrelevant matter prevented the orderly presentation of his chosen theme. There was an excessive and even specious display of erudition, and not infrequently a sententious obscurity, born of a desire to play the oracle in the manner of Montesquieu.

The choice of French also was a mark of youthful and rather perverse vanity. To use a foreign language with mastery had been a seduction in every age—the parallel of Cicero composing his memoirs in Greek and anxious for their fame was significant—but while other nations, the Germans especially, had 'seized the opportunity of speaking to Europe in this common dialect', Englishmen had been so backward and insular that after allowing for what Temple and Bolingbroke, Chesterfield and Hamilton had written, the young exile felt that it might be accorded to him to say *Primus ego in patriam* as being the first Englishman to domesticate French in the manner of Leibnitz or King Frederick. It was a foible which persisted for some years and was no doubt strengthened by the reception which he deservedly got in Paris in 1763.

The subject chosen was equally naturally the reaction of his predilections to the current atmosphere of French intellectual life. In the early eighteenth century there was a popular appetite for natural science and its possibilities contributed to the intellectual optimism of the time. Men whose talents lay in other fields were tempted to change their allegiances. Montesquieu even had projected a physical history of the earth. The name of savant was becoming appropriated to scientists, and scholars of the older learning were termed contemptuously *Érudits*. It was, Gibbon records, especially d'Alembert's *Discours préliminaire à l'Encyclopédie* which provoked him to champion the cause of ancient literature as a worthy field in which all the faculties of the mind could be fully and usefully expended. The scholar was no mere compiler of facts. All facts were precious, even if their immediate significance or use was not obvious.

> 'Imitons les botanistes', he says. 'Toutes les plantes ne sont pas utiles dans la médecine, cependant ils ne cessent d'en découvrir de nouvelles. Ils espèrent que le génie et les travaux heureux y verront des propriétés jusqu'à présent cachées.'

But the scholar must bring to the interpretation of facts judgment and imagination not inferior to those of the scientist. History was for a philosophic mind what play was for the Marquis de Dangeau, who discerned a co-ordinated system where others saw only the caprice of fortune. In the following paragraphs Gibbon discusses the relative value of facts, the use which should be made of them and the rarity of that type of mind which can select the Essential out of the chaos of events. But perhaps his most illuminating remark is that which opens Chapter L: 'Déférez plutôt aux faits qui viennent d'eux mêmes vous former un système, qu'à ceux que vous découvrez après avoir conçu ce système'.

There would be fewer dead histories if this simple advice had been more often remembered.

In a number of reflexions of this kind the *Essai* preserves for us some value and interest and we may agree with Gibbon himself that it was a creditable performance for a young Englishman of twenty-two. It also marks a period in his intellectual life. The inconsequence of the ideas, Robertson has remarked, already indicates a lukewarm zeal for theorising. But so far as they go, they are the product of genuine and hardy speculation.

> 'It is indeed almost startling to find him touching on problems which are still baffling; solving them, indeed, quite prematurely, but really facing them. "Beauty", he writes, "is perhaps founded on utility alone. The human form is beautiful only because it so perfectly answers the ends for which it was designed." The solution visibly fails; but Spencer had got no further a hundred years later. This is a thinker as well as a student. If he dismisses Mandeville in the Autobiography with a cool concern to be on the respectable side of things, he shows in the *Essai* that he had pondered him even as he had ruminated Montesquieu.' [1]

If the *Essai* did not make the sensation at home that such a *tour de force* might be expected to do, it was well received abroad, and the *Bibliothèque des Sciences et des Beaux Arts* said that there was no need for the author to claim indulgence for his youth, and prophesied that sooner or later he would rank with d'Alembert, de la Bletterie, Lyttelton and Warburton.

[1] J. M. Robertson, *Gibbon*, p. 39.

Chapter 8

THE MILITIA

1760–1763

YET in the midst of his newly found happiness and congenial occupations Gibbon could hardly forget that his independence was specious. He was tethered by his £300 a year at short length within the range of his father's ambitions. A long and elaborate letter addressed early in 1760 to his father while they were under the same roof gives the measure of his uneasiness. He was clearly afraid of being talked down.

His father wished to see him in Parliament, and was willing to provide fifteen hundred pounds to that end. Gibbon had no wish to enter the House. He felt that he was not the man to seek to convince others of anything which he understood only imperfectly himself. The title would not be worth the outlay. But if his father was prepared to spend so much money, could he not apply it not to making his son great, but to rendering him happy? To avoid keeping his father in suspense he opened his full plan. He wished to travel; France was inaccessible, but not so Italy, 'a country which every scholar must long to see'. He proposed to set out in the autumn and pass the winter at Lausanne

'with M. de Voltaire and my old friends. The armies no longer obstruct my passage and it must be indifferent to you, whether I am at Lausanne or at London during the winter, since I shall not be at Beriton. In the spring I would cross the Alps and after some stay in Italy, as the war must then be terminated, return home thro' France, to live happily with you and my dear Mother.'

He added that 'the man who does not travel early, runs a great risk of not travelling at all'. He was now nearly twenty-three and need not be accused of inconsistency with his previously expressed dislike of young travellers.

It is remarkable that he should have proposed to return to Lausanne, mentioning Voltaire whom he hardly knew, though a weighty name to press on his father. The affair with Mlle Curchod was evidently to be regarded as finished. We do not know what his thoughts or feelings were at this time. Neither the Letters nor the Journal, which he was to begin in a year's time, contain any reference. On the other hand the Journal does reveal a Gibbon whom we have not seen before, one who may be called on to make a marriage approved of by his father and whose heart is meanwhile free and not a little susceptible, but protected by a very alert mind.

In August 1761—to jump forward a moment into Gibbon's military career—a Miss Chetwynd, though not perhaps perfectly handsome, was causing him some uneasiness. 'This girl grows on me', he exclaims and determines to seek other occasions of seeing her than the assemblies where his inability to dance is humiliating.

> 'Tho' she has said nothing extraordinary, I am convinced she is sensible, perhaps it is an illusion of passion, perhaps an effect of that sympathy by which people of understanding discover one another from the meerest trifles.'

But after an evening at the theatre, where she could not but notice his assiduity in looking at her from a distance, this lady is heard of no more.

The case of the Misses Page was more formidable. The elder was 'that dangerous female character called a wit'. But Fanny, 'a pretty meek (but I am afraid) insipid girl', was talked of for the heir of Buriton, and even invited to stay there. What stories would not that produce! She would have a fine fortune, and her father had some influence under government. But Gibbon postulated a wife he could talk to, and after sacrificing a morning, mainly from curiosity, to Miss Fanny, his verdict was that she was cheerful and chatty but without much intelligence, while her education, like her sister's, had been totally neglected. He was not likely to find another Suzanne in Hampshire.

However, Gibbon and his father were on the brink of events which were to put travel out of the question for two years, and though neither the idea of marriage, as we have just seen, was completely dismissed, nor did Mr Gibbon abandon his parliamentary plan during these years, yet at the end of them it was not either of these projects that held the field but the patiently cherished tour.

Gibbon himself was surprised at the ease with which he finally won his father's consent to a tour,[1] and it does not seem improbable that his concession was a reward for the indispensable services which the inexperienced, bookish, half-foreign young man rendered to the Major and his Colonel during these two years of unexpected bustle and constraint.

By Hawke's victory in Quiberon Bay in November 1759 the fear of invasion which had reigned when the Gibbons accepted their commissions had disappeared. Early in 1760 it was even possible to plan going abroad in the following winter. But as so often happens, the impetus given to the military machine continued after the need for it had gone, and in May 1760 more militia battalions were called out, in addition to the thirty-six already in being. Among these was the South Battalion

[1] *Gibbon's Journal*, p. 196.

of Hampshire, and Captain Gibbon went to Alton to put his company 'in proper order to march'.

At the beginning of his service Gibbon was so far taken with the novelty of it as to think of transferring into the Regular Army. By the end of eight months he was disillusioned. Yet he carried on with spirit and application for the rest of the time, and when at last he was free he expressed his exultation temperately enough in saying that he was glad the Militia had been and glad that it was no more. He even allowed himself a slight regret that they had not continued another year, for they could promise themselves that they would be one of the best militia corps by next summer.

There was everything to tempt a man who had little taste for soldiering to let things go. Little interest was taken in these corps by the powers above. They moved about at the 'capricious and arbitrary' directions of the War Office for no very obvious purposes, and the only practical service they rendered was the occasional guarding of French prisoners, a depressing and exhausting duty which involved the men in conditions only less disgusting than that of their unfortunate captives. In such circumstances it was impossible to expect any enthusiasm among the officers.

Nominally this constitutional army was officered by the nobility and gentry of England. Actually the battalions fell away from this high ideal, and, as Gibbon complains, instead of men of property, raw boys were taken without a shilling. Sometimes they were worse than that. One of Gibbon's brother officers had been tried for theft at Dorchester Assizes and only narrowly acquitted. The adjutant forced on them by the Duke of Bolton had been a prize-fighter and an ale-house keeper. Moreover, men of property or not, they were not congenial society: 'No manners, no conversation, they were only a set of fellowes, all whose behavior was low and most of whose characters were despicable. Luckily I was their superior in every sense.' One friendship was formed with a brother officer, John Butler Harrison, 'a young man of honour, spirit and good nature. The virtues of his heart make amends for his having none of the head.' Once in a drunken day Gibbon nearly quarrelled with him; but he kept up with him in after-years and amid divergent interests, and felt his death keenly in 1767.

Gibbon is severe and perhaps priggish about his companions. He might have blamed them less for having 'neither the knowledge of scholars nor the manners of gentlemen' if they had surpassed him as soldiers. They clearly did not.

The Colonel did not give them a good lead. Sir Thomas Worsley might be admired as 'a man of fashion and entertainment', yet his presence in the mess was the signal for heavy drinking, and the men's clothing, his special interest, was reduced to a chaotic state. Fortunately he absented himself for long periods. When he went to Spa in 1762 he entertained Gibbon the whole day with a long detail of sensible schemes he would never execute and schemes he would execute which were highly ridiculous.

Then there was the Major, as Gibbon generally refers to his father, especially when he has to criticise him. The Major's weakness was at drill. 'We had a most wretched field day. Major, officers and men seemed to try which should do worst.' But like the Colonel, he too was a frequent absentee, and at one time thought of resigning his majority, provided his son could have it. Yet with characteristic inconsistency, when the hour of demobilisation approached he was as full of regrets as the young adventurers who had everything to lose by the peace.

Pavillard had remarked that anything that Gibbon took

up he did thoroughly. If the young man was now conscious of his superior talents he did not hesitate to apply them to the work to which he had committed himself. That work was by no means confined to the captaincy—first of an ordinary company, then of the Grenadiers—which was his official status throughout. At the outset of their mobilisation a quarrel destined to be 'prolix and passionate' broke out between Sir Thomas and the Duke of Bolton, the Lord-Lieutenant of the County and Colonel of the North Battalion, who claimed the colonelcy of the South as well. It was largely a matter of politics and patronage. The Duke was a Whig; Sir Thomas with the Gibbons in support was a Tory. Correspondence and memorials ensued, and young Captain Gibbon as the scholar of the regiment had to undertake this task entirely. In a short time it would seem that everything connected with the administration of the battalion came to him and was accepted not unwillingly. To use his own words, he became 'Sir Thomas's prime minister and in fact commanded the Battalion'.

Whatever depressed reflexions he might make on the life there can be no question of the closeness and liveliness of his attention. He can write of their doings with evident enthusiasm:

> 'We had a field day by Mr. Kneller's desire, who came over to see us, and I never desire to see a better. The weather was charming and the ground good. After going thro' the manual which they did with great spirit I put them . . . thro' a variety of evolutions. . . . At the volley I made them recover their arms, not a piece went off. We ended as usual by marching by to salute. Upon that occasion the men marched and the officers saluted, better than ever I saw them.'

Equally unmistakable is his wounded self-esteem in the following:

> 'The Battalion was out, officers but no powder. It was the worst field day we had had a good while, the men were very unsteady, the officers very inatentive and I myself made several mistakes.'

And what a true militiaman he showed himself when the chance came of criticising the regulars. There were Oswald's Green Hunters—men and discipline equally bad. The Queen's Rangers 'marched in very good order, and considering circumstances were very tolerable men. Their Grenadier company indeed was but indifferent.' And in the very last days of service he makes a triumphant comparison with the 14th Foot:

> 'They an old Corps of regulars——We, part of a young body of Militia. Every advantage was on their side, and yet our superiority, both as to appearance and discipline was so striking, that the most prejudiced regular could not have hesitated a moment.'

In addition to their disputes and the accompanying court-martials, the uncertain moves of the first eight months, from Winchester to Blandford, then to Hillsea and finally to Cranbrook and Dover, and the pernicious duty of guarding French prisoners at Portchester were enough to damp enthusiasm. But the winter passed pleasantly at Dover. Entertaining the officers of the 14th and their wives was expensive. But there was plenty of time for reading and writing. An interruption came in March when Gibbon went back to Buriton for the Petersfield election.

The only reference to Gibbon's candidature on this occasion is in his Journal. We have also a copy published after his death by a Petersfield printer of the speech which he made declining a poll. But it does not throw more light on the matter than to promise that the candidate would have been an admirable member.

Some freeholders of Petersfield had persuaded Gibbon's father to stand against the interest of Jolliffe, whom Gibbon often refers to in his letters as the king of Petersfield. The Major declined in his son's favour. Gibbon records:

> 'I had never any opinion of the affair and was only comforted by the reflexion that it cost hardly any thing. One Barnard of Alresford made me lose the Election or rather gave me an opportunity of giving it up with honor.'

On the 1st April 'The Election came on. I, in a set speech, thanked my friends, abused Barnard and declined a poll.'

After this escape a quiet month was spent at home reading and preparing the *Essai* for the press, until Gibbon set out with his father and Mrs Gibbon to rejoin the battalion by easy stages. At Dover he had the pleasure of seeing his father at the head of a deputation receiving Richelieu's secretary on his way to open negotiations in London. In the spring there were parties on Captain Blyke's yacht. On an excursion to see the *Newark* in the Downs they were becalmed, eventually getting to Margate at two in the morning, 'where we dined and the weather proving rough, returned to Dover by land thro' Sandwich. I read severall odes of Horace and compared them critically with Dryden's translations.'

In the following summer came the most splendid period of the corps when they joined the great camp on Flowerdown at Winchester. The season culminated in a grand review of the line by the young Duke of York, when the South Hants 'distinguished themselves by their dirty appearance and excellent fires far beyond the rest of the line'. When they arrived in a camp consisting of far more experienced units, it was apprehended that they could never take their place in the line. But the Dorsets lent them N.C.O.'s, and the men being willing great progress was made by them and also by the officers, with the exception, alas, of the Major, the adjutant and a captain. But their appearance was on more than one occasion a sore disappointment to Gibbon who cared now, as later, considerably for such things.

But clothes or no clothes Winchester camp was a

> 'new and lively scene during the summer, a charming dry spot of ground, our tents convenient and agreable by their novelty. Five counties assembled and living in a mighty free friendly way; except some slight jealousies between the right and left wings.'

There was also more varied and more brilliant society—Sir George Saville, Sir Willoughby and Lady Aston, Lord and Lady Tracy, Colonel and Lady Harriet Conyers—to grace their assemblies and parties in the mess. There was the zest of preparing for the review:

> 'The whole line was out for the first time but only with sergeants and wooden snappers. As this was the only time I was a Spectator, I must say they made a very fine appearance.'

And at last on the 29th September the Duke of York came. The review was prudently very simple and the troops much commended, though Gibbon thought they had done better before Lord Effingham on the previous day. This was attributable to the Duke's childish behaviour. He upset the men and slighted the officers. 'Phelps, the Brigade Major, appeared likewise very little to his honor.'

Three days later came a further climax for the Captain and an event certainly unique in the militia camp. The scheming Major saw a chance for advertising his son. If he could not or would not go into Parliament, diplomacy should be open to a young man who had just published a book in French. He should present it to the Duke. It looks as if he acted on the spur of the moment. The battalion had just returned from a field day, and Gibbon, book in hand but 'somewhat disordered with sweat and dust, in the cap, dress, and acoutrements of a captain of Grenadiers', was passed into Colonel Pitt's tent where the Duke was at breakfast.

> 'He received it courteously, asked me whether I had wrote it since I was in the militia, and how long I had been about it; promised to read it and gave it to Sir William Boothby.'

Gibbon was glad to have been in camp once. But they were kept there too long. It was another matter when the cold weather began and the officers were crowded into the suttling booth where noise and nonsense reigned all day long. In such conditions it was something to have read a treatise on the Roman Legion, Soame Jenyns on the *Origin of Evil* and an essay on ancient painting. At last in October, when they thought they were forgotten, they were sent to Devizes for the winter. The gentlemen of Wiltshire proved inhospitable; in two months Gibbon did not remember dining or sleeping away from quarters. In December he passed six weeks of leave at home, during which he never went visiting, hunting or walking. 'My only resources were myself, my books and family conversation. But to me these were great resources.'

When Gibbon returned early in 1762 he found discipline had gone to pieces largely through the presence of a regular unit, the Black Musketeers. He promptly ordered Ensign Smith extra duty for being absent without leave, and twenty-one court-martials in four months against ten in five at Dover tell their tale. But the war was coming to an end and the Militia was almost forgotten. Gibbon himself was on leave for a great part of the year, and when present was frequently commanding officer. Their movements were few. The battalion remained at Devizes until February. After a short stay at Salisbury they returned 'to our beloved Blandford a second time [March 9], and finally to the fashionable resort of Southampton [June 2], where the colours were fixed till our final dissolution [December 23]'.

In the absence of instructions from above, they passed the time at Blandford in holding field days for the entertainment of wealthy West Indians and passing lords. At Southampton once more came the loathed task of guarding prisoners. But Gibbon had little to do with that, and in the remainder of the summer was able to do his duty from home. It consisted almost entirely of trying to apply the recruitment clauses of the Militia Acts to a reluctant population. Whole days were wasted. On one occasion Gibbon was out from seven in the morning till ten at night. It was pretty good to have read about a hundred lines of the *Iliad* as well.

A call to sit on a general court-martial at Reading in April of this year was a diversion and a valuable experience. Among others Gibbon made the acquaintance of Wilkes. He had scarcely ever met a better companion; one of inexhaustible spirits, infinite wit and humour and a great deal of knowledge. But his character and conversation were scandalising, and Gibbon is careful to note that when later the colonel of the Buckinghamshire dined with them he was not one with Sir Thomas and others who broke into Wilkes' room and made him drink a bottle of claret in bed.[1]

It was all in keeping that when disbandment became a certainty the battalion should be thrown into new confusions. Young Ensign Hall, aged sixteen, had to be

[1] *Op. cit.* p. 145. Sheffield carefully edited the account of this evening in *Misc. Wks.*, 1796. According to Maltby, Wilkes then said that Gibbon must have been drunk when he wrote this account. Maltby said Wilkes would have called Sheffield out if he had seen what was printed in the 1814 edition. Rogers, *Table Talk*, p. 351.

sent away hurriedly for fear that he should be arrested for debt after he had lost an officer's privilege.

> 'Sir Thomas came down from London. When he was absent we differed settling our affairs till he came, and when he came we found he was of no use to us. Indeed everything was in a strange confusion.'

Gibbon was not present at the final disembodiment of the companies, when the men fired three volleys, received their money, partook of a dinner at the Major's expense, and then separated with great cheerfulness and regularity.

When Gibbon had been in the Militia about fourteen months he began what was proposed to be an exact journal of his actions and studies. This was intended both to assist his memory and to accustom himself to set a due value on his time. As it turned out his memory had frequently to assist his journal, since he fell far behindhand with it more than once.[1] Nevertheless he kept it with increasing fullness down to his arrival in Paris, 28th January 1763. Henceforward he wrote in French.

The greater part of the English portion is taken up with recording and discussing his reading and his own literary projects. In fact during his periods of leave at Buriton there is very little else. In spite of long periods when duty and dissipation, which was almost a duty, left time for nothing else, the balancing of the account —'not of money but of time'—at the end of each year was not unsatisfactory 'after making proper allowances'; a favourite phrase. 1760, it is true, was almost a total loss. But for the next year 'four books of Homer in Greek, six of Strabo in Latin, Cicero *De Natura Deorum*

[1] See *Gibbon's Journal*, Introduction, pp. xix *sqq.*

and the great philosophical and theological work of M. de Beausobre', besides a number of smaller books and articles, was not unsatisfactory considering the many distractions. Naturally the following year showed a far more gratifying profit, and his choice of reading was directed by more settled aims. He read most of the *Iliad* twice and consulted a great number of authorities on Greek antiquities connected with it. Longinus was read too, with Burke's *Essay on the Sublime and Beautiful* and Hurd's *Horace*, and he records some meditations on the subject of prose rhythm.

At the same time he had not forgotten his ambition to write history. In the summer of 1761, after considering the potentialities of Charles VIII's expedition into Italy, Richard I's Crusade, the war of King John and the Barons, the Black Prince, a comparison of Titus and Henry V, lives of Sir Philip Sidney or Montrose, he had at last fixed on Sir Walter Raleigh. But in the following summer he felt obliged to drop his hero. He found that he could add little to the existing life by Oldys, poor performance though that might be, while he would hesitate to eke out his work by digressions into contemporary history which had already occupied such men as Walpole, Robertson and Hume. Moreover, he foresaw two special dangers. He shrank from a topic which would be modern enough for his readers to expect him 'to hoist a flag of party'; a more potent fear was that Raleigh was a domestic subject which would be received with an indifference abroad 'far more bitter than censure or reproach'.

With such ambitions in view he reviewed two other subjects. The most attractive would be the History of the Liberty of the Swiss.

'From such a subject, so full of real virtue, public spirit, military glory, and great lessons of gouvernment, the meanest writer would catch fire. What might not I hope for, who to some

> talents perhaps add an affection for the nation which would make me labour the composition *con amore*.'

But his enthusiasm was checked on reflecting that his materials were 'fast locked in the obscurity of an old barbarous German dialect', which he could not make up his mind to learn for that purpose alone. The passage is typical of Gibbon's ethical and aesthetic approach to history. So too are his reflexions on the alternative—a History of Florence under the Medici. He contrasts the rise of the Swiss, a poor virtuous state, to glory and liberty with the republic which in wealth and corruption loses its independence and sinks into the arms of a master. 'Both lessons equally useful.' And he adds:

> 'what makes this subject still more precious are two fine *morceaux* for a Philosophical historian, and which are essential parts of it, the Restoration of Learning in Europe by Lorenzo de Medicis and the character and fate of Savonarola. The Medicis employed letters to strengthen their power and their enemies opposed them with religion.'

Not the least significant are the books which are classified as the amusements of his leisure hours. They include besides a mass of learned journals such diversions as Barclay's *Argenis*, a Latin allegorical novel which entertained Cowper, a Life of Erasmus and some of his books, and especially Voltaire's *Siècle de Louis XIV* and the works of Fontenelle.

It is often assumed rather easily that Gibbon was a disciple of Voltaire; it is even said that his acquaintance with the actor of Mon Repos was the starting point of his religious scepticism. Such a statement is very wide of the mark, and Voltaire's influence either on Gibbon's philosophy or history should be admitted with great reserve. Gibbon admired Voltaire as a dramatist immensely. He thought part of *Merope* was equal to Racine. He valued him much less as a historian, finding him superficially brilliant but unwilling to undertake severe research and at the same time an indifferent narrator. These opinions, expressed in the Journal, are reinforced by a mass of pugnacious notes in *The Decline and Fall.* In these Voltaire is repeatedly assailed for his want of logic and for his partiality. 'In his way Voltaire was a bigot, an intolerant bigot.' He could lavish praise on a philosophical Turk who retired from the world, which he would have refused to a Christian prince retiring to a monastery.[1] Far deeper went the impression made by Fontenelle.

At Blandford in May 1762 Gibbon read six volumes of Fontenelle 'with great pleasure'. This remarkable man, whose life came within a month of a hundred years, has been likened to the old man in Virgil's *Eclogues* who, having been admitted into the secrets of the gods, sang to a golden lyre of the creation of the world and its laws while young shepherds and shepherdesses crowned him with flowers. He was in fact the lady's man of science, the first to popularise abstruse knowledge which he made acceptable to the *marquises* by adorning it with the *bel esprit* of a vanishing period. For in his long life he had seen the world pass from a state of indifference and even hostility towards the sciences into the dawn of the *philosophes* whose spiritual father he himself was. He was cold and equable in temperament, unusually free from prejudice, a single-hearted champion of reason and rigorous method, who discerned and expressed for the various sciences their common goal in the rational explanation of the universe. The random curios which the Ashmoles of the last age had assembled must be ultimately transformed into a select and classified museum. Such a mind would

[1] *The Decline and Fall,* c. lxvii. n. 13, also xlvii. n. 118, lviii. n. 65, lxviii. n. 25. There are probably more references to Voltaire than to any other modern writer in *The Decline and Fall,* and most are combative.

be naturally stimulating to a young man designing to win the world's ear. But Fontenelle had something particular to offer to a historian.

In France as in England the debate had raged upon the comparative merits of the ancient and modern worlds. It had been largely a Battle of the Books. Fontenelle raised and disposed of a deeper issue than that of rival literary values. With his conception of the progress of knowledge he combined a belief in the constancy of human nature based on a general acceptance of the stability and continuity of natural forces. Man neither degenerated essentially from one age to another nor improved. If centuries and peoples varied strikingly in their degrees of barbarism or culture it was to be explained by the accident of time and other external conditions. A man famous for his discoveries may be luckier than others in preceding them in time; he is not necessarily of superior ability. 'Refinement or coarseness,' Fontenelle makes Socrates say in his dialogue with Montaigne, 'knowledge or ignorance, the varying degrees of a certain naivety, a serious or frivolous outlook of mind are merely the externals of man, and all that changes. But the heart never changes, and the whole man is in his heart.' The influence of this conception is visible at large in Gibbon's work.[1]

In his *Histoire des Oracles*, Fontenelle starts a line of historical enquiry which runs very close to that of the once shocking Dr. Middleton. Christians had long held that the ancient oracles had been genuine in so far as they were the work of demons. Fontenelle destroys this notion and disposes of the oracles as so much quackery and imposture. Gibbon was right in judging the work superficial. The essay nevertheless was daring enough in its criticism of some of the Fathers, to be an adventure

[1] Fontenelle, *Dialogues des Morts; Socrate, Montaigne*. See also Bury, *The Idea of Progress*, pp. 98 *sqq.*, and Sainte-Beuve, *Lundis*, iii. 320.

which was never repeated. There can be little doubt that Fontenelle's influence on Gibbon would entitle him to be mentioned not far behind those to whom the historian has avowed his debt explicitly.

Gibbon is revealed with an eye for country and a turn for concise characterisation in this regrettably brief Journal.

He sees the world, it is true, through the glasses of contemporary taste. Nature is subservient to man's designs. From the terrace at Cliveden 'you command a most glorious prospect of the adjacent country, thro' which the Thames serpentines in a manner on purpose for this house'. His most complete landscape is a setting for some quiet comedy:

> 'Mr. and Mrs. Porteman, young Chafin the Clergyman, my father, Mrs. Gibbon and myself set out one way, the Battalion marched under Captain Eyer's command to Winbourn, and Sir Thomas went up to London. We first drove to Lord Shaftesbury's, as fine as a flat well can be. The winding river is beautiful, tho' the Chinese bridge is criticised as too high and too near one end of it. The house appears excessively large but very irregular. We did not see the inside. His Lordship came out to ask us in, but the invitation was so faint that we declined it. One of the great artificial beauties here is the Grotto, containing a vast variety of curious shells, disposed with great taste. From this place to Mr. Sturt's, where we saw an artificial piece of water of two hundred acres, and an elegant turret a hundred and forty foot high; but such is the character of the man, that he keeps his place in no order, sells his fish and makes a granary of his turret. From thence we drove to a pretty little place of Mr. Fitch's, Mrs. Porteman's brother. There we eat a very agreeable cold dinner at a seat in the garden just by a Cascade, and after we had passed a most agreable day, they set us down at Winbourne and carried Mrs. Gibbon back to Bryanstone.'[1]

[1] *Gibbon's Journal*, p. 78, 31st May 1762.

It was the characters that he encountered who interested him most. A succession of shrewdly touched sketches are scattered through these pages. He was particularly interested in the country gentlemen and what they were likely to achieve. Sir Gerard Napier is found to be 'a proud ill-tempered fool', from which it is deduced that the improvements he contemplates for his estates are likely to be 'a mixture of grandness and littleness with more expence than taste'. The portrait of Mr Pleydwell is kinder:

> 'He is a very good-natured country gentleman, affable to everybody, indifferent as to his company and ready to do whatever they please. In a word a most excellent candidate for a County. His wife is a little ill-natured thing that seems to torment him continually.'

Gibbon was fond of posing husband and wife together and viewing them with a bachelor's relish. His masterpiece is that of Mr Crop, the Mayor of Southampton, and his wife:

> 'Crop is an honest fellow in the Tory sense of the word; he drinks hard, rails against all ministers and keeps alive the small remains of Jacobitism at Southampton. Even Sir Thomas thinks him too violent. *À cela près*, he is most impenetrably stupid. His wife is a merry, good-natured woman, but one who, in her conversation, respects altogether as little the laws of truth as the patience of her hearers.' [1]

If only the diarist had persevered with his art, what portraits might not his sketch-book have contained of Johnson and Boswell, Goldsmith, Reynolds and Garrick and a score of others.

What of the artist's portrait of himself? We have seen him going about duties which he disliked but was incapable of neglecting, all too conscious of his superiority to his fellow officers. He was conceited certainly, but

[1] *Op. cit.* p. 144. Cf. too the portrait of Sir Matthew and Lady Featherston.

only at the price of setting the highest standards for himself. 'While every one looks on me as a prodigy of application,' he wrote in August 1762 with reference to his studies, 'I know myself how strong a propensity I have to indolence.' He has an almost religious sense of the value of time. Once when on a rare occasion he indulged himself in 'the pleasure of rambling about that fine cliff of Porteman's' and lost most of the morning, he felt the reproach, which no one but himself could have inflicted, of having reviewed no more than four hundred and fifty lines of the *Iliad*.

This rare relaxation had occurred on his twenty-sixth birthday and he sets down what he claims to be an impartial examination. He could have had no consciousness of having wronged anyone when he wrote that his character was 'incapable of a base action, and formed for generous ones'. But he finds 'that it was proud, violent and disagreeable in society'. This is severe, and though he mentions a drunken quarrel with Jack Harrison, his only close friend in the Militia, he gives no hint otherwise that he did not get on well with those with whom he had to associate. In the crowded suttling booth one can imagine the stupid questions and perhaps mock reverence about things they did not understand when the young Captain produced those incomprehensible books of his. He entrenched himself behind a disdainful reserve.

Of the benefits of the service he makes no concealment. The active life established his health. He learnt a great deal about his fellow men and their affairs, and was made an Englishman once more. He never forgot that he had been a soldier, and though he could smile at his 'bloodless campaign', was none the less proud of it, and one cannot help feeling that amid all the tedium the zealous Captain was unconsciously satisfying that tribal instinct which will often make a man acquiesce in belonging to some corporate society even if he has hardly a good word to say for it.

Within a week of demobilisation Gibbon had obtained his father's consent to spending two years abroad and lost no time about his preparations, going over to Goodwood at once to obtain from the Duke of Richmond an introduction to the Duke of Bedford, the British Ambassador in Paris. This consent was obtained easily enough in the end; in fact the Major had opened the subject in September, at a time when Gibbon was nerving himself to propose it. A foreign tour had also been in contemplation still earlier in the year, when the Major had offered to raise his son's annuity to £400 a year, with a further £100 a year for two years abroad. But the transaction on which this offer was based fell through, and Gibbon reflected philosophically on the loss of his prospective increase that it was not the sort of misfortune he felt very greatly.[1]

Yet the state of dependency in which he was, arising especially from his father's uncertain nature both in regard to making plans and to carrying out what he had undertaken, was to remain intermittently embarrassing for a long while to come.

In June he had received a letter from his friend Deyverdun. Gibbon had not forgotten him but was afraid he was forgotten. Deyverdun was now governor to a German prince's son, but was regretting he had not accepted some offer that Gibbon had made of bringing him to England.

> 'Deyverdun', Gibbon writes in his Journal, 'from his character and way of thinking is the only friend I ever had who deserved that name. I wish I could find out any scheme of our living

[1] *Op. cit.* pp. 46, 66, 137, 196.

> together, but I am afraid it is impossible in my present state of dependance.'

A month later the entry runs:

> 'I finished my letter of eight pages to Deyverdun, it is a kind of pleasure I have not had a great while, that of pouring out my whole soul to a real friend. *Why* I deferred writing and the *schemes* I proposed to him are not to be trusted even to this paper.' [1]

In a little over a month from his liberation from the Militia Gibbon was in Paris. Once his father's consent was gained he did not waste time. Leave was taken of Mrs Gibbon 'with the mixture of joy and grief which one always feels upon those occasions'. During three weeks spent in London with his father, a variety of diversions were enjoyed—snug parties with Aunt Porten—a night at Captain Crookshank's, where 'the supper was so elegant and the wines so various and powerful that I could but just walk home at four a clock in the morning'—a brilliant party at Lady Hervey's, where he was not in spirits and had a very small share in the conversation. Lady Hervey gave him introductions for Mme Geoffrin and the Comte de Caylus, and through Dr. Maty he was presented to the Duc de Nivernois, who gave him letters to various French scholars. Nivernois, who had asked Maty to present the author of the *Essai*, not unnaturally treated him 'more as a man of letters than as a man of fashion' and wrote his letters in the same tone.

On the 23rd of January 1763 Gibbon set out on his travels and reached Canterbury. At Dover he fell in with the Duke of Bridgewater and Lords Tavistock and Ossory and they agreed to his going with them on a yacht they had hired. Setting sail at five in the morning they were unable to make Calais, their intended port, and only got to Boulogne at three in the afternoon.

[1] *Op. cit.* pp. 82 and 92.

The road to Paris was already overcharged with Englishmen hastening to enjoy the first-fruits of the peace. There were not horses to go round. So Gibbon set out alone and got to Abbeville. He visited Van Robais' cloth factory there, and after passing Amiens and stopping at Bertueil reached Paris about five in the afternoon of 28th January. Busbequius' travels in the Near East, in Latin, entertained him on the road.

Chapter 9

PARIS

1763

THE unpublished portion of a Paris letter depicts Gibbon's new situation:

PARIS, *February 24th*, 1763

'DEAR SIR,

'I received your letter about 12 days after its date owing as I apprehend to Mr. Foley's negligence. As I am now settled there is no farther occasion to make use of that Channel. My direction is *A Monsieur, Monsieur Gibbon Gentilhomme Anglais a l'hôtel de Londres rue du Colombier, Fauxbourg St Germain à Paris.*[1] You see I am still in that part of the town and indeed from all the intelligence I could collect I saw no reason to change either upon [the score] of cheapness or pleasantness. Madame Bontems, Mrs. Mallet's friend and a Marquis de Mirabeau I got acquainted with at her house have acted a very friendly part, tho' all their endeavours have only served to convince me that Paris is unavoidably a very dear place. My apartement (up two pair of stairs) consists in an Antichamber, a dining room, a bed chamber and a servant's room, and stands me in six Guineas a month! Apropos of servants Suess turns out an exceedingly good one and I have all the reason in the world to be highly satisfied with him. But the most expensive article is my coach. There is at present such a concourse of strangers at Paris that the hirers of coaches hardly know what to ask. In spite of all the enquiries of my friends I have not been able to get mine under sixteen guineas a month. It is indeed a very elegant

[1] The rue du Colombier is now rue de l'Université. Gibbon was not doing so badly with his arrangement. William Cole paid four guineas a month for one room and a servant's room in the same quarter: *Cole's Paris Journal*, p. 35. Gibbon in 1777 paid 364 francs for a month's lodging, *i.e.* about £22: *Magd. Coll. Papers.*

vis-à-vis and I have seen a great deal more given for equipages inferior to it. I have made one suit here, a velvet of three colours, the ground blue. I am sorry to find my English cloaths look very foreign here. The French ones are all excessively long waisted. At present we are in mourning for the Bishop of Liège, the King's Uncle, and expect soon another of a singular nature, that of the Old Pretender, who is very ill. They mourn for him not as a crowned head but as a relation of the King's. I am doubtfull how the English here will behave. Indeed we can have no difficulties since we need only follow the example of the Duke of Bedford.' [1]

The postscript, also unpublished, gives what was almost his only cause of dissatisfaction:

'P.S.—I have seen very little of the English noblemen I came over with, beyond an exchange of visits. I have not yet had one invitation from the D. of B. I wish you would tell the D. of R. of it. Tho' indeed it is a general complaint.'

That is not the only reference to the British Ambassador's neglect. But wounded vanity was but a scratch on the surface of Gibbon's deep satisfaction. In three weeks he had heard more memorable conversation and had met 'more men of letters among the people of fashion' than he had in all his months in London. He was absorbed into Parisian society at its freest and most hospitable period and the number of his acquaintance was increasing daily. He could pick and choose among them. 'Next Sunday for instance I have only three invitations to dinner.'

It was said in those days that a foreigner did not know Paris until he had been received at Mme Geoffrin's, and it was one of Mme Geoffrin's innovations in the ways of the salon that she admitted foreigners regardless of their social rank provided they had some claim to be noticed.[2] Gibbon lost no time in presenting himself,

[1] The beginning of Letter XVI, *Misc. Wks.* ii. 54. From Captain G. C. Onslow's papers.
[2] P. de Ségur, *Le Royaume de la rue St. Honoré*, p. 51.

armed not only with Lady Hervey's letter but with the reputation of the *Essai*. This he considered his best recommendation. He felt here, as he so often liked to feel, that he was indebted only to himself.

'My book was very useful to me. I had the pleasure of seeing that it was my best recommendation and of feeling that I was only indebted to myself. It would savour of vanity to record in this writing all the eulogies and compliments that it brought me. It decided my status. I was a recognised man of letters, and it is only in Paris that this quality forms a distinct status. I have not sufficient vanity to believe myself free from it. I admit unaffectedly that after discounting these compliments and exaggerations I can flatter myself that these eulogies were founded on some degree of truth. The favourable way in which the greatest part of the reviewers have spoken of me convinces me that it is creditable to a young author and can inspire me with some confidence for the future. But even if my Essay had not much merit in itself, it was naturally bound to have some in the eyes of the French. They love their own language and prefer it unaffectedly to all others. Could one better court them than by a homage as public as it was unique. The Germans have often neglected their own language to write in French. No Englishman has ever done so unless one includes Count Hamilton and Ramsay, who though a Scotchman by birth had been naturalised by a long residence in France.

'This reputation nevertheless caused me one small dissatisfaction. It resulted in my being regarded solely as a man of letters. That quality may be in itself the first in society, but I should have liked to add to it that of a man of rank for which I have such indisputable claims. I did not want the writer to eclipse the gentleman entirely. Perhaps such vanity does me little honour but I am not writing a panegyric. Perhaps too my pride deceived me and I fancied I saw some attitude towards me which only existed in my jealous imagination. In that case this is the avowal of one more fault.' [1]

Writer or gentleman, Gibbon was received with a kindness which should have laid to rest his uneasy

[1] In this and the next three chapters extracts from Gibbon's Journal are translated from the unpublished French MS.

vanity. Let us hope that he entered Mme Geoffrin's house with proper awe. His masters Montesquieu and Fontenelle had been familiar here not so long ago, and the company he found merited Sainte-Beuve's description of it as the great centre and rendezvous of the eighteenth century. Here were men on whose criticism of the past and belief in man's perfectibility a new age might have been founded—d'Alembert and Diderot, d'Holbach and Helvétius. Helvétius took particular notice of the young essayist, and at his house and d'Holbach's was to be found the freer conversation and the company of certain advanced spirits such as the motherly Mme Geoffrin's 'capricious tryanny' would not admit. Nor was talk the sole attraction. d'Holbach gave excellent dinners, and Helvétius had 'a very pretty wife'. Gibbon may have been less concerned than Morellet, who thought Mme Helvétius 'upset philosophical discussions badly with her sparkling beauty and wit'.[1] But neither these impressive talkers nor their agreeable setting dethroned the critic in Gibbon. He refused to be intoxicated with their ideas and could not 'approve the intolerant zeal of the philosophers and the Encyclopaedists the friends of d'Holbach and Helvétius; they laughed at the scepticism of Hume, preached the tenets of Atheism with the bigotry of dogmatists', and 'damned all believers with ridicule and contempt'.[2] An eclipse of the sun at Lausanne in the following April was the occasion of a similar reflexion. 'One rightly smiles at eclipses nowadays, yet the incredulity of this age is often as blind as the faith of its ancestors.'[3]

A greater satisfaction was to be found in less austere atmospheres. The breadth of Gibbon's acquaintance is recited in a proud succession of names, and for us they

[1] Morellet, *Mémoires*, p. 136, quoted by W. H. Wickwar, *Baron d'Holbach*, p. 26.

[2] *Murray*, p. 204.

[3] MS. Journal, 1st April 1764.

are little else but names, of the Count de Caylus, the Abbés de la Bletterie, Barthélemy, Raynal, Arnaud, Messieurs de la Condamine, Duclos, de Ste. Palaye, de Bougainville, Caperonnier, de Guignes, Suard, etc.; some were old friends through their books, all were distinguished in fields of knowledge especially dear to Gibbon—Greek and Roman history, Oriental travel, archaeology and history. Here his highest expectations were not disappointed. It is true that the Count de Caylus, the supreme archaeologist among them, had become too much of a recluse to help him much. Somewhat oddly and to his own subsequent regret he neglected to make Buffon's acquaintance. But there were many compensations. Barthélemy, whose *Voyage du jeune Anarcharsis en Grèce* was a popular forerunner of Hellenism, accompanied him to see the King's collection of medals.

> 'The society of Madame du Bocage was more soft and moderate than that of her rivals and the evening conversations of Mr. de Foncemagne were supported by the good sense and learning of the principal members of the Academy of Inscriptions.'

Here he found good sense and enlightenment combined with ease and candour. 'Je commence à m'y établir,' he entered in his Journal, and a rare corroboration comes in a letter from Mme de Verdelin to Rousseau recommending Gibbon, whom she had met at de Foncemagne's, as having had a reputation for intelligence and other good qualities.[1] It was a testimonial, as it happened, that Gibbon might have preferred to have remained unwritten.

Gibbon had neither the money nor the inclination to enter the more frivolously brilliant salons of the financiers such as Pelletier or La Popelinière. He was assiduous at the Théâtre Français, where he preferred

[1] Dufour, *Corr.-Gén. de J. J. Rousseau,* ix. 289, dated 14 mai 1763.

'the consummate art of the Clairon to the intemperate sallies of the Dumesnil'. The opera and *Les Italiens* were visited less often, for he had little taste for music. At the beginning of his stay he did a little sober sight-seeing. The modern tourist may compare his morning's programme with his own. Gibbon made the round of the library at St. Germain des Près, les Invalides and l'École Militaire; then a glance at St. Sulpice. The full horror of its façade was not finished. Gibbon thought it nevertheless one of the finest structures in Paris, a judgment which follows rather disconcertingly close to the dictum that 'the Catholic superstition which is always the enemy of reason, is often the parent of taste'. And finally to the Carmelite church, where a close examination of the monuments and pictures revealed Gibbon's curiously matter-of-fact views of art. He admired among other things

> 'a picture of the apparition of an angel to Joseph, father of Jesus Christ. The dignity, sweetness and serenity of the envoy from heaven are very well portrayed, also the state of Joseph, who is buried in a deep slumber. Perhaps even his sleep is too profound. He appears to feel nothing, and evinces none of those agitations common to those whose senses are in truth at rest while the soul is struck by some singular dream.'

He approved also of Le Brun's portrait of Mlle de la Vallière as the Magdalen, which contrived to depict penitence without sacrificing beauty. And so to dinner with Helvétius and to Mme Boyer's evening.[1]

His guide on this occasion was M. d'Augny, a young officer of the Guards but an exceptional one, for

> 'he is as reserved, as little a man of the world, and as awkward as I can be. But he has a fine natural understanding—a clear unprejudiced head, and a heart which seems to be full of the noblest sentiments of honor, probity and friendship. I will not decide too hastily, but I believe and hope that I am forming a connection which will last as long as my life.'[2]

[1] Journal, 21 fév. [2] *Prothero*, i. 31.

This was in a letter to Mrs Gibbon. In his Journal he wrote:

> 'The better I know d'Augny the more I like him. I will wait a little before attempting his portrait. But it seems we are suited to one another. Already I begin to take on with him that tone of intimacy and those confidences of heart and mind which are not frequent in me.'

But the portrait was never written and M. d'Augny is mentioned no more. Soon Gibbon's time and thoughts were taken up with another friendship, this time with a lady whom he describes to his family in the same letter smugly enough:

> 'Madam Bontems is a very good sort of a woman, agreeable and *sans pretensions*. She seems to have conceived a real motherly attachment for me. I generally sup there three or four times a week quite in a friendly family way.' [1]

The motherly relation seems to have been interpreted generously and both Gibbon's Memoirs and Journal tell a different and somewhat ambiguous story. In the first we learn that

> 'in the middle season of life' [she was about forty-five] 'her beauty was still an object of desire; the Marquis de Mirabeau, a celebrated name, was neither her first nor her last lover; but if her heart was tender, if her passions were warm, a veil of decency was cast over her frailties.'

Sheffield suppressed this and Birkbeck Hill, on reading it, took his chance to say with Victorian zest that Gibbon 'indulged in a guilty passion'. Perhaps he did, but this seems hardly the phrase to be given to the amorous pottering which the Journal reveals.

There we find Gibbon very much in leading-strings in the hands of this agreeable lady. She took him on pleasant excursions to St. Denys, St. Germain or Ver-

[1] *Prothero*, i. 31; 'family' is omitted there, but see Add. MSS. 34883.

sailles or still more decorously to church. At the church of St. Roche in the rue St. Honoré they listened to Père Elysée on the uncertainty and futility of deathbed repentances. We may imagine this odd pair coming out of the church and standing on the steps in the rue St. Honoré just where, some thirty years later, Napoleon was to fire 'the whiff of grape-shot' which ended the Revolution. Gibbon was full of reflexions on the father's eloquence, and ready to compare it with the cold discourse which English preachers coldly delivered. Mme Bontemps was a good Catholic and 'believed firmly in the most contradictory mysteries and humbly followed the most popular superstitions'. Yet her heart, which had led her to this acquiescence, rebelled against its conclusions. Her faith was especially troubled by the notion that heretics were damned, and she told her young Protestant as much a hundred times.

She had her place in literature as the translator of Thomson's *Seasons*, but was without vanity or ambition and refused to be drawn into literary discussions. She preferred to confide her secrets to the young man, and in return to advise and even scold him over his own affairs. Their attraction was mutual, but the young man did not or would not understand her advances. Was it in despair perhaps that she made him read La Fontaine's *Tales* to her? Alas for her, he respected her feeble resistance to the freedom engendered by this elegant titillation. 'With a little more boldness', he recorded, 'I might perhaps have succeeded.' He did not want to. He preferred 'a delicious friendship' with the sermons and the suppers sometimes *tête-à-tête*, sometimes with M. Bontemps and M. de Mirabeau, whom he admired considerably, judging him to have enough imagination for ten men and not enough cool-headedness for one.

These reflexions appear to have been written at the close of his visit. On his return from Italy after a fortnight's stay he says 'he tore himself from the embraces of Paris'. Sheffield again suppressed this, and those who have in mind the ambiguous phrases of the Memoir already quoted may, if they like, put an extreme interpretation on the words. But they must remember that Gibbon at this time was much in attendance on Mme Necker safely wedded from every point of view. It does not seem to matter very much whether he was Mme Bontemps' lover or not. He had learned one lesson clearly enough. It was a lesson which he had begun with his stepmother, though in that relationship its full significance naturally could not be seen. It was that his need for feminine companionship which was constant throughout his life was best satisfied in the temperate zone of friendship. We are as we are made in these matters.

This friendship was perhaps the principal reason for prolonging his stay to fourteen weeks, and Gibbon does not deny that had he been rich and independent he might have remained there indefinitely. But Paris was expensive and he had to account for his doings at home. He had already given Mrs Gibbon the agreeable task of informing his father that he had drawn for another hundred pounds, and we find him at last at bay to questions and criticisms. He had not written to friends of the family; he had written to Lord Lichfield; both actions in their way having caused dissatisfaction. What was he doing? Gambling? He could assure his father that he had only lost seven livres, and that in one night at picquet. Clothes of course he had to buy—ruffles and silk stockings in this capital of the fashionable world. That was an expense now done with, and as he had pretty well seen Paris he thought of setting out, if his father had no objection, by way of Dijon and Besançon for Lausanne, where he would spend two or three cheap months and prepare for his entry into Italy.

Chapter 10

SUZANNE CURCHOD AGAIN

1760–1763

IN FIVE years fortune had dealt Suzanne Curchod some hard blows. Her father had died in 1760. The smiling hillsides of Crassy were exchanged for Geneva, where the pension allowed to the widow by the government of Berne was supplemented by the daughter's earnings. She gave lessons sometimes for seven hours in one day, she was often ill and consumption was feared; they were poor and without interest.[1]

At Geneva Suzanne was drawn into the ardent correspondence and confidences which teemed among the friends and admirers of Rousseau. In 1761–2 she was corresponding with Julie de Bondeli on the subject of *La Nouvelle Héloise*, and Julie was creating an interest among her correspondents about the orphan girl;[2] an interest enhanced by mystery, since Suzanne's letters contained confidences which could not be shown round. Were they confidences concerning Gibbon? Probably not, I think. Suzanne had sent Julie a précis of Gibbon's *Essai*, and later Julie is reading the book when she recounts the anecdote already mentioned of Gibbon's passionate absurdity and adds that neither this extravagance nor his extreme ugliness will affect the merit of his book. She writes as if the affair was well known and done with, and she can hardly have got the impression

[1] P. Kohler, *Mme de Staël et la Suisse*, c. i.
[2] E. Bodeman, *Julie von Bondeli und ihr Freundeskreis*.

about Gibbon's looks from Mlle Curchod. The book interested her and her friends. Her only complaint about it was that it was too short. At the end of 1762 she assures a correspondent, on the strength of Mlle Curchod's authority, that M. Gibbon has written nothing else. But whatever the confidences may have been, she passes on one of her pen portraits as an example of her friend's penetration and *tour d'esprit*. It was of the minister, Paul Moultou.

This young Genevan clergyman—he was about six years younger than Suzanne—was an enthusiastic and faithful friend of Rousseau. He had married the daughter of a merchant named Cayla, and it was through this family that he became acquainted with the Curchods. A close and confidential friendship was formed, but one must not be misled into imagining these disciples of Rousseau felt anything more than friendship.[1] 'Ses amis sont bien ses amis, mais que le nombre en est petit! Ah, que je voudrais être du nombre' is the frank conclusion of Suzanne's portrait of Moultou. She did not have to wait long to experience the worth of his regard.

Her mother died in January 1763, and the pension from Berne came to an end. There was a frail hope of recovering some of Mme Curchod's property in France, but in the meantime this girl, so attractive and accomplished, whose prospects had seemed so bright a few years ago, was now only a little above the level of destitution, dependent on her friends until she could make her way in the only honourable occupation open to her, the uninviting status of governess or *dame de compagnie*.

There were offers of marriage, it is true. There had been a M. de Montplaisir; there was a M. Correvon, a

[1] As d'Haussonville *op. cit.* did. Moultou was an active intelligent man. He corresponded with Voltaire in 1762–3 over *l'affaire Calas*.

lawyer who was humbly persistent. It seems fairly certain that Montplaisir had been rejected in favour of Gibbon. It is not so clear whether the same reason sufficed to dismiss Correvon or if his offer was not good enough. Far less serious, but they must be mentioned, were the attentions of a Genevese savant, G. L. Le Sage, who is said to have equated his inability to finish his treatises with innocent affairs with girls—he called them *amouritiés*. He sometimes proposed, but if 'yes' was the answer, would disentangle himself the next day. Manon, Margot, Jacqueline and Sophie—none of them took the old gentleman seriously any more, no doubt, than did Suzette, who must be added to the list and who was Mlle Curchod. He even noted in his diary that she told him he was not rich enough to marry her. Too much weight must not be put upon these diversions, but they cannot be dismissed entirely,[1] and it may be that the flirtation with Le Sage took place after her return from France in 1763. But he was at least aware and interested in her departure in that autumn.

Meanwhile Suzanne lived for some time in Cayla's house looking after Moultou's children. It was Moultou who wrote to Julie de Bondeli and others on her behalf to announce her bereavement, who suggested and looked into the prospects of a position in England, and who finally attempted to interest Rousseau on her behalf.

Moultou was staying with Rousseau at Motiers-Travers, not far from Neuchâtel, when Mme de Verdelin's letter arrived announcing the imminent departure from Paris of some Englishmen who wished to see Rousseau. Among them might be M. Gibbon, whom she specially recommended. Moultou saw this letter and immediately

[1] Kohler, *op. cit.* pp. 18-19, 22-3; also *Meredith Read,* ii. p. 347. Moultou in the letter to Rousseau cited below, p. 140, mentions that his father had forwarded letters from Mlle Curchod and Le Sage unsealed so that Rousseau could read them.

wrote to Mlle Curchod. He gave the gist of Mme de Verdelin's encomium in different words.[1] 'Si M. Gibbon est du nombre, recevez-le bien car c'est un homme d'un très grand mérite et fort instruit.' Upon that he tells her he had acquainted Rousseau with her story and obtained from him a promise to speak to Gibbon if he came. Not content with that, as soon as he left Rousseau, he wrote to him on the 31st May having had from Suzanne a letter which made his heart bleed. Gibbon had arrived at Lausanne, cold and unfeeling, as cured of his old passion as Mlle Curchod was far from being. An Englishman who fancied himself in love with this charming creature but was incapable of knowing true love, had tried to prejudice Gibbon against her. With touching faith in the power of the master's words Moultou implored him to speak to Gibbon on Suzanne's behalf. He must say how well known she was in Geneva for her knowledge, her wit and above all her virtues, for Moultou knew nothing more pure or celestial than her soul, and guaranteed the purity of his own motives by his desire to settle her for good in England. Rousseau, he adds, must be assumed to know nothing of what had passed between the young people. He has heard that Gibbon is starting at any moment to visit Rousseau. The letter ends after a page of other matter with a final appeal not to forget Mlle Curchod.

He enclosed a copy of this in a letter written on the same day to Mlle Curchod, in which he told her sensibly enough that 'if this man is worthy of you he will return; if he is no good leave him alone, his loss is not worth one of your regrets'.

[1] d'Haussonville, *op. cit.* i. 65 *sqq.* Mme de Verdelin wrote, 14 mai 1763: 'Si M. Gibbon est du nombre, mon voisin, traitez-le bien; il est dit-on plein d'esprit et beaucoup de bonnes qualités; il a beaucoup vu ici M. de Foncemagne chez qui je l'ai rencontré' (Dufour, *Corr. Gén de J. J. Rousseau*, ix. 290).

How did they know so much about Gibbon's state of heart, his intended movements, or the other young Englishman's intervention? No correspondence survives between 1759 and 1763. Probably he wrote when he sent her his *Essai*. Meredith Read gives a translation of a long high-flown epistle and thinks that Gibbon had wished to dedicate the *Essai* to Mlle Curchod and that she declined the honour.[1] This is very likely, and the letter in Read is probably a dedicatory epistle sent for her approval and consent. It has some close resemblances to the dedication to his father finally printed. It is impossible, I think, to infer anything very definite from Suzanne's references to some correspondence in her letter of 23rd June which we are coming to. Gibbon may have written from Paris announcing his coming. He could not expect it to be a secret. Nor could he have suspected the activity in the other camp which the news of his coming aroused. It has been asked why he returned to Lausanne at this time. The simple answer seems to be that he had many ties with the place, and thought that he was safe so far as Mlle Curchod was concerned. He knew his own mind even if he did not know hers.

He reached Lausanne on the 25th May. On the 30th Suzanne wrote a rather hysterical letter in which she implored him to put her out of her misery by avowing his indifference. She blushed deeply for this step and implored him to secrecy.[2] She directed it to 'M. Gibbon gentilhomme anglais, chez M. de Mézery, à Lausanne'.

Whether there was any reply to this we do not know, but in five days it was followed by another. In this she tells him at length with calm reproach that his letter has

[1] *Meredith Read*, ii. p. 333. Read says d'Haussonville gave him a copy of this letter from the Duc de Broglie's archives.

[2] d'Haussonville, *op. cit.* i. 61. When this letter, with the other which d'Haussonville quotes, was returned to Mlle Curchod she wrote on it, 'A thinking soul is punishment enough, and every thought draws blood'.

disabused her.[1] He has returned to the ordinary rank of men. Her romantic imagination had caused her to sacrifice herself for a fictitious being who will never exist. In future she will be as kind and as indifferent as she is to all her friends and there will be no further question of their old story. She will end it by some necessary remarks.

These consist in asking for information on the prospects of a *dame de compagnie* in England; in enclosing some comments on his *Essai* as a first token of her new friendship for him, together with an invitation to Geneva to hear his praises from her mouth; and finally in a conscious echo of Mme de Verdelin's letter. She has heard that a number of English are leaving Paris for Motiers. If that is his goal, and he would like a letter for Rousseau, let him write to her for one since her best friends are in close friendship with Rousseau, and she would gladly prove her regard for him with such a service.

The manœuvre was too ingenuous, and had Gibbon exposed himself to Rousseau's admonitions he could not but have detected the conspiracy. But he did not go; to Rousseau's relief if to no one else's. On the 4th June, the same day that Mlle Curchod was writing to Gibbon, Rousseau sent a letter to Moultou disclaiming his ability to help. He did not like Gibbon's coldness. He did not like his book, finding in it a straining after wit and affectation. Therefore Gibbon was not his man.

> 'I do not think he can be Mlle. Curchod's. Who does not realise her value is not worthy of her, but he who has known it and can break off is a man to despise. She does not know what she wants. This man serves her better than her own heart. I would rather a hundred times that he should leave her poor and

[1] The question is whether the letters referred to here are those written in 1758–9 or later ones. *Birkbeck Hill*, p. 294, assumes that his answer to her note of 30th May had given her great pain. But this seems far from clear.

free in your midst, than to take her away to be unhappy and rich in England. In truth I hope Mr. Gibbon will not come. I should like to disguise my feelings, but I could not. I should like to be of use, and I feel that I shall spoil everything.'[1]

This letter was published with initials only in Gibbon's lifetime. He did not shrink from calling attention to it in his Memoirs, giving the exact reference and adding:

'as an author I shall not appeal from the judgement or taste or caprice of *Jean Jacques*; but that extraordinary man, whom I admire and pity, should have been less precipitate in condemning the moral character and conduct of a stranger'.[2]

This revelation at the end of his life cannot but have confirmed his impression that he had been the object of a designing girl, which, as J. M. Robertson suggested, may well account for his complete silence about her in this part of his Autobiography.

In his reply, written on the 23rd June, to Suzanne's letter there is no mention of her offer concerning Rousseau. He attributes his delay in answering to his desire to study carefully her notes on his *Essai*, and with solemn compliment assures her that perhaps for the first time an author has enjoyed reading a criticism of his works. He can give her no assurance about her prospects in England beyond another solemn compliment that she must earn esteem wherever she goes. In all essential circumstances she would find him her friend but firmly, perhaps coldly, certainly not ungently, he declines her suggestion of a correspondence. Judging by himself he has come to the conclusion that it would be dangerous for both of them.[3]

Five days before he wrote this he had assured his stepmother, upon disclosing his desire to pass the winter in Lausanne, that no woman was in the least concerned in

[1] Dufour, *op. cit.* ix. 327. [2] *Murray*, p. 298.
[3] d'Haussonville, *op. cit.* i. 68.

this project and that he was cured of his old passion, upon his word of honour.

If that was his state of mind, for whatever reasons, his attitude towards Suzanne's proposals was only wise and honourable.

An accident produced an unhappy epilogue. In the next letter to Mrs Gibbon is a vivid and witty account of a visit to Voltaire at Ferney. The great man in his new rôle of country gentleman and even farmer had not forgotten his old hobby. 'His playhouse is very neat and well contrived, situated just by his Chappel, which is far inferior to it, tho' he says himself "que son Christ est du meilleur faiseur de tout le pays de Gex".' The piece was the *Orphan of China*, an old favourite, and Gibbon, fresh from the Paris theatres, sat quizzing the hollow-voiced old ranter of seventy as he played the Tartar Conqueror opposite his ugly old niece. The play began at eight. A hundred people sat down to supper from twelve to two. Then they danced till four, and their coaches returned to the gates of Geneva just as they were opening. Was there anything in history or fable to compare with it?

Neither in this letter nor in his Journal does he mention that he encountered Mlle Curchod at Ferney. Nor apparently did he think very much of the meeting, for he was genuinely surprised to find some two months later that he had set a train to a magazine which was only then exploding.[1]

[1] The Swiss poet Bonstetten says that during a year he used to go to Ferney every Saturday with Mlle Curchod and Moultou: *Souvenirs de Ch. V. de Bonstetten*, 1832. Voltaire was not generally reticent about his dramatic activities. But at this period there are only two references. In a letter of 26th July (*Œuvres*, 1881, xlii. 525) he says, 'J'ai voulu jouer un rôle de vieux bonhomme sur mon petit théâtre; mais on ne m'entendait plus. Je suis obligé de renoncer à cet agréable amusement, qui me consolait.' In a letter to the Comte d'Argental of 6th August he says: 'J'ai joué à l'âge de soixante-dix ans Gengis-kan avec un applaudissement universel—Mme. Denis jouait encore mieux que moi, s'il est possible'. Voltaire was writing to d'Argental

Perhaps Gibbon did behave coldly or pertly on this occasion. Did not Mlle Curchod very likely make some mistakes on her side? Was she perhaps too eager, too ready to rally him as we know she did on occasions? One of these long August nights was the most unhappy moment for them to meet after their long separation. Amid the distractions of the play, the supper, the dance, the throng of guests, the posing even more inseparable from a social gathering then than now, the true self of neither was likely to be apparent. But whatever passed between them on that evening, it was not until the 21st September that Mlle Curchod launched a very long and passionately angry letter.[1]

She was on the point of leaving for Montélimar and later Paris in the hope of salving her mother's fortune. Her return as well as her whole future was uncertain. Gibbon might well be leaving before then, never to revisit Lausanne. Pent-up feelings could and need be restrained no longer.

> 'Intimidated and overcome at Ferney', she writes, 'by the continual play of forced gaiety and the hard-heartedness of your replies, my trembling lips absolutely refused to serve me; you assured me in other words that you blushed for me for the rôle I sustained; Monsieur, I have never been able to confuse the rights of honesty with those of vanity. You have taught me at times to forget the one. As for the other—you are not a dishonest man and what sort of a criminal would be the man who should dare to accuse me of ever having harmed——'

almost every other day, and it is hardly likely that he would omit this great event in the letter immediately following it. Therefore the performance was probably on 4th or 5th August, and in any case in the first week of that month. Gibbon's letter to Mrs Gibbon was written on 6th August. In his Journal, 31st December 1763, cited *Misc. Wks.* i. 173, Gibbon implies that he went to Geneva in July. The only important point for us is that he encountered Suzanne Curchod before 6th August and she did not write to him till 21st September.

[1] d'Haussonville, *op. cit.* i. 70-76. The dates take the wind out of d'Haussonville's sails, who says that after her cruel treatment at Ferney *le vase déborda* the next day.

Over five pages flows the tumultuous justification of her conduct from their first meetings; in her constancy, in her independence and disinterestedness in view of his position and prospects, in her relations with M. de Montplaisir and Deyverdun her conscience is proudly clear. He might see any of her letters if he cared. And in truth a surviving letter to Deyverdun is innocent enough, a rigmarole of girlish wit.[1] As for Montplaisir, she relates that it was in order to let Gibbon see that she would not sacrifice her heart to a fortune that she revealed the fact of his offers. Gibbon himself surprised her by declaring his own passion. Mr Gibbon's refusal had brought her 'au bord du tombeau'. But such was her infatuation with an imaginary figure, that she had interpreted Gibbon's silence as proof of his constancy throughout the painful years which followed. Her visits to Lausanne had been an escape from the slavery of lessons, and if her conduct had drawn people's jealousy and censure, it was only that she was enjoying the little triumphs of vanity; no one else had taken his place in her heart.

> 'I acted', she concludes, 'with you as an honest man of the world, incapable of failing in his promise, of seducing or betraying, but who has amused himself in tearing my soul with tortures most deliberately conceived and carried out. I will not threaten you any more with the vengeance of heaven, an expression which escaped me in a first access, but I can assure you here, without any prophetic wisdom, that you will one day regret the irreparable loss which you have made in alienating for ever the too tender, too frank heart of S.C.
>
> 'GENÈVE *ce* 21^{e} *septembre.*'

This is the entry in his Journal for 22nd September:

> 'The second volume of the letters of Baron de Bielfeld diverted me from Nardini. His character interests me. I find in his

[1] MS. in the possession of Mme Grenier-Brandebourg.

letters a naive enough picture of the courts of Germany. I should have preferred in truth some details of the character and history of the King of Prussia and of his suppers at Potsdam to all these galas and marriages. But discretion and fear impose very rigorous laws in Germany.

'I have received a most unexpected letter. It was from Mademoiselle C. Dangerous and artificial Girl! At this air of candour which reigns in your letter, at these sentiments of affection and straightforwardness which you display, I felt some regrets and almost remorse. She makes a defence of her conduct from the first moment that she knew me, her constancy to me, her scorn for M. de Montplaisir, and the tender and firm faithfulness which she believed she saw in the letter in which I told her there was no more hope. The journeys to Lausanne, the adorers whom she has had and the complacence with which she has listened to them form the most difficult article to justify. Neither d'Eyverdun (she says) nor any body have for a moment effaced my image from her heart. She was amusing herself at Lausanne without becoming attached. Granted. But these amusements convict her all along of the most odious dissimulation, and if unfaithfulness is sometimes a weakness, duplicity is always a vice. It was during the month of July 1758 that she wrote me from Crassie that remarkable letter full of tenderness and despair her eyes filled with tears and her health enfeebled by grief. In that same month of July she was at Lausanne full of health and charm. *The object of the women's jealousy and the men's sighs* (   )[1] enjoying all the pleasures, founding Académies, distributing prizes, herself composing jeux d'esprit and playing with love even if she was not engaging herself seriously. Is not this contrast enough to enlighten me on her account? I say enlighten. It is only a question now of ideas and not at all of feelings. The most complete justification, in restoring my esteem for her, could no longer rekindle fires so completely put out. As she tells me that she must soon leave Geneva I shall not see her again any more and all is finished. This remarkable affair in all its aspects has been very useful to me. It has opened my eyes upon the character of women and will serve me for a long time as a preservative against the seductions of love.

'I went to dine at Mesery where I found myself almost alone

[1] Gibbon left this bracketed space in his MS. intending apparently to insert a reference.

with Madame. After dinner I returned to town and supped with Guise and Clarke.'[1]

Lovers are not the best judges of evidence. Who would now pledge his verdict on the rights of this matter on their testimony alone? Who on the other hand can doubt that Gibbon and Suzanne Curchod were not made to marry one another? Not for the last time would that tide of eloquence have swept vainly over the smooth well-constructed breakwater. Perhaps one is rather appalled to see it stand so unshaken when the wave has passed. Rousseau was right. The grave balancing of the phrases, the cool subordination of all experience to himself, show that the lover has gone, the historian remains, and if he sighs at all now, it is a sigh of relief.

[1] Part of this was printed in a footnote, *Prothero*, i. 41, but with very serious omissions.

Chapter II

LOVE AND FRIENDSHIP

1763–1764

'A PARIS j'étois un sage.' Gibbon's rueful comment on his dissipations was written in February 1764 when his stay in Lausanne was drawing to an end. It is the text of the contrast between the brief complacent account of this period in his Autobiography and the detailed often uneasy record of the contemporary Journal.

The prospect in the previous May had been bright enough. His return had been welcomed by old friends to whom he was anxious to display himself in his new rôles of soldier and author. Pavillard had shed tears over him and had shown him how he carried about the gold snuff-box, with his pupil's miniature on the lid, in a wooden case to protect it.[1] This was gratifying; it was also satisfactory that without offending the good man it had been possible to secure lodgings more suitable to the young captain's tastes and position.

Henri de Crousaz de Mézery kept what was known as the Academy. He had two houses, one in the rue du Bourg,[2] the other a château at Mézery, about three miles out of the town to the north-west. According to the

[1] *Prothero*, i. 40. Gibbon's father had given Pavillard this snuff-box. Many years later Gibbon discovered that the family had cut the box up and divided it. He recovered the portrait from them and gave it to Sheffield. The miniature was painted by Miss Carwarden, afterwards Mrs Butler. Add. MSS. 34887, f. 40.

[2] The Hôtel Central stands on its site.

season of the year his guests could be put up at either house; in the height of summer indeed they had the run of both. Most of the inmates were young Englishmen, Germans or Dutch, who were nominally at least pursuing various studies and could engage what masters they pleased. M. de Mézery was a gentleman who, to Gibbon's satisfaction, successfully maintained the fiction that he was entertaining for his pleasure, and Mme de Mézery was a lady of charm and ability.

Their hospitality was not confined to young men, and Gibbon on his arrival found established there an old militia friend with his family. Sir Willoughby Aston and his wife were respectively enjoying unlimited whist and wine, and they all had a good talk about Winchester camp and the great court-martial at Reading. There was also Count Golovkin and his wife, who were bringing up their children on Rousseau's advice.

In such staid and agreeable surroundings Gibbon settled down in June to a course of hard study. When he was out at Mézery he read Latin poetry. In Lausanne he made use of the libraries in order to begin an elaborate analysis of the geography of ancient Italy.

But when his Journal begins again on 17th August we find him a prey to various distractions and moving with an idle crowd between Mézery and the town. Some of the young men had rooms in the Lausanne house but came out to Mézery to dine, and in the afternoon Gibbon's room would be the 'Caffé reglé de ces desœuvrés'. From time to time these young men would haunt his rooms, chattering there until half-past midnight, and he complains with all the severity of an over-anxious undergraduate whose schools are less than a year ahead. Yet having already found the château at Mézery boring, he was ready at any time to go into town with them were it for a supper party or to improve their French by hearing a sermon on despising the world. There was a long bill for cabriolets, and it was a relief when the family moved to the rue du Bourg in September. Unfortunately the young men were not satisfied with these mild diversions, and the militia captain was involved and perhaps led the way, for the honour of the service, in some boisterous escapades which he soon regretted and learned to avoid.

They were noisy young men. There was Sidney, 'a meer boy', but of a violent nature, and Mr Guise, 'a Sir John Guise of Gloucestershire's son—a very sensible well-bred man', and Clarke and Victor de Saussure, a Swiss. On the other side were the town watch, honest fellows somewhat puzzled how to deal with high-spirited gentlemen, and the authorities themselves a little puzzled too, because it was not certain how far foreign students, whether fully matriculated or not, were answerable only to the Bernese government. Somewhere between the parties were men like M. Frey, the man who had brought Gibbon out from London ten years ago and was now Guise's governor.[1]

One Sunday night in June Sidney and Guise caused a small riot at Ouchy. The next month Clarke and Saussure lodged a complaint about their treatment by the watchmen, and the magistrates felt bound to establish a patrol to watch the watch. Nevertheless a few days later there was another uproar, and this time the Council received a circumstantial letter signed by 'Messieurs Clarke, Guise, Guibon et Sidney'. The watchman, Jacob Corbaz, had demonstrated with a bayonet and threatened the said gentlemen. They demanded justice and promised to appeal to the Bailli and to the government of Berne. This was Gibbon's first appearance in these troubles and he must have been a useful fellow in distress, with his knowledge of French, and of the ins and

[1] Later Sidney's, but he refused to take him to Italy because of his uncontrollable behaviour.

outs of the local government. It is significant that in the next mention in the minutes his name has moved up to the first place in the list of complainants.

The Council pondered the problem and enquired for facts, and at last named 23rd August for a hearing. Gibbon appeared at the head of his party and laid their case in a speech of a quarter of an hour. The threat to go to Berne proved successful. The Council found on the facts for the Englishmen, and it was agreed that the watch should get off with a reprimand in their presence.

> 'Thus', comments Gibbon, 'our case ended, an unhappy business which showed on the magistrates' part an obstinacy, bad faith and incapacity which renders them very contemptible, and on ours too much desire to hold on to a trifle.' [1]

That was enough for the watch, and they kept out of the way on other occasions when the wine of Burgundy had marched to some purpose.[2] The disgraceful climax came on the 14th September. Gibbon had visited one of those innocent and perhaps tame gatherings of young people, *la société du Château*, and had played with Catherine Crousaz, whom he much admired. Then, after two pages left blank for no stated reason, he continues the sad story of the same day:

> 'On leaving this assembly why did I not go home at once instead of supping with Clarke? There we were Guise, Clarke, Captain Clarke, Sidney, Manners, de Salis and I; councillor d'Illens, Major Grand, Corsier and de Saussure. Clarke made the bottle pass with such speed that after having emptied five and twenty of Burgundy we went down the town in an uproar, falling and picking ourselves up again twenty times and waking everybody. At three o'clock in the morning I reached my apartment with the help of Manners, who is never so sensible as

[1] Lausanne, Hotel de Ville, *Manuel de Conseil de 1761–64*, ff. 245-451, sittings for 21st to 26th July, 16th and 23rd August, also 28th June, 1st, 4th and 8th July, and Gibbon's MS. Journal, 23 août.

[2] 'Le vin de Bourgogne a marché et nous nous sommes trouvés passablement gris.' Journal, 8th September.

when he is drunk. The others flung themselves into Sidney's apartment where there were nearly some fearful scenes; Sidney and Saussure at each other's throats; a gun went off under Guise's arm and the ball broke the window. But what is bound to make a noise is the visit Guise and Clarke made to Corsier who had gone home. They threatened to break the door, and when Mlle. Corsier appeared at the window, she was not treated with all the respect possible. I would give much that all this *tintamarre* had not happened in a town as small and consequently as censorious as this one.'

The morning had its inevitable physical consequences. More disastrous, as Gibbon foresaw, was the blow to his reputation. Although he had the sense to avoid the risk of cold looks or worse, he knew what was thought of him when, in eleven days' time, he ventured to call on Mme du Bochat and she said nothing and made no comment on his absence.

'Her silence gave me pain. My manners had a very good reputation here but I can see that people are beginning to identify me with my compatriots and to look on me as a man who likes wine and riot. Are they altogether wrong?'

He never erred to this extent again, but more than one reference in the diary indicates that his disgrace was not quickly wiped out.

Gibbon, as has been already seen, was ready at making friendships and optimistic for their future, undeterred by the transience of many of them. Huntingtower and d'Augny had gone their ways. John Butler Harrison was no companion away from the militia. Gibbon had a letter from him this autumn and pondered regretfully on the illiteracy of this good fellow. The bond with Deyverdun remained firm in spite of absence. But he was away now tutoring in Germany. They corresponded, but at the moment were a little at cross purposes.

Deyverdun had rejected some plans for living together which Gibbon had made the previous year. Now he wanted to accept them; but Gibbon's plans were already in great uncertainty once more through disturbing letters from home, and this news from Deyverdun was but an added embarrassment. Meanwhile in his absence Deyverdun had obligingly recommended Victor de Saussure. This idle but engaging young man had made a great way in Gibbon's regard, and by the end of September they were sitting up till one in the morning in deep conversation. But Saussure was soon sent packing to Göttingen. He had offended his family's pride and expectations by falling in love with Marianne de Illens, whose place was in La Palud rather than in the exclusive Bourg. Gibbon later, 1766, wrote him a letter of Chesterfieldian cynicism recommending the pursuit of married women.[1] A boyish effusion.

Gibbon confided his regrets to his Journal:

> 'I have lost this friend almost as soon as I had gained him. It happens rarely enough that one can count in advance on forming a close tie with some one quite unknown and still more rarely that such expectation should not be in vain. That is the history of our connection. D'Eyverdun's letters had introduced this young man to me, and from the moment that I formed the plan of coming to Lausanne I always reckoned on compensating myself with his company for the loss of my friend. He viewed me seemingly with the same predilections. We took a mutual liking for one another and passed rapidly to familiarity to confidence to friendship, and in six weeks we had nothing more to hide from one another.'

The diarist then gives of Saussure one of his most elaborate pen portraits. The claims of other candidates for his favour are reviewed more briefly but with unfailing interest. A young man, de Cheseaux, who had been *fort lié* years ago makes a passing appearance.

[1] *Meredith Read*, ii. p. 353.

Gibbon spends a day with him at his country place and sizes up his position. A good deal of time is spent with Wuest, but finally he is relegated with almost girlish pedantry to the second class of friendship. He cannot be ranked with Victor de Saussure or Deyverdun. In the same class perhaps was Clarke, Godfrey Bagnall Clarke, with whom Gibbon kept up after their return to England and lived to execute his will. Of the other Englishmen Guise is well liked, and converses with Gibbon 'sur un ton d'amité'. Lord Palmerston is well-informed and likely to profit by his tour. He is shy, but that will wear off with experience. He has distinguished himself by visiting the Alps. Nevertheless a few days later, after an evening spent in his company, Gibbon concludes that, though they appreciated each other's merits, they would never become friends in a year spent together. Meanwhile there had arrived at M. de Mézery's house a young Englishman who after an unpromising beginning was destined to hold first place above them all, not excepting even Georges Deyverdun.

Captain John Baker Holroyd, with his friend Captain Edward Manners of the 21st Light Dragoons, the Royal Foresters, a regiment raised by the Marquis of Granby for the war and recently disbanded, had visited Germany and now, in the course of a tour which was not to be taken too seriously, arrived in Lausanne in August and settled at M. de Mézery's, where, to their great entertainment, a small and consequential young man announced himself as Captain of Grenadiers in the Hampshire Militia. But this was Major Sturgeon to the life! The military cit of Foote's farce *The Mayor of Garratt*, who had made the town laugh with his swelling tale of marchings and counter-marchings between Ealing and Uxbridge, and of casualties on Hounslow Heath. And here he was again, gossiping of duty at Dover or Devizes, and ready to show his eye for the fine points of drill when Major Grand's Swiss grenadiers turned out. The likeness was too much for the young cavalrymen and they hailed him as such. This was too much in turn for the young grenadier and he demanded explanations. It was incredible. A British government would never allow so valuable an institution as the militia to be made game of on the stage. No civilised nation would allow it. The impertinent young regulars must be drawing on their prejudiced imaginations. Encouraged by his indignation, they were delighted to return to the attack and assure him it was all too true.[1] Gibbon accepted this as philosophically as he did heavier blows. Slowly but cautiously he admitted them to his society and to his Journal. But there it is Manners who receives the fullest portraiture: 'C'est le meilleur garçon du monde, vif, enjoué, sans soucis et sans science quelconque'. Holroyd, on the other hand, 'ne manque pas d'esprit, ni de connoissance mais il paroît très suffisant'. Four days later, 5th September, the entry runs, 'je commence à goûter Holroyd et Manners plus qu'au commencement. La suffisance du premier diminue tous les jours et je me faits à l'étourderie du second.' Their irreverence was forgiven, and twenty-five years later Gibbon could equably promise to record his marches and counter-marches like his brother, Major Sturgeon.[2]

An acquaintance begun thus cautiously and almost against expectation developed slowly, and Holroyd's name makes but few and brief appearances in the Journal. The Italian tour was planned and begun in Guise's company; it is of Guise that Gibbon writes home with constant approval, announcing once again

[1] Memorandum by Lord Sheffield, see Brit. Mus. 11909. dd. 25 (1). From a letter of Holroyd's in Add. MSS. 34887 it appears that he was at Lausanne before 9th August. Gibbon does not mention him till 31st August, and on 1st September refers to him as 'un des nouveaux débarqués'.

[2] *Murray*, p. 184.

his hopes of a friendship formed for life. Only in the last days at Lausanne is the progress made by Holroyd revealed.

Guise and a young Dutchman quarrelled at a dance over Nanette de Illens. A duel was imminent. Pavillard and Holroyd, an odd alliance, knocked up Gibbon in the morning to invoke his aid. With them Gibbon spent the day running to and fro, to succeed finally in pacifying both parties. He concludes his record by reflecting on the insight into his friends' characters afforded by this small crisis: 'I have conceived a real friendship for Holroyd. He has plenty of sense and feelings of honour, with a heart in the right place.' He follows this up in a letter in May from the Borromean Islands addressing him familiarly as 'dear Leger' and calling him his best friend, and in his Journal for 1st July he notes receiving a letter in Florence and anticipates the pleasure of meeting Holroyd in Rome in the winter.

The temperament and habits of this new friend were very different from those of Gibbon or his previous friends. Holroyd bathed in the lake every morning until it became too cold, and had intended, with what seems strangely modern optimism, to go on all through the winter. Four mornings a week he was at the riding school. Sometimes he would go shooting in the afternoon, and would then spend the evening in his rooms.[1] He was not a scholar and seems to have had little Latin.[2] If he was well-informed it was for practical purposes;

[1] Letters of Holroyd in Add. MSS. 34887.

[2] When he received Dr. Parr's inscription for Gibbon's tomb with the phrase *decessit XVII CAL. FEB.* he hastened to inform the learned doctor that Gibbon had died in January. Add. MSS. 34887. Probably the quotation from Tacitus which adorns the closing paragraph of his continuation of the Autobiography was supplied by one of the scholars whom he called in to help with his editorial task. *Misc. Wks.* i. 425. Gibbon, it must be said, often quotes Latin in his letters to him. Holroyd had been at school in Dublin with Malone. His family had migrated to Ireland from Yorkshire in Charles II's reign.

in time to come he was to be a progressive agriculturist. It is unlikely that he was introspective, or the man to sit up half the night exchanging confidences. His portrait by Reynolds shows a frank energetic countenance with 'an eagle eye', and we know him to have been quick-tempered and given to damning and cursing in his letters. Though like Gibbon and the other young men he was a whole-hearted dangler, to use their own word, on his record he was a marrying man, being destined to have had in the end three wives, though only one during Gibbon's lifetime. This friendship was one of the happiest unions of opposites, and Gibbon at least was lucky, and very likely wise in securing the devotion of a man who supplied some essential qualities which he himself lacked.

But such differences do not exhaust the significance of these men's relation, a significance apparent from their earliest days together. In that first autumn Holroyd is seen as a rule in the company of such active fellows as Guise and Manners and Clarke. They made up a party in October to see Switzerland and reached the sources of the Danube. Gibbon was asked to go with them. But he apprehended expense and racket mainly on the part of Manners and Clarke. Besides it was getting late in the year and they were going on horseback. His mind was ready to support the loss of interests to which his slight frame was unequal. Gibbon's feeling for nature has been underestimated in some ways, but he never quite understood the attraction of the mountains. He liked to send home awe-inspiring references to the snow-capped peaks which surrounded Lake Leman. But Lord Palmerston's curiosity to go fairly near them was another matter, and here was Holroyd at it too. In Gibbon's last days in Switzerland the 'tour of the glaciers' had become incomprehensibly popular, and when Lord Sheffield was induced at last to bring his family out to view 'the highly respectable situation of Mr. Gibbon' [1] in Lausanne, he must needs also take his daughters to Chamouny and adventure them over the Col de Balme, and they too must go and sign their names in Rousseau's bedroom. They were true children of their father in that. Gibbon was destined to advance half unawares into a new age of ideas and achievements with his eyes still comfortably fixed upon a receding world, and this contrast is strikingly illustrated in the greatest intimacy of his life, and even in the neo-Gothic setting which Holroyd provided at Sheffield Place with the assistance of Wyatt's genius.

An angry lover, a new friendship—nor must that regrettable *tintamarre* of the 14th be forgotten—were enough to make that September memorable. But there is one more agitation to be recorded, one which went near to making the merest trifle of any other matter. The Italian tour, the thing which after all lay nearest to Gibbon's heart, for which he was preparing so solidly through every other distraction, was seriously threatened. Letters from home conveyed his father's dissatisfaction over his expenditure, revealing the very uncertain state of the family finances. Another mortgage was spoken of. Gibbon deplored such a step and proposed an alternative. If his annuity was made into a perpetual rent charge, Gibbon would sell that for an annuity on his life. By that he would be able to double his present allowance. He was willing to make almost any concession to his father, provided he could go to Italy, barring if possible the raising of another mortgage. He had made up his mind that he would never marry now, but he was bound to take the long view for his own lifetime. He already foresaw interminable em-

[1] *Misc. Wks.* i. p. xxvi.

barrassments. An injudicious phrase in one of his letters annoyed his father still more. Gibbon is seen anxiously and eloquently trying to explain it away, and still eloquently and persistently holding on to the Italian tour.

Month by month the correspondence went on with the long-drawn suspense of the tardy posts. At one time—if the mortgage was persisted in—Gibbon was holding himself ready for a quick journey to London and back, always *incognito* in order that the town might not know that the Gibbons were in any difficulties. But eventually the threat was removed. Mr Gibbon agreed to the tour of Italy. There would be no need for him to come home. This glad news arrived at the end of October, and the Journal relates how its writer in the full flush of his relief made a very dull and unpromising party go with spirit. Yet this was not the end of his troubles. His father appears to have played a cat-and-mouse game. On 1st February Gibbon desperately recorded after receiving a letter that he must make an end of these *tracasseries*. Either he must go on to Italy with a peace of mind which he had not so far enjoyed, or return to England and wait for a favourable opportunity to make a third journey on the Continent. He thereupon sat down and wrote a temperate and persuasive letter, not arguing about their financial plans, but calmly setting out the scale of inevitable expenses. He had been assured that Italy could not be visited, and proper company kept, except at the rate of £700 or £800 a year at the lowest. He was concerned to know that he had already spent about half of his father's income.

'If it was possible for you, Dear Sir, to make such an effort for *only one year*, I should consider it as an obligation which it ought to be my study to repay by the most exact economy upon all other occasions and by coming (if necessary) into any schemes which might be thought of to make us both easy. But in case you cannot do it, I had rather give up a scheme (I have indeed always set my heart upon) than it should be the occasion of perpetual uneasinesses and inconveniences to us both.'

The reply was favourable at last. Mr Gibbon agreed to let his son have £700 a year and left him in peace of mind until the middle of his stay in Rome.

A brief idyllic picture of Lausanne society is painted by Gibbon in his Autobiography. By the light of his Journal it appears neither quite so simple nor satisfactory. But first let Holroyd sketch the scene in his more direct way.

'All the world is come to town and we are eminently brilliant, not an evening scarce without one or two Assemblies. We are not troubled with Playhouses Ridottos or such like. There is a sort of Club Coffee House the Members of which are chosen by ballot. The Number is confined to Eighty and is at present full. It is a very good collection. There are persons from all parts and several very sensible men. The Prince of Würtemberg and the Governor of the town are members. . . . There is another society which pleases me very much. It is called the Spring because it consists of Young Women. It is held every Sunday at the house of one of the young ladies. I attend most devoutly. After cards we generally amuse ourselves with some innocent recreations which are nearly the same as what is called in your country Blind Man's Buff, Questions and Commands, etc. etc. At the same time I must observe that notwithstanding the Gayety of the Misses there never happen any improprieties. Occasionally they have balls. They are much addicted to English country dances.'

Elsewhere he remarks, 'they are not so reserved as English misses, but are extremely shy of pawing and handling'.[1]

The young Englishmen enjoyed themselves in these various coteries, and none the less for knowing that

[1] Some letters of Holroyd, 19th December 1763, in Add. MSS. 34887.

they were regarded as good catches and the nets were out. Besides the *Printemps*, there were the *Mercredi* and the *Château*. Gibbon tasted them all in turn, and when their members were judged provincial, foolish and insipid, and altogether company unworthy of him, he turned his eyes on the exclusive houses of the rue du Bourg. Presently he was to be found in the inner circle of Mesdames d'Hermanches, de St. Cierge, and d'Aubonne. M. de Chandieu Villars, the father of the girl with whom as Madame de Sévery he was so closely associated in later years, called and paid him particular attention. Here were to be found the ease and usage of the highest society.

Yet in a short while this aristocratic group proved unsatisfactory. It was dull and pretentious, aping ways that were foreign to the Swiss, and, out pops the ultimate truth, they had not paid M. Gibbon all the attention he looked for. '*Je me suis faufilé dans le Printems.*' The truant was warmly welcomed with a shower of invitations. He could play the fool there at his ease.

Among his other criticisms Gibbon did not spare himself. He owned up to his appetite for flattery, bemoaned his laziness, wondering when he would get a solid year devoted to useful occupations. Then he gives himself a good mark for being less *maussade* in society. But at the Club he had a serious set-back in being rejected in favour of a young Dutchman to represent the foreigners on the committee. He had also lost forty pounds, an event which gave rise to some sound reflexions on the folly of gambling, with an emphasis on the barrenness of the satisfaction brought by winning.

But on the whole it was a series of enjoyable episodes. First there was dangling agreeably between 'ma bonne amie Catherine Crousaz' and Mlle de Wufflens—a Macheathian situation only spoilt by the presence of a disagreeable fellow, Juste Constant de Rebecque, who four years later was to have a son known as Benjamin Constant. Then there were the Grands and the de Illens of La Palud, overbidding one another for popularity. What a weapon to break a rival's party was Nanette de Illens! Guise, Holroyd and Clarke, the rogues, forsook a previous engagement for her sake. The cautious Gibbon attended both parties, and was rewarded by enjoying the frosty discomfiture of the first before he joined the second in its hour of crowded hilarity. He found Blind Man's Buff rather boisterous. But he enjoyed the comic operas in which Nanette shone with the rest, even when they did not know their parts or the music, and was not a little, though no doubt agreeably, shocked at seeing nice girls in breeches; actresses were different. It was as well at times to make a sober jaunt to Lutry in Pavillard's company on a visit to the *pasteur* there.

After Christmas the fun became faster than ever with parties and plays and *veillés* every day and night, and for Gibbon especially so by reason of two predicaments which, unexpected in themselves and in their mutual relation, afforded a feverish and rather disgraceful climax.

On 2nd February at a party somewhat marred by Constant's presence he met a Mme Seigneux and plunged headlong into a warm flirtation.

> 'J'ai beaucoup causé avec une petite Allemande qui a épousé le jeune Seigneux. Sans être jolie sa vivacité et son petit air mutin et chiffonné la rendent très interéssante. Elle se laisse agacer fort bien; elle agace à son tour. Elle entend tout sans se formaliser, et y répond de même. Qu'elle a de tempérament! C'est la lubricité la plus décidée qui perce dans ses yeux, dans ses gestes et dans tous ses propos. Aussi l'a-t-il fallu marier à quinze ans, parceque—etc.'

It was in the idyllic *Printemps* that he pursued *La Petite Femme* with a calculated mixture of ardour and restraint. Within a week it was the established order that they should be at the same table at these parties, and invitations from the great Mme d'Hermanches were neglected that he might be there. 'Tout comme a l'ordinaire', it went on from day to day. 'Le Printems, le Whist et la Petite Femme.' He was gleefully playing with fire. 'La petite étoit de mauvaise humeur. Est-ce que son mari ne l'avoit pas assez—etc.' Gibbon at any rate had fixed his limit. It was to be an affair of badinage without any serious element.

Then news came of Mlle Curchod's arrival, and he notes, and perhaps the fact that he did note it betrays some uneasiness, that he felt how far his cure was completed by the indifference with which he learnt of it. Once more he meets *La Petite Femme*. She seeks him out, so he says, and they whisper together in a corner until 'Le Mari commence à s'en formaliser un peu', and comes to interrupt them more than ten times. The next day a formal visit to Mlle Curchod was made under the safe escort of Pavillard.

> 'To begin with I was a bit confused, but recovered myself and we talked for a quarter of an hour with all the freedom of people who have understood one another. How instructive for me is this tranquillity on her part! I passed the afternoon with la Petite Femme at Madame Fornerey's. Nothing new.'

The next few days were devoted to *La Petite Femme*, who was in and out of humour, and an invitation to walk after the sermon draws the reflexion that Gibbon preferred his old authors. He turns from this 'goût passager et sans principes' to consider his old affair.

> '21st. I could not help thinking a good deal about Mlle Curchod. She betrayed me, since d'Eyverdun had no motive to do so. There is however something sly in her story. She could only have founded her Academy in 1759. It is true that is enough for me. I ventured to call on her. We talked with all the freedom in the world. Her mind has gained a great deal and

if we can forget the past, her company is charming. I took her to a big gathering at Mme Sachli's but without paying her marked attention.

'22nd. As I was settling down to work, a bit late if the truth were told, la Petite Femme walked in the derrière Bourg.[1] Guise went and joined her under his window and I was obliged to go down and lose the morning with her.

'After dinner I went up to the Cité and had a tête-à-tête of two hours with la Curchod. An inclination draws me thither. I note with pleasure that she does not talk at all of the past except for some allusions which I am not obliged to understand.'

So he went on with both of them. 'Toujours la Petite Femme et moi nous sommes bons amis', and if he had *views* the opportunity would not be wanting. Then he is present at an afternoon given in Mlle Curchod's honour by Mme la docteuse d'Apples. He did not play. De Brenles and his wife, Mme Sachli and Gibbon talked to La Belle, who was very witty with her pleasantry. Gibbon began to be bored.

The next day—

'28th. I spent the afternoon and supper at Madame de Brenles by invitation. It was for Mlle. Curchod. I paid little attention to her, talking with a number of other ladies. She acted on her side with a great deal of freedom and rallied me on my tone of *petit maître* and my liking for La Seigneux. I took her after supper to a dance at the de Illens where Guise had invited her at my request, but she must have seen a hundred times that everything was irrevocably ended. Decency kept me sometimes near her, but I was always making for la Petite Femme, and for this time at least my senses have triumphed over my mind. In truth la Petite often spared me the trouble of looking for her. Never have we got on better together. She has admitted to me that she dislikes being married. These two women that I had on my hands amused me much. I saw every one else leave and saw la Curchod home. She had abandoned herself wholeheartedly to her taste for pleasure.'

Gibbon could not keep away from Suzanne, and yet

[1] What is now Avenue Benjamin Constant.

when he was with her he could only be rude. It was a sign that his cure was not as complete as he wished to believe. He could not let the past alone.

> 'We rallied very freely on our departed affection and I made her see quite clearly that I knew all about her inconstancy. She defended herself very well and maintained that she had always kept d'Eyverdun off. What is one to believe? I admit my friend's conduct seems sly and I almost suspect that he pushed matters on. I gave la Belle back the letters which she wrote to me after my return to Switzerland. She asked me for them.'

The next scene is in Voltaire's old theatre at Mon Repos. Once more *Zaïre* was on the stage. The only Englishmen in the audience were Holroyd, de Salis, Ridley, Manners and Gibbon, who had brought Suzanne with him.

> 'In the most interesting places of *Zayre* she sobbed enough to draw the eyes of all upon her. But when she removed her handkerchief one only saw a fresh and cheerful face without a trace of tears. Everyone noticed such gross affectation. How this girl plays Sensibility.'

And the next day he has Bourgeois in to read over *Zaïre* together. Gibbon wished to acquire the good French style of declamation and flattered himself that he had succeeded to some extent, especially in the passages of grandeur, power and passion. And so once more to the de Illens', where he gave the preference to *La Petite Femme*, excusing himself because the odious Constant was with Mlle Curchod.

The ridiculous affair goes on; with *La Petite Femme* behaving demurely under the eyes of her disapproving in-laws; with *La Petite* allowing an arm round her waist and lips to hers; with her and another couple ensconced in a *cabinet* where they talked, etc. etc., until the husband 'formalising himself of it' outside, at last sat down bleakly in their midst. The affair was plainly heading towards one if not two dénouements, were not Gibbon determined to avoid them both.

People who had smiled and connived began to frown. Nanette de Illens took Gibbon to task, reproaching him for preferring Mme Seigneux to Suzanne. Suzanne herself, when Gibbon for once dropped his bantering tone with her—how irritating he must have been!—gave him a sound warning of what his enemies were saying on the score of this flirtation as well as the unforgotten 14th September. Gibbon heard reason and, although he did not altogether tear himself away, we hear no more of these tousings.

As for Suzanne herself, he continued to visit or see her, and she received him until her departure early in April. Gibbon reiterates tiresomely the care he took to show her that all was over. Could this tiresome reiteration have been necessary? He goes further: 'No more question with her of the pure love of angels, my senses were stirred and hers were not at all undisturbed'—and on another day: 'J'ai fait visite à la C. J'y suis sur un pied très amusant. Beaucoup de badinage, quelques licences lui faisant sentir beaucoup de goût et peu de considération. Je vois que mon procédé la déroute.'

It was time they all parted. Mlle Curchod went first early in April. Gibbon saw her the day before.

> 'There was a tone of pleasantry about our talk which I increased without difficulty to let her see that I saw her go with indifference. This feeling was not rehearsed. Time, absence, above all the knowledge of the false and affected character of this girl have extinguished the last sparks of my passion.'

Sacred and Profane Love, Gibbon had not proved himself very impressive with either. Love is a matter in which one should be thorough or leave it alone. But it is not enough to be indignant with what may appear a rather odious little man. Suppose we all kept a diary with the same unrelenting frankness. It is rather late in the day to be angry with Gibbon when others more nearly concerned could forgive him, and it is after all more a question of manners than anything. Probably few of these young men would pass as unexceptionable by the current code of good form. And it must indeed be somewhat surprising for those who have their own conception of this full-blooded century to find this provincial pottering holding so large a place in the grand tour.

Chapter 12

THE TOUR OF ITALY

1764–1765

THE farewell dinners had been given and received, *les petites* embraced and told a hundred foolish things—Gibbon was leaving Lausanne this time with few regrets and no dreams of felicity—and on Wednesday, 18th April 1764, he set out in Guise's company well equipped for the great adventure of Italy, and not least by the presence of the closely written folios of his *Nomina Gentesque Antiquae Italiae* in his baggage. Their host de Mézery accompanied them as far as Geneva, showering attentions on them to the point of embarrassment.

They were entertained in Geneva by the English, with Lord Mount Stuart at their head. At each city they were to visit, there would be the same welcoming and passing on in the grand chain of 'the pilgrims of the year' coming and going anywhere between Geneva and Naples, making and losing friends, pausing to greet old acquaintances on the return route, and noting the progress each had made.

On the 20th they left Geneva to approach the still unpierced barrier of the Alps. Now their adventures were beginning. 'We have exchanged the most beautiful countryside perhaps which exists under the sun, the delicious banks of Lake Leman, for the sheer and barren mountains of Savoy.'

'Tuesday 24th. We dined at Modane and lay at Lannebourg[1] at the foot of the Mont Cenis. Always the same spectacle. Steep and very narrow roads lead us up the side of the mountains whose summits, bare or covered with snow, rise one above the other and only end in the clouds. Below the precipices we see the Arc whose white foaming waves plunge down the valley with a roar, and form perpetual cascades on the rocks and big boulders which the torrents bring down from the mountains. The most lovely sunshine in the world gilded this romantic scene and gave it a sombre colouring which disposes the soul to an agreeable melancholy. Lannebourg is so buried under the mountains that the inhabitants do not see the sun from the beginning of November to the end of April.

'Wednesday 25th. After crossing the mountain we arrived in very good time at Susa. One can cross in more than one way. One can go à la Ramasse; for that you get in a little sledge with a peasant for guide who steers it and stops it as he wishes. Its own weight and the incline of the mountain carry it down with such momentum that the descent from the Maison de la Ramasse to Lannebourg is made in a quarter of an hour though it must be a good league. This method is most used on this side of the mountain where the descent is straighter than the other. Guise wanted to ride a mule, but he did not find this animal as sure as had been represented. As for me I made the whole journey in a chair from Lannebourg to Novalise. These chairs made of rush and cords have a very low little back and a board on which to rest the feet. Underneath it is entirely flat so that nothing under it can stop it. I had four porters who took it in turns and who made the five leagues across the mountain without stopping at all. The ascent is slow and painful but on the level and coming down they ran rather than walked. Their quick short little steps are superior in these places to that of a mule and are very like the double of our soldiers. The king taxes them at fifty sous a porter. It is however the favourite occupation of the peasants. They reckon there are a hundred and twenty porters at Lannebourg, and a hundred and fifty at Novalise. In any case it is the only work they can do in the mountains during seven months of the year. My humane feelings caused me some repugnance to being carried over a fearful mountain by my

[1] *I.e.* Lanslebourg.

fellows but this repugnance yielded to necessity; and that all the more easily that I flatter myself that their trade is not harmful though it may be irksome. They certainly told me themselves that it shortened their days. But among my porters there was one vigorous fellow in spite of his fifty-two years during thirty-four of which he had been following this occupation.

'The side of the mountain towards Lannebourg offers a remarkable view. No rocks or precipices are visible. An immense covering of snow presents a uniform surface like an iced cake. The ascent is over a path a foot wide, very rough and at this season very slippery from the ice on it. This path winds almost continually. But one is very safe on it and the only inconvenience felt by us was the excessive cold. When we were at the top, a slight fog arose which soon dispersed to allow the most beautiful sun in the world to reappear; the reflexion on the snow made us feel a very uncomfortable heat for some moments. The plain at the summit of the Mont Cenis is only a pretty narrow valley which may be two leagues wide from the Maison de la Ramasse to the Grande Croix. It is bordered by mountains on both sides of still greater height, among which one can make out the little Mont Cenis on the right. This pass is shorter, but as it is very dangerous it is little frequented. This plain is covered with snow to a depth of twenty to thirty feet; but they assured us that for some months of the summer it is a charming place covered with grass and flowers, which furnish excellent pasture to a number of herds from which the owner derives a considerable revenue. There is a small lake there too. When it is thawed it provides small but good trout. The descent on the Piedmontese side is two leagues from the Grande Croix to Novalise. It is very difficult and bordered with very deep precipices; but to diminish the steepness a zigzag road has been made known as the Chemin de l'Échelle. I counted about thirty turns myself and think there must be more than fifty. One sees already that it is Italy. For while the other side of the mountain is covered with snow, there is almost none on this side. The great and almost only danger of the mountain is the avalanche; masses of snow which break loose from the summit and fall into the plain with the noise of thunder. Men, houses and even whole villages are often buried in them. We saw the remains of an avalanche which had fallen on the plateau from the Mont Cenis. It had choked the valley and mounted high enough up the opposite side to block the path. As it is not unknown for men to live a considerable time buried in the snow, the porters take care to provide themselves with bread so as not to die of hunger before they can be got out. Such is the force of education and of familiarity to inure man and to make him prepare coolly for the most frightful dangers.'

They were in Italy now, for they were surrounded by a crowd of people who demanded payment for the slightest service. Gibbon had tipped his porters a guinea to their apparent satisfaction, yet a moment later one of them demanded more money for having lent him some gloves.

Seven days after leaving Geneva they were in Turin. Reading and conversation had passed the time, but it would be difficult, so Gibbon commented, to make a less agreeable journey than this one over the mountains of Savoy.

In Italy Gibbon was at last really a foreigner on the Continent. Not merely the strange language but the manners and outlook of society brought home to him that he was in a different world from Paris and Lausanne. He soon concluded that Turin was not the town for amusements. The pretty women—they were uncommon—were all taken up with their *cicisbei*. Of an evening in Mme de St. Gilles' drawing-room he writes with heavy sarcasm:

'If there is any pleasure in watching play which one does not understand, in listening to a Piedmontese jargon of which one does not take in a word, and in finding oneself in the midst of a proud nobility who will not speak a word to you, we had a most amusing time in this assembly.'

After absurdly formal delays they made their bow to the King as he went to mass. His Majesty put some simple questions to the travellers about their coming and going, and Gibbon noted that he was a little old man whose uneasy manners indicated a bourgeois of

SILHOUETTES OF GIBBON *After the originals by Mrs. Brown*

very poor style. The sight of this unimpressive royalty gave rise to some reflexions.

> 'A court is for me simultaneously an object of interest and disgust. The servility of the courtiers revolts me and I view with horror the magnificence of the palaces which have been cemented with the blood of the people. In a small and poor kingdom like this they must grind the people in order to be equal with the other crowned heads, and to keep up the air of grandeur and the long series of apartments filled with guards and officers whom one sees in the palaces of Turin. In each gilded ornament I seem to see a village of Savoyards ready to die of hunger, cold and misery.'

These are sentiments which are frequently repeated in *The Decline and Fall.*

It is in describing to Holroyd a later scene at court that Gibbon gives an amusing sketch of himself. One not merely sees how he was already prepared in the smallest details to make a figure in the world when the time came, but it is possible to divine here as in other letters that if the Grand Gibbon became something of a legend in his own life, the legend was in great degree of his own making.

> 'The most sociable women I have met with are the King's daughters. I chatted for about a quarter of an hour with them, talked about Lausanne, and grew so very free and easy, that I drew my snuff-box, rapped it, took snuff twice (a crime never known before in the presence chamber), and continued my discourse in my usual attitude of my body bent forwards, and my forefinger stretched out.'

Nearly three weeks passed in these unexhilarating entertainments, combined with some laborious sight-seeing, and relieved by Italian lessons at seven in the morning.

So without much reluctance the travellers went on to Milan, which they reached on 13th May after passing over 'the most beautiful plain in the world, rich, fertile and well cultivated, watered by a number of streams without being flooded'.

Their stay at Milan was short, and Gibbon has therefore little to say of the people beyond noting that they were not so rich nor so superstitious as the Torinese. The city was vast rather than beautiful. A visit was made to Lake Maggiore, where it rained all day and they camped out in the *palazzo* on Isola Bella, meals being sent in from a *trattoria*. On the way back the energetic Guise climbed up inside the colossal statue of S. Carlo Borromeo at Arona.

Venice had been their next aim for the sake of the Carnival, which the presence of the Duke of York was expected to make more brilliant than usual. But already the tale of their expenses was ominous and they still felt the handicap of their lack of Italian. It was decided, therefore, to go to Genoa and thence by sea to Leghorn, and to master the language in the course of a summer spent in Florence.

Genoa was made more agreeable by the presence of M. and Mme Celesia. Experience of the world had cured Mallet's daughter of her romantic notions. She was intelligent and good-natured, and Gibbon confessed to a friendship with a strain of tenderness in it. Now both husband and wife showered entertainments on the young men for which Gibbon took all the credit to himself. They took them out to their country house where nature obliged them with an Italian thunderstorm sharp and short, and where acquaintance was made with a new and more agreeable class of Italians. Walking in the woods Gibbon saw many *contadini*, and though most of them went barefoot he observed with some surprise their healthy appearance and cheerful air. Celesia told him that they were virtuous, good, extremely responsive to kind treatment or the reverse, and happy without many reasons for being so.

It was nearly the end of May, and Gibbon lamented that the heat made him inconceivably lazy. Nevertheless he made a study of Genoese history and visited the great *palazzi* indefatigably, and churches too, where they anticipated the manners of much-scolded humbler tourists by pushing through the crowd during a sermon, and training their glasses on the pictures in the midst of the preacher's most moving expressions.

June had now come, but not the favourable wind that should carry their felucca down the coast to Lerici. There was nothing more to see. It was existence lost, and the Journal died for want of nourishment. Gibbon passed the time in reading Horace, in translating some of his own collections and in reflecting upon the idioms of the two languages. One morning his mind was full of the problems of ancient money; but want of books prevented him from doing much.

At last they could wait no longer. They must face the loss of time and money and go round by way of Parma and Bologna. So on the 12th June they set out for a few days' hard travelling; making their way with difficulty over the pass to Lombardy; posting from Piacenza to reach Parma before the gates shut; getting to Reggio after a short drive in the cool of the evening, and sending out at once for dominoes for the Ridotto, where the company was large and the play high; going to the opera the next night and setting out at half-past one in the morning to reach Modena at dawn; then one more drive in the evening and Bologna at nine o'clock.

The flat vine-chained landscape where one brown campanile quickly succeeds another was altogether to Gibbon's taste. It was one garden, he said, from Piacenza onwards, 'and as the town and even the capitals touch one another, it is less a journey than an agreeable promenade'.

Bologna and its school of painting deserved a fortnight or three weeks, and Gibbon hoped to devote some time there on his way back. A traveller's tale or experience is embalmed in *The Decline and Fall*. 'The famous Bologna sausages are said to be made of ass-flesh.'[1] Meanwhile they pushed on the next day, the 19th June.

> 'We left Bologna at three in the morning to cross the Apennines for the third time. These Mountains are not high; they are rather wide and extensive hills covering a deal of territory. I know nothing more melancholy than their general view. At long intervals you come on a poor village, and you do not even see those pastures covered with flocks which do something to brighten the sight of most mountains. We had been so badly provided with horses that we did not reach Florence till nine in the evening. We stopped at a certain Charles Hatfield's an innkeeper well known among the English who speak very well of him. To judge by our supper it would appear he deserves it.'

The next day the English called on them. There was Lord Fordwich, 'who has become almost a Florentine'; Ponsonby, an old friend; Captain Hatsel, who had come from Gibraltar with his friend, Captain Parry. Mr Lyttelton, later to be known as the bad Lord, did not call, but they were told that was just like his eccentric ways.

> 'In the evening we drove to the Porta San Gallo. It is the general and boring rendezvous of the Florentine nobility who come there to take the air or rather the dust. I did not notice much beauty or magnificence.'

In a few days they learnt with the other English to prefer the Cascine, 'a fine meadow surrounded by trees'. 'If only the Florentines would realise how very much a gathering of society would enhance it!'

They were now taken charge of by Sir Horace Mann, the indispensable minister whose task for thirty years had been as much to restrain or retrieve young men

[1] *The Decline and Fall*, c. xli. n. 88.

from their scrapes as to represent his nation at the Tuscan court. Gibbon found him 'an agreeable man, quiet and polished, but somewhat wrapped up in a round of important trifles'. He had become altogether Italian.

Mann's house on the Lungarno[1] stood open to all respectable comers, and Gibbon notes that he and Guise dined or spent the evening there so frequently that he does not always record the fact. Not content with giving excellent dinners, the minister was at pains to introduce his visitors to the best society and to every entertainment that was afoot. One of his first services to Gibbon and Guise was to secure them places in the Regent's box for the horse-race through the Corso—a narrow main street—which, though in honour of St. John, was held on St. Peter's Day.

The Journal contains an elaborate description of this race, as also of the ceremony of homage to the Emperor, Grand Duke of Tuscany in the Piazza Signoria, and the chariot races the next day in the Piazza Santa Maria Novella. The noise and colour; the elaborate pageantry combined with haphazard organisation; the old English horse of twenty-three years who was generally expected to win; the system of flashing the winner's number from the top of Giotto's Campanile; the crowd docilely taking the buffetings of the Austrian soldiers—are vividly detailed. The chariot race was a less fashionable assembly, and as the horses all belonged to one jobmaster the competition was nominal. In any case the racing was not to be compared with the meetings at home. But it was worth observing that not only were these entertainments of venerable antiquity but

'the presence of the prince and even of religion give it a much more dignified air. Plainly the Florentines cherish this custom as the sole relic of their ancient liberty . . . and since the ancient games it is perhaps the only spectacle of the pleasure of a whole

[1] Now the Hôtel Gran Bretagna.

state gathered for amusement by the care and under the eyes of its magistrates.'

Italian was practised assiduously under an abbé, and Gibbon soon tried his jargon on the polite Florentines; with some success, particularly with a Madame Antinori. But generally the assemblies to which the indefatigable Mann shepherded his young friends, sometimes to three in one evening, were insupportable unless there were enough of the nation, as Gibbon always calls the English, to make up some tables of whist. In these hot evenings the parties were sometimes held in the courtyards of the houses, which were lit up and hung with tapestries. Mann himself gave a party in August which surpassed all others. Not only did the illuminations shine on the best society of Florence, but 'there were plenty of refreshments and the scene was enlivened by several French horns posted in the garden'. The men did not lend themselves to conversation, and the women once more were rendered inaccessible by these strange Italian ways. With the help of Madame Minorbetti, Mann's '*maîtresse sans consequence*', Gibbon made a fresh investigation of the *Cicisbeo*, an institution which intrigued most Englishmen and was even a topic of the guide-books. For a military man in transit it had to be realised there was little prospect. Madame Antinori had been gracious, the Contessa Acciaiuoli, 'famous for the size of her nose', was an acquaintance worth mentioning, and near the end of his stay he began to be attracted to Mme Gianni. She was very suitable for a historian's attention,

'as she was born a Medici and her branch should have succeeded to the Grand Duchy on the extinction of Cosimo's line, if violence could have allowed them to claim the constitution of Charles the Fifth. They are . . .'

The manuscript breaks off, but one cannot help feeling that the blank pages following were left rather to continue his reflexions on the Medici, than to record his campaign with one of their latest daughters.

Gibbon even welcomed the opera because of the opportunity it gave of a freer mingling of society. He appreciated the novelty of the Italian theatre, 'where the boxes are small separate apartments open only on the side of the stage where one amuses oneself with anything rather than the performance'. Sir Horace's box was at the disposal of the nation and there would be a gathering of the English and ladies there. But each box was the scene of a little reception which one was at liberty to join or leave at the first approach of boredom.

> 'The piece is only one more amusement. It serves like a table as the gathering point of a company and some distraction for a society which it renders more lively and free.'

Of drinking there is no mention. It is unlikely that, under Sir Horace's surveillance and with the strict policing of Florence, the echoes were raised in the midnight streets as once in Lausanne. Yet it may not be vain to conjecture that at least once the young travellers encountered Bacchus in Tuscany.

The grand chain of young men came and went and their record was duly set down. Lord Palmerston returned from the south having finished his tour, and was adjudged to have done very well. Lord Ossory, with whom Gibbon had crossed the Channel eighteen months previously, arrived. He had certainly developed from the callow stage he was in then, but might have done better. Gibbon suspected that there was really little in him; but he was at least a great lover of pictures and had an artist travelling with him. The chief figure, however, among the English was the eccentric Mr Lyttelton, who went his own way, taking little notice of the other English, though dominating the conversation, when he was present, with a stream of talk on poetry, politics and chemistry. He appears to have taken a fancy to Gibbon and Guise and treated them to somewhat embarrassing attention. Gibbon observed with quiet amusement that his ideas of economy amounted to limitless extravagance. He was vain and ambitious and sought to combine the two characters of philosopher and libertine. He had no interest in art or antiquities and said that one could see Rome in twenty days. 'That is enough for me', is Gibbon's comment.[1]

Another traveller was about to sail for Constantinople with the Venetian ambassador. Gibbon would have liked to be going too. 'Un voyage de la Grèce ne peut que piquer la curiosité.' Fate did not intend that he should be deflected from his true goal. But we should be careful not to under-estimate Gibbon's interest in Hellenism.

Fourteen visits to the Uffizi alone indicate the difference between Gibbon and his wild acquaintance. The antiquities were studied with minute care. The interest in the fine arts does not seem very spontaneous; but Gibbon went through the business conscientiously, adhering pretty closely to the official taste of the day.

He betrays a curious literalness and prosaic desire for illusion. This perhaps is the cause of a greater interest in sculpture. But the precarious postures of Dawn and Night in the Medici Chapel were very disturbing, and there is a characteristic confusion of sensual and aesthetic perceptions in a long note on the *Venus dei Medici*. He could not get over the absence of correct drawing in the primitives. But the one master whom he really disliked was the accomplished Veronese. His

[1] He was also the hero of an extraordinary scene at Lucca. See passages from the Journal printed with the names suppressed in *Misc. Wks.* v. 484-5. Among other young Englishmen in Florence was Henry Swinburne, whose books on travel are referred to in *The Decline and Fall.*

style and colouring displeased; and he was intellectually incapable of blending the divine and human elements in the Infant Jesus.

But servile imitation was not enough. On this score and for their choice of the lowest subjects, he is compelled to dismiss the Flemish artists, though it is clear he was much attracted by them. Similarly he had little interest in portraiture, since the close copying of the particular excluded any ideal generalisations. Nevertheless he abandons his own principles in front of Raphael's *Julius II.* Raphael was the first of painters, and his *Transfiguration* in S. Pietro in Montorio in Rome the finest picture in the world. But the painter to whom Gibbon really warms is Rubens.

Gibbon's remarks on architecture are of no great interest. Gothic was only suggestive of ruin and weakness; while to other buildings he applied the classic rules of proportions with minute pedantry. But he was responsive to the aura of famous buildings, and before he had left Florence he had recorded some impressions which unconsciously foreshadow the conclusion of his history and are a true prelude to the supreme moment that was to come in Rome.

Of the Palazzo Riccardi he says:

'I could not enter without secret awe this cradle of the arts in a house whence the light has spread all over the West, where under the eyes of Lorenzo the Magnificent, a Politian, a Lascaris, a Gaza, a Pico della Mirandola and a Marsilius Ficinus made the great men of Greece and Rome live once more for the instruction of their contemporaries.'

Again, these words on Santa Croce foreshadow the style and sentiment of *The Decline and Fall*:

'The architecture is undistinguished; but it was not without a secret respect that I looked upon the tombs of Galileo and Michael Angelo, the restorer of the arts and of philosophy respectively; truly powerful and original geniuses. They have shed greater glory on their country than conquerors or politicians. The Tartars have had a Jenghiz Khan and the Goths an Alaric, but we turn our eyes from the bloodstained plains of Scythia to fix them with pleasure on Athens and Florence.'

It was now September, an Italian September, but the great heat of summer was over. The crown of the tour was approaching. On the 22nd Gibbon left Florence and 'the sharp and barren ridge of the hills of Faesulae',[1] promising himself to keep a shorter but not less interesting journal. The road led first to Pistoia, with reflexions on Sulla's veterans; thence to Lucca, where the opera was said to be the best in Italy, and was artfully put on at a time when the season in other cities was over. At Pisa Gibbon found some relatives, Commodore Acton and his nephew, and with them crossed 'the dreary unwholesome uncultivated Maremme of modern Tuscany'[2] to reach Leghorn.

The elder Acton had joined the Roman Church in his old age, thus cutting himself off from his compatriots in Leghorn and prejudicing his nephew's position. It was a definite scandal to the English colony and Gibbon had to explain to Parson Burnaby and others that he could not neglect relations from whom he had received nothing but kindness. In consequence the interest of their visit was considerably impaired. Gibbon had had one more instance at first hand of the foolish estrangements that can be brought about by religious disagreements.

Thence to Siena where they fell in with Lord Mount Stuart once more, who took them to an assembly. 'The women were so ugly and the men so ignorant that I had

[1] *The Decline and Fall,* c. xxx. (4-48).
[2] *The Decline and Fall,* c. xxxi. n. 57.

not the slightest desire to stay in a town whose society I had heard praised up so much.'

The last stage approached and was duly headed in the Journal:

'*October 1764. On the road from Siena to Rome.*

'September 30th. I have got as far as Radicofani, a small frontier town of Tuscany. The country is really frightful. I have never seen barer or more unproductive mountains.

'Monday 1st. From Radicofani to Viterbo. The country is already better. We are in the Papal States. I saw from a distance the Lake of Bolsena.[1] Volsinii was actually situated at the bottom of the woods which rise from the lakeside.

'Tuesday 2nd. The Campagna of Rome! A beautiful plain once the mountain of Viterbo is passed. It seems in this country that the more nature has done for men the more they neglect her gifts. We reached Rome at five in the evening. From the Pons Milvius I was in a dream of antiquity which was only interrupted by the Customs officers, a very modern race who obliged us to go on foot to look for a lodging, for there are no inns, while they took our chaise to the customs house. The approach to Rome is not pleasing.'

Gibbon gives a delicious account of his impressions to his father on 9th October:

'I am now, Dear Sir, at Rome. If it was difficult before to give you or Mrs. Gibbon any account of what I saw, it is impossible here. I have already such a fund of entertainment for a mind somewhat prepared for it by an acquaintance with the Romans, that I am really almost in a dream. Whatever ideas books may have given us of the greatness of that people, their accounts of the most flourishing state of Rome fall infinitely short of the picture of its ruins. I am convinced there never, never existed such a nation, and I hope for the happiness of mankind there never will again. I was this morning upon the top of Trajan's pillar. I shall not attempt a description of it. Only figure to yourself a column 140 feet high of the purest white marble, composed only of about 30 blocks and wrought into

[1] 'It is surrounded with white rocks and stored with fish and wild-fowl' (*The Decline and Fall,* c. xli. n. 55).

bas-reliefs with as much taste and delicacy as any chimney-piece at Up-park.'

In a letter from Florence, Gibbon, eager as always to justify his travels, had said that the solid foundations laid at Lausanne were not forgotten, and he did not despair of producing something by way of a description of ancient Italy which might be of some use to the public and of some credit to himself. Now his impressions were both narrowing that idea, and at the same time sowing for an ultimate expansion as yet undreamt of. Six days after this letter the supreme moment came. The date, the hour and the moment could be remembered precisely and always with emotion. The record of it is unforgettable. It would be foolish to omit it here on the score of familiarity; but I quote from one of Gibbon's original versions:

'It was on the fifteenth of October in the gloom of evening, as I sat musing on the Capitol, while the barefooted fryars were chanting their litanies in the temple of Jupiter, that I conceived the first thought of my history. My original plan was confined to the decay of the City; my reading and reflection pointed to that aim; but several years elapsed, and several avocations intervened, before I grappled with the decline and fall of the Roman Empire.[1]

Only a little less familiar but if anything more significant is the recorded impression made by the Forum, then at the height of its romantic appeal when cattle grazed near the capitals of its buried columns:

'After a sleepless night, I trod, with a lofty step, the ruins of the Forum; each memorable spot where Romulus *stood*, or

[1] Memoir D, *Murray*, p. 405. The vulgate text is a conflation of Memoirs C, E and D. In Memoir C, *Murray*, p. 270, Gibbon says he sat musing *in the church* of the Zoccolanti or Franciscan fryars. This is the church of Santa Maria in Ara Coeli, built not on the site of a temple of Jupiter but of Juno. Gibbon was misled by his authority Nardini. It is in this Memoir that Gibbon refers to his Journal for the record of the date. But the extant Journal ends with his arrival in Rome except for a few notes on works of art written in December 1764.

Tully spoke, or Caesar fell, was at once present to my eye; and several days of intoxication were lost or enjoyed before I could descend to a cool and minute investigation.'

A fundamental inspiration of his history is implicit in these words. Gibbon never forgets that he is writing of a decline and fall from an age in which political freedom and great literature had flourished together. That they were almost necessary complements of one another, is an assumption that has been drawn from an idealised and partial view of those two conspicuous periods of history, fifth-century Athens and Republican Rome. It is still one which the world might be wise to gamble on. For Gibbon at any rate the proof lay in the scene before him: 'In Rome the voice of freedom and discord is no longer heard; and instead of the foaming torrent, a smooth and stagnant lake reflects the image of idleness and servitude'.[1] He surveyed the scene with a practical eye and its poetry seems to enter his writing in spite of himself. Unlike some modern sentimentalists he would have admired Mussolini's reclaimed acres even if he detested his principles. His canvas is at once mellow and trenchant.

'The first and most natural root of a great city is the labour and populousness of the adjacent country. But the greater part of the Campagna of Rome is reduced to a dreary and desolate wilderness: the overgrown estates of the princes and the clergy are cultivated by the lazy hands of indigent and hopeless vassals; and the scanty harvests are confined or exported for the benefit of a monopoly. A second and more artificial cause of the growth of a metropolis is the residence of a monarch, the expense of a luxurious court, and the tributes of dependent provinces. Those provinces and tributes had been lost in the fall of the empire; and if some streams of the silver of Peru and the gold of Brazil have been attracted by the Vatican, the revenues of the cardinals, the fees of office, the oblations of pilgrims and clients, and the remnant of ecclesiastical taxes, afford a poor and precarious

[1] *The Decline and Fall*, c. lxx. (8-264).

supply, which maintains, however, the idleness of the court and city. The population of Rome, far below the measure of the great capitals of Europe, does not exceed one hundred and seventy thousand inhabitants; and within the spacious enclosure of the walls, the largest portion of the seven hills is overspread with vineyards and ruins. The beauty and splendour of the modern city may be ascribed to the abuses of the government, to the influence of superstition. Each reign (the exceptions are rare) has been marked by the rapid elevation of a new family, enriched by the childless pontiff at the expense of the church and country. The palaces of these fortunate nephews are the most costly monuments of elegance and servitude: the perfect arts of architecture, painting and sculpture, have been prostituted in their service; and their galleries and gardens are decorated with the most precious works of antiquity. The ecclesiastical revenues were more decently employed by the popes themselves in the pomp of the Catholic worship; but it is superfluous to enumerate their pious foundations since these lesser stars are eclipsed by the sun of the Vatican, by the dome of St. Peter, the most glorious structure that ever has been applied to the use of religion. The fame of Julius the Second, Leo the Tenth and Sixtus the Fifth, is accompanied by the superior merit of Bramante and Fontana, of Raphael and Michael Angelo; and the same munificence which had been displayed in palaces and temples was directed with equal zeal to revive and emulate the labours of antiquity. Prostrate obelisks were raised from the ground; of the eleven aqueducts of the Caesars and consuls three were restored; the artificial rivers were conducted over a long series of old or of new arches, to discharge into marble basins a flood of salubrious and refreshing waters; and the spectator impatient to ascend the steps of St. Peter's, is detained by a column of Egyptian granite, which rises between two lofty and perpetual fountains to the height of one hundred and twenty feet.' [1]

Such was the scene through which Gibbon moved during 'this winter of enchantment'. During the first two months he was under the care of James Byers, a true forerunner of modern agencies, who combined the

[1] *The Decline and Fall,* c. lxxi. (8-287). The extract has been slightly shortened; apologies are offered to any ears offended by mutilated rhythms.

valuable functions of banker, art-dealer and guide. Of his social life there we know hardly anything. From Holroyd who joined his friends there come a few gleanings. An Irishman, Meighan, was their tailor, and at the Carnival a ballet was performed called *Voxhall, Giardino Inglese*. But Rome was still a place of real awe to a Protestant, and circumspection of behaviour was probably accepted as inevitable.[1] Moreover, Roman society could not have been so accessible as Florentine. Naturally and inevitably therefore Gibbon could say that

> 'my conversation was with the dead rather than the living, and the whole college of Cardinals was of less value in my eyes than the transfiguration of Raphael, the Apollo of the Vatican, or the massy greatness of the Coliseum.'[2]

Nor could his eye be accused of idle straying when he noted that 'the matrons from beyond the Tiber still represent the features and character of antiquity'.[3]

After some five weeks the dream of antiquity was expelled by a nightmare that had become too familiar. In August, Gibbon had commented in his Journal on the occasion of writing to his father,

> 'it is strange that I have not had any letters from there since the end of March. I know them; so I am not alarmed. I know that it is a sign that they are not displeased with me. Practically only a fit of bad temper can overcome their laziness and put a pen in their hands.'

Now Mr Gibbon made himself felt once more in a peculiarly aggravating and baffling manner. He had written a letter to which his son in reply refers in words which had almost become a formula in their corre-

[1] Gibbon was very likely in Rome in March 1765 when his acquaintances, the two Damers, were involved in a brawl resulting in the death of an Italian coachman. Doran, *Mann and Manners at the Court of Florence*, ii. p. 132.

[2] *Murray*, p. 302.

[3] *The Decline and Fall*, c. lxxi. (8-282).

spondence: 'I . . . could scarcely have thought that any one from you could give me so much uneasiness as this has done'. The £10,000 raised six years ago had apparently gone, with £1200 after it. So Mr Gibbon was proposing to sell the Lenborough estate in Bucks, which his son had been taught to look on as the fairest portion of their estate. Where was this going to end? In real dismay but not without a sly touch of irony Gibbon foresees the day when, left alone without half his father's knowledge of business, he might very well find himself in gaol.

Meanwhile he proposed that it would be better to sell the Putney property, and repeated his plan for raising a fund for his father, with the reward of a further increase of his own annuity. Since he was fairly certain that he would now never marry, he had no wish to look beyond the lives of Mr and Mrs Gibbon and himself.

What was for the moment a worse stroke was to follow in less than a month. Gibbon was travelling with a general credit all over Italy given by his banker at Lausanne. Early in December this was mysteriously stopped. Barazzi, his banker in Rome, showed him the letter he had received. No doubt it was circulated to all the big towns and Gibbon might well believe that his character in Italy was ruined, more particularly as he had just drawn for £100 which would probably be protested. Meanwhile he could not stir from Rome and was in danger of being suspected for a rogue and adventurer. The trouble must have started from his last Florentine draft's having been protested, and he asks his father with great pertinence how could a letter have had time to go from London to Florence, from Florence to Lausanne and thence again to Rome, without the smallest intimation meanwhile from Mr Gibbon to his son.

The matter was set right, and when Gibbon was able

to draw again he drew for a considerable amount for fear of renewed difficulties. The precaution was justified. When the travellers reached Venice in April 1765, the banker there, 'a sour suspicious old fellow', made such difficulties, in spite of the assurance of renewed credit, that Gibbon told him at last he wanted neither his money nor his company. He was thankful to be in a position to talk so. What makes the incident of especial interest to a later age is that the banker humiliated Gibbon especially by raking up the history of the protested letter in Guise's presence, and Gibbon had spent several months of very real distress in his company without saying a word about his troubles.

A short excursion to Naples in the first quarter of 1765 served to render Gibbon a better Englishman, so he told his stepmother, without adopting all the honest prejudices of a Hampshire farmer. 'Racked and battered on the broken remains of the old Appian way' and reaching inns only to wish they could leave immediately, they surveyed 'the wretched state of this fine country and the misery of its idle and oppressed inhabitants'. At Naples they looked to Mr Hamilton to present them to the boy king, anticipating that 'It must be a most ridiculous farce of Majesty'. They had now reached the ordinary limit of the tourists' grand chain—'our only Peer is Lord Berkeley with whom we are just going to dine'—and by March they had returned to Rome, thence to cross the Apennines to Loretto, and follow the Aemilian Way along the Adriatic, reaching Venice in April. Venice came in for some hard words: 'old and in general ill built houses, ruined pictures and stinking ditches . . . a fine bridge spoilt by two Rows of houses upon it, and a large square decorated with the worst Architecture I ever yet saw'. But Gibbon admits he was out of humour with the place. Apart from the disagreeable incident of the banker, there were no

English in residence, and communication with the natives was strictly forbidden.

Regarding the final stage of the tour, it had been left uncertain whether he should go to Germany, or work his way back through France. Now he learned that the family would like to see him back in May, ostensibly on account of a militia meeting. Pleading for an extension of six weeks or so, he proposed to return over the Mont Cenis, see something of Provence and Languedoc and take ship home from Bordeaux. A more peremptory summons, however, led to the curtailment of this pleasant project. 'After a pretty troublesome passage of the Mont Cenis', Lyons was reached at the end of May. Here Gibbon saw Guise leave 'to swim down the Rhone' —it must have been sadly tantalising—but as he himself had had letters convincing him that he ought no longer to deprive his country of one of its greatest ornaments, he reluctantly turned north, and after 'about ten delicious days at Paris', reached England at the end of June 1765. He was not to go abroad again for twelve years.

The last act of Gibbon's romantic comedy coincided neatly with the final stage of his tour.

In the early months of 1764 Suzanne Curchod's friends had remained sadly concerned about her future. What she had recovered of her mother's estate was trifling. On the other hand, she had refused a post in England,[1] and another in Switzerland. Julie de Bondeli did not shrink from accusing her of false delicacy.[2] Suzanne herself seems to have fallen into a state of inertia, nursing 'son cœur désespéré du mérite des morts et des défauts des vivants'.[3]

[1] A note in Add. MSS. 34887 says she was offered a post by the Duke of Grafton; the matter fell through as she demanded a separate table for herself.
[2] Bodemann, *op. cit.* p. 325.
[3] F. Golowkin, *Lettres diverses recueillies en Suisse*, 1821, pp. 232 *sqq*.

Meanwhile the Moultou household had another interesting inmate. Madame de Vermenoux was a young widow by no means averse from male society, who had been spending some time in Geneva to be near the celebrated Dr. Tronchin. She liked Suzanne and offered to take her back to Paris as *dame de compagnie*. Moultou and others apparently urged acceptance, and Suzanne left in June, complaining that her friends had uprooted her unnecessarily from Switzerland where all her interests lay. She would not conceal her ill-humour. Within six months news was going round Geneva again, and the flirtatious old Le Sage entered in his journal for 1st December, 'Mlle Suzette Curchod épouse M. Jacques Necker, banquier à Paris'. This was extremely satisfactory for everyone.

M. Necker was assuredly *sérieux*. One of the founders of Thelusson Necker et Cie, he had long been eminent for his unremitting industry and speculative astuteness. A man of blameless life in the ordinary sense, for he had had no life outside his office. He was not uneducated. He had read his Cicero at college in Geneva, where he had been born, being the son of a German who had married into the aristocratic bourgeoisie. Now at the age of thirty-two he had made a fortune and at the same time was, in his daughter's words of enthusiastic sympathy, 'si jeune, si aimable, si seul'.[1]

His one taste of the pleasures of life had been apparently to dangle after Mme de Vermenoux. It is not known why she did not become Mme Necker or if either desired such a change. But a sense of comedy is reluctant to believe other than that the lady was forestalled by her *dame de compagnie*. At least the stock ingredients were there: the charming homeless girl a paid servant, not altogether happy or at home in Paris, if reports are to be accepted, exposed even to reproof

[1] Mme de Staël, *Œuvres*, ii. 262, cited by Kohler, *op. cit.* p. 6.

before visitors for her provincial manners; and then her compatriot hitherto heart-whole, ready to be sympathetic, to be interested and impressed, and so to offer her the wealth and position which he, an exile too, had won. He was quickly at her feet. Suzanne's proper hesitation lasted a few weeks. Necker was inspired to make a hasty trip to Geneva and consult the invaluable Moultou. Soon afterwards Mlle Curchod was informing a friend in Switzerland that she was uniting herself with a man who was an angel except for his weakness in choosing her. His qualities were of more worth than his 80,000 *livres de rente*.[1]

Mme Necker did not dissemble the gratification of receiving her old lover amid the new splendour of the rue Michel le Comte. Gibbon reached Paris in June; five months later she was dilating upon the event to Mme de Brenles. It had been an unspeakable pleasure. Not that she had any feeling for a man who scarcely deserved it. But feminine vanity had never had a more complete or honourable triumph. During two weeks in Paris Gibbon had been at her house every day. He had become gentle, submissive and a model of propriety. He had seen what a clever devoted husband she had, and with his ardent admiration of wealth he had made her for the first time take notice of that with which she was surrounded; or at least till then it had only made a disagreeable impression on her.[2] May not Mme de Brenles have smiled to herself?

Gibbon had his confidant too and the comedy was in no danger of falling flat. To 'Leger' he wrote waggishly, though with some slips of the pen which possibly betray

[1] Golowkin, *op. cit.*

[2] Golowkin, *op. cit.* pp. 265-6. The letter is dated 7th November 1765. The passage is printed in *Letters*, i. 81, n. 1. One sentence omitted by Golowkin may be added from the MS. in the Bibliothèque Cantonale of Lausanne. After saying 'j'ai vu Gibbon' she adds: 'et en verité il y jouoit un Rôle assez mince'.

a nervous excitement which he would have disclaimed:

'The Curchod [Mme Necker] I saw at Paris. She was very fond of me and the husband particularly civil. Could they insult me more cruelly? Ask me every evening to supper; go to bed and leave me alone with his wife—what an impertinent security! It is making an old lover of mighty little consequence. She is as handsome as ever and much genteeler, seems pleased with her fortune rather than proud of it.' [1]

But what joy to trip her up on this delicate point:

'I was (perhaps indiscreetly enough)', he continues artfully, 'exalting Nanette de Illens's good luck and fortune. "What fortune?" said she with an air of contempt,—"not above 20,000 livres a year." I smiled, and she caught herself immediately. "What airs I give myself in despising twenty thousand livres a year, who a year ago looked upon 800 as the summit of my wishes." '

[1] *Prothero*, i. 81, 'supper', 'handsome as ever'. Actually the MS. indubitably has 'summer' and 'handsome as every'. It must be admitted that this particular kind of slip is found several times in Gibbon's MSS.

Chapter 13

MANY DISTRACTIONS

1765–1770

THE great tour finished, Gibbon was prepared to acknowledge his obligations by settling down with his father and stepmother in the mixed state of liberty and dependence which he had already known.

The programme was to be much as formerly, a free alternation between London and Buriton, subject only to the limits of his annuity and the demands of filial duty. No more appears to have been said about Parliament, and the only public service required of him was the yearly attendance with the militia. This entailed a residence of four weeks at Southampton. Gibbon was now, as he sometimes facetiously signs himself, the Major, and in 1768 he became Lieut.-Colonel commanding. Each year he was 'more disgusted with the inn, the wine, the company, and the tiresome repetition of annual attendance and daily exercise'. He resigned finally in 1770.

In town the returned traveller might expect to profit by the acquaintance made abroad. There were clubs: the Cocoa Tree, the School of Vice, 'as innocent a Club as any in town', and Boodle's or the *Savoir Faire*. There was too the Romans, a weekly convivial meeting for those who had made the great pilgrimage.[1] Gibbon himself had instituted this club and looked forward to the meetings eagerly. It was still existing in 1773. Of

[1] A list of the members is given by Sheffield in *Misc. Wks.* i. 200.

Guise, the constant companion of the Italian journey, Gibbon saw little in after-days. His connexions were with men rather than women, and they, 'though far from contemptible in rank and fortune, were not of the first eminence in the literary and political world'.[1] The context, fairly judged, implies by 'women' drawing-room society. In spite of increased acquaintance he still found 'the avenues of society fortified', and hardly knew himself in the immense city; though invitations multiplied he disliked the formality, and regretted 'the small parties of Lausanne where one might pass an evening without form or invitation'. Yet among the bachelors he had not the means to stand the pace. It was not so much that his 'virtues of temperance and sobriety had not completely recovered themselves from the wounds of the militia'. That would be the least damaging of their diversions. Amid the reckless gambling of those days Gibbon could take only a moderate part. He had some slight leaning towards play in spite of his many protestations. As for general conversation, he had not yet established himself as an oracle of learning and anecdotes. Perhaps from this period comes the experience which gave rise to the gibe of 'the proud ignorance so dear and familiar to a polished people'.[2]

Whatever temptations he had to be extravagant, he resisted them, and was able to tell Mrs Gibbon after his father's death that he had always lived within his allowance of £300 a year, that the only other money he had from his father was once £400, nearly £100 of which were arrears of his allowance; he had returned most of this to his father when he needed it. He had not got into debt and had not lost £100 at any one time; perhaps not in the course of his life, so he said.

The qualified independence which had been pleasing at the age of twenty-one, fell far short of satisfying a man

[1] *Murray*, p. 273. [2] *The Decline and Fall*, c. lviii. n. 76.

of thirty. Gibbon had determined to achieve something memorable; but meanwhile the goal was far off and vaguely discerned, and the route to it filled with uncertainties. Part of the price of his ambition was the humiliation of standing still while others were advancing in one or other of the professions that he too might have chosen. He need not have been too severe on himself for that. His physique, the accidents of his life and, above all, his father's way of ordering things cannot be left out of the account. His father having brought him up to live as an independent gentleman, was now likely to ruin the achievement of this ideal if his own not conspicuously useful life was prolonged. The son's position was ignominious and might have been embittering.

Winter by winter these invasions of the town were repeated with decreasing frequency. The growing embarrassment of the estate and Mr Gibbon's declining health were the reasons. Finally such visits as were made were chiefly devoted to conferring with lawyers and trustees. Gibbon became charged with the management of a chaos for which he was not responsible and which he could not clear up. Not merely were Mr Gibbon's debts still such that it was proposed to sell the Putney and Hampshire estates, while some of the remaining property was to be vested in Gibbon though charged with annuity and jointure for his parents, but the bulk of his correspondence during these years reveals a dreary tale of time spent in search for lost deeds, of his father's obstruction and suspicion and last-minute rebellions against proposals which had been painfully explained to him, and lastly of the false gentility by which Mr Gibbon was led to oppose advertising the Putney estate. A stirring rebuke from James Scott gives a spontaneous and independent corroboration of Gibbon's dutifulness:

'. . . You look all on your own side and nothing on your Sons, you seem to forget how much he has given up and how much he dos now, it is not a Son in a thousand that would have don as much, he says that instead of your acknowledging it, he receives nothing but angry letters, and that you are very angry with him because he dos not do everything you want him to do, and in your own manner and that you seam to have no regard for him but everything for yourself. I daresay Sir that when you think coolly and put yourself in his place, you will alter your way of thinking and will not drive him to do that he would not willingly do without your forceing him to it. My Dear Sir, I do'nt write this out of any disregard to you, far from it, but what I really think is right, and I dare say if all circumstances were to be laid before the world, which God forbid it ever should—it would think the same.' [1]

Meetings with Holroyd do not appear to have been frequent. But the friendship begun abroad was only waiting suitable circumstances to develop. Holroyd had prolonged his tour into Germany and after returning appears to have been away, probably on the family properties in Ireland and Yorkshire.[2] Gibbon was left—and expresses no surprise at it—to hear of his friend's marriage in 1767 to Abigail Way, from a notice in the *St. James's Chronicle*. Thereafter there is little evidence of intercourse between them until 1769, when Holroyd bought Sheffield Place in Sussex from Lord de la Warr. At once Gibbon was getting more invitations to visit there than he could accept in those perturbed days. The real blossoming of this friendship belongs to the time after Mr Gibbon's death. In the years before that, a great deal of interest and consolation was found in Georges Deyverdun's company.

After four years (1761–5) of tutoring the Margrave of Schavedt, the young Swiss came to London in 1765, and

[1] Brit. Mus. 11907, dd. 25 (2).

[2] There is no letter extant to Holroyd between 31st October 1765 and 29th April 1767. There are in any case only two other letters of Gibbon surviving from this period.

spent the summer of that year and the three following at Buriton. His position was like Gibbon's in so far as his present means were negligible, though he had prospects of a considerable inheritance. Meanwhile, unlike Gibbon, he had to find a living. After some time a clerkship was obtained for him in the Secretary of State's office, where David Hume was Under-Secretary. It was an appointment which Gibbon claims to have had a part in securing. His influence was more likely to have been exerted through someone like his uncle Stanier Porten than through Hume.[1] It is doubtful whether he knew the historian at this time, and the later relations of these three men point to Deyverdun's being nearer to Hume than his friend.

Hume had only received his own appointment a month before Deyverdun.[2] The coincidence is curious, because Deyverdun had been brought to Hume's notice for the first time in 1766 through his meddling in the absurd quarrel with Rousseau.[3]

The position indeed was felt to be unequal both to Deyverdun's rank and to his powers. At any rate he had time on his hands. The friends could look about for other means of advancing either the one or the other.

The first enterprise was one which only concerned

[1] Porten had been appointed Secretary to Lord Rochford's extraordinary embassy to France in 1766. In 1768 he himself was appointed Under-Secretary when Rochford became Secretary of State Northern Department. *Home Office Papers* (1766–9), p. 435; Hist. MSS. Comm. 3rd Rep. App. p. 138.

[2] Hume's appointment was 21st February and Deyverdun's 4th March 1767, 'in Mr. Secretary Conway's office'. On 20th January 1768, when Lord Weymouth was sworn in as Secretary of State, Deyverdun appears among his clerks. Weymouth changed to the Southern Department on 21st October and took his clerks with him. In *Royal Kalendar*, 1767, 'De Verdun' is a clerk in the Northern Department; *Court and City Register*, 1769, gives 'Geo. Dryverdun' in the Southern Department. See also *Home Office Papers*, vol. ii. (1766–69), pp. 161, 162, 293.

[3] Deyverdun's letter, dated 'Londres le 18 novembre 1766 at M. Mennet's in Denmark Street, Soho Square', is in *Letters of Eminent Persons to David Hume* (1849), pp. 297 *sqq.* See also Hume's letter to Davenport of 27th November 1766, J. Y. T. Greig, *Letters of D. Hume*, ii. p. 113.

Gibbon, but which was impossible without Deyverdun's help. A history of the Swiss Republics had long been planned and much of the sources that were in Latin or French had been surveyed. Further progress was barred by ignorance of German. It was here that Deyverdun could and did help Gibbon by translating copiously from chronicles and earlier historians. In the summer of 1767 Gibbon was able to begin composing and wrote forty-three folio pages. Deyverdun's presence again fortified early predilections and Gibbon wrote in French. Anxious to have an early opinion on the work they contrived to have it read aloud to a literary society of foreigners in London. Gibbon sat among the audience, the unknown author, and had the mortification of hearing his work freely criticised and condemned. On reflexion he owned that they were right and abandoned the work.

Hume, on the other hand, to whom the manuscript had been shown through Deyverdun's mediation, exhorted Gibbon to go on with his design. He had only one objection to make. Why did Gibbon compose in French and carry faggots into the wood, as Horace said with regard to Romans who wrote in Greek? Hume compared the fates of Latin and Greek in Western Europe and went on to apply the lesson. The present supremacy of French might be allowed. But 'our solid and increasing establishments in America, where we needlessly dread the inundation of Barbarians, promise a superior stability and duration to the English language'.[1]

Gibbon very properly replied to the honour of this letter with unusual promptness:

'Sir,

'Your approbation will always flatter me infinitely more

[1] *Misc. Wks.* i. 204, and Greig, *op. cit.* ii. p. 170; Burton, *Life of Hume*, ii. 410 *sqq.*

than the applause of an undistinguishing multitude. I am persuaded that your judgement is sincere, and if sincere I am well assured it is just. I could wish to have avoided your general objection to the language I have made use of. It is really more the effect of accident than of choice. The five years (from sixteen to twenty-one) which I passed in Switzerland formed my style as well as my ideas. I write in French because I think in French and strange as it may seem, I can say with some shame but with no affectation, that it would be a matter of difficulty to me to compose in my native language. I must indeed acknowledge that a desire of being more generally read, invited me to indulge my taste for the French tongue. Your prophesy though extremely probable, concerns me but little. A Hume (if you will excuse the instance) may leave a κτῆμα ἐς ἀεί, but the ambition of us plebeian writers is limited to a much narrower term, both of space and of duration. My vanity will be gratified if I am read with some pleasure by a few of my contemporaries, without aiming to instruct or amuse our posterity on the other side of the Atlantick ocean. Your opinion will however, Sir, have always so great a weight with me that when I have finished the work which your kind approbation encourages me to pursue, I will endeavour to put it into an English dress; at the risque perhaps of appearing a foreigner to my own countrymen, and of betraying myself to foreigners for an Englishman.

'I fear that the *Ambitiosa ornamenta* which you censure so tenderly deserve a much severer sentence, and that many of them are not even entitled to the poor excuse of fashion or custom. Were I not sensible how precious your time is to yourself and to the publick, I could wish you would point out some of those which offended you the most. Your corrections would serve to guide me in the remainder of my course.

'I propose myself the honour of waiting on you on my arrival in town, and of assuring you of the esteem and gratitude with which I am,

'Dear Sir,

'Your most obedient humble servant,

'E. GIBBON, Junior

'BERITON, *October 25th*, 1767.'[1]

[1] Communicated to me by Prof. C. K. Webster.

In spite of this encouragement Gibbon was wise not to continue this history either in French or English. He was mistaken—rather oddly—in saying in his Autobiography that he burnt what he had written. The manuscript survives and was printed by Lord Sheffield. Although the writing and composition reveal a great advance on the *Essai*, the writer has not done more than embroider, sometimes too floridly as Hume remarked in his letter, an agreeable narrative on the framework of his authorities. The critical and creative mind is absent. Gibbon came to the conclusion that French had not yet yielded the ideal style 'to sustain the vigour and dignity of an important narrative' and it would not be for a foreigner to evolve it. Moreover his narrative was not important, and that would have been fatally seen had he translated it into English.

It may be supposed that during this winter of 1767–8 Gibbon took the opportunity of seeing something of Hume. He says that it was the *Mémoires Littéraires* that brought both him and Deyverdun to Hume's notice.[1] That is clearly incorrect. But the scantiest record of the acquaintance remains. When Holroyd was visiting Edinburgh in 1773, Gibbon hoped that he would not fail to visit the sty of that fattest of Epicurus's Hogs and inform himself whether there remained no hope of its recovering the use of its right paw.[2] But he suggests no personal message. That may be an accident. Of their actual meetings only one small testimony remains. Among the annotations in Gibbon's hand in the first volume of *The Decline and Fall* in the British Museum we read: 'N.B.—Mr. Hume told me that in correcting his history he always laboured to reduce superlatives and soften positives'. That Gibbon should have thought of noting this some time after 1782 is as real an expression of regard as his reflexion that the letter Hume

[1] *Murray*, p. 280. [2] *Prothero*, i. p. 190.

wrote him on the appearance of his first volume overpaid the labour of ten years.

The *Mémoires Littéraires de la Grande-Bretagne* [1] were designed for and carried on primarily by Deyverdun. But Gibbon, who could aid his friend with his pen though not with his purse, had a considerable part in it. The plan was to supply the Continent with a review not only of contemporary English literature but with surveys of the drama, fine arts and the general state of society, in annual volumes. The hope of a profit might appear dubious and proved illusory. Yet their precursor and model, *Le Journal Britannique* of Gibbon's old friend Matthew Maty, had lasted for six years, from 1750 to 1755. That venture, however, had the advantage of being carried on from the Hague. The *Mémoires Littéraires* were published in London, and it does not appear that any trouble was taken to disseminate it on the Continent.

Self-advertisement is the other advantage which young men who found reviews look for. Of this Deyverdun reaped something, for it brought him to the notice of Lord Chesterfield, whose cousin and heir Philip Stanhope he subsequently took abroad. It also brought Gibbon acquainted with Chesterfield. But neither got the reward or penalty of publicity, through the extreme anonymity of their proceedings. Gibbon in particular, in two extant letters, enjoins a profound secrecy on his correspondents.[2] How far his share in it ever came out is an interesting point. Deyverdun's connexion with it was well known to Walpole. For at

[1] This section is much indebted to V. P. Helming's *Edward Gibbon and Georges Deyverdun Collaborators in the 'Mémoires Littéraires de la Grande-Bretagne'*. Publications of the Modern Language Association of America, xlvii. (1932), p. 1028 *sqq*. Mr Helming if anything, I think, underestimates Gibbon's share in the work.

[2] Letter to G. L. Scott, *Misc. Wks.* ii. 68, and in an unpublished letter to Becket of 20th September 1767.

Hume's request he lent Deyverdun *The Life of Lord Herbert of Cherbury* to review, and thought himself ill repaid by the notice of his *Historic Doubts on the Life and Reign of King Richard III.*[1] Gibbon wrote this with an epilogue of notes supplied by Hume.[2] But Walpole was quite unaware of Gibbon's authorship or of his connexion with the *Mémoires*, when he hailed the first volume of *The Decline and Fall* with such enthusiasm.

Only two volumes appeared; the first on 18th April 1768 to cover the previous year. Becket and De Hondt published it, and the change to Heydinger for the second, which came out in 1769, no doubt indicates a want of success. Only a dozen copies of the second volume were sold in England, and about fifty abroad. Materials for a third nevertheless were nearly complete; but by the middle of 1769 Deyverdun had gone away again, this time in charge of Sir Richard Worsley, the son of Gibbon's old colonel. The unpaid bill pursued Deyverdun across the Continent. He evidently was solely answerable, for the bookseller could have applied to Gibbon.[3]

The reviewing does not rise above the standards of the day. Long extracts from works are given; some over-smart short notices are probably Deyverdun's. At a distance of twenty years Gibbon was unable or unwilling to distinguish their respective shares, so complete in thought and style had been their collaboration. He acknowledged the article on Lyttelton's *Henry II*, and competent criticisms of Adam Ferguson's *Civil Society* (with a reference to *L'Essai sur la Littérature par Mr. G.*) and of Lardner's *Credibility of the Gospel History* are probably his. Reviews of the *Life of Lord Herbert*,

[1] Hume's letter to Walpole, 11th November 1768, Greig, ii. p. 193, and Walpole, *Short Notes of My Life*, under date May 1769, quoted in *B. Hill*, p. 176, n. 2.

[2] *Misc. Wks.* iii.

[3] *Meredith Read*, ii. p. 381.

Sterne's *Works*, and Baretti's *Manners and Customs of Italy* support the claim of giving a comprehensive view of contemporary letters. The most vivacious and militant notice is on Boswell's *Journal of a Tour to Corsica*.

Mr Helming ascribes this to Deyverdun. But Gibbon must have had a hand in it, if only for the painstaking correction of Boswell's errors of scholarship. The charm and novelty of the work are missed, and the author's naïveties come in for some pert banter. There is too a strong anti-Johnsonian tone. Boswell's devotion is laughed at and Johnson is reported to have compared truth to a cow—an impish condensation of a not very wise remark on the vanity of infidels.[1]

The reviewers took their tone from another hostile pamphlet[2] and borrowed an absurd pseudo-Plutarchian parallel between Paoli and Wilkes, adding an item of their own. Paoli had not the conjugal virtues, no more had Wilkes. That implies such a gross perversion of what Paoli said as to be funny.[3] It would certainly have annoyed Boswell. It is impossible to say if he ever saw this rare volume or had any inkling of Gibbon's connexion with it. But Gibbon was probably prudent in refusing to give anything away.

Another piece of anonymous writing was acknowledged by Gibbon in after-years with some complacency, in spite of professed contrition for 'the cowardly concealment of my name and character'. This was a pamphlet, *Critical Observations on the Sixth Book of the Aeneid*, published in 1770. The object of the attack was

[1] 'Sir, these men are all vain men, and will gratify themselves at any expence. Truth will not afford sufficient food for their vanity; so they have betaken themselves to error. Truth, sir, is a cow which will yield such people no more milk; and so they are gone to milk the bull '(*A Tour of Corsica*, ed. S. C. Roberts, 1923, p. 68).

[2] J. Kenrick's *An Epistle to James Boswell Esq.; occasioned by his having transmitted the moral writings of Dr Samuel Johnson to Pascal Paoli, General of the Corsicans.*

[3] *A Tour of Corsica*, ed. cit. p. 41.

the redoubtable Bishop Warburton, and the ground chosen was his contention in *The Divine Legation* that the vision of the underworld in Virgil was founded on the Eleusinian Mysteries. Gibbon's argument was praised by Hayley—a doubtful ally—and also by the great Virgilian scholar Heyne, and was reprinted by an admiring Mr Green of Ipswich shortly after his death; but both Conington and Nettleship held that the honours of scholarship lay with Warburton, and the subject has not yet been dismissed by scholars. *Critical Observations* do not reveal the real Gibbon and have nothing to add to his fame. The chief interest in this sally for us is psychological, as Cotter Morison very truly discerned. It was in fact the outward expression of the dissatisfaction which Gibbon was feeling at this time.

> 'That inward unrest', says Morison, 'easily produces an aggressive spirit is a matter of common observation, and it may well have been that in attacking Warburton he sought a diversion from the worry of domestic cares.' [1]

It may seem hardly necessary to mention that the *Letters of Junius* have been claimed for Gibbon. The argument that the pause in the series coincides with Gibbon's attendance on his father at Buriton in the summer of 1770 proves too much. For if Gibbon was unable for that reason to send more than one letter (in August) between May and November, how is it that the letter of 14th November appeared only two days after his father's death? [2]

Amid these divagations the inspiration of the Roman Capitol had not been forgotten. It is not necessary to

[1] J. C. Morison, *Gibbon*, p. 63. Morison has some valuable comments on the *Critical Observations*.

[2] For this theory see an anonymous *Junius Unmasked*, 1819, and J. Smith, *Junius Unveiled*, 1909; also a letter to Lord Sheffield of 22nd March 1819 in Add. MSS. 34887, f. 376; and Clayden, *Early Life of S. Rogers*, p. 95.

repeat here the account which Gibbon gives of his studies. It is a picture of omnivorous and at the same time systematic reading which must always stand among the supreme achievements of scholars.

> 'I began gradually to advance', he says, 'from the wish to the hope, from the hope to the design, from the design to the execution, of my historical work, of whose limits and extent I had yet a very inadequate notion.'

From the classics with which he was familiar, he advanced gradually into the unknown and almost uncharted seas of what is still known as Low Latin, and passed on through the darkness of the middle age 'till I almost grasped the ruins of Rome in the fourteenth century, without suspecting that this final chapter must be obtained by the labour of six quartos and twenty years'. *The Decline and Fall* is also the history of the death and resurrection of Learning and the Arts. Thus the nature and scope of his work, the object of so much anxious questioning, took shape almost as inevitably as the events of history themselves.

In a very remarkable incursion into Oriental history belonging to this period Gibbon shows how deeply he had meditated on both the style and method of historical composition.[1]

Very significant also is his summary of his religious and ecclesiastical studies. He had come to the conclusion, which no one can deny however different their views may be, that the progress of Christianity was inseparably connected with the decline of the Empire. In the light of that conception he reviewed exhaustively all the sources, Christian, Hebrew and Pagan, that bore on the history of the Church. 'In an ample dissertation

[1] 'Sur la Monarchie des Mèdes', *Misc. Wks.* iii. It is dated there between 1758 and 1763. But it mentions the death of J. P. Bougainville. That happened in 1763. The essay must have taken some time to write.

on the miraculous darkness of the Passion I privately drew my conclusions from the silence of an unbelieving age.' In no superficial or question-begging manner he had made the long journey from his youthful acceptance of the third century miracles to a solidly based scepticism.

The account of these preparatory studies is carried beyond the date of his father's death into the years 1771 and 1772. When the work of composition was begun Gibbon had ranged far beyond the scope of his first volume. In one revealing note to the thirtieth chapter we learn that a rough draft of it was composed as early as 1771.[1]

The end of Mr Gibbon's life, declining through the stages of blindness, dropsy and general decay, could only be a relief. Yet Gibbon sincerely claimed that the spectacle of his father's last days prevented any other interests from absorbing his attention. Mr Gibbon died on 12th November 1770, and, as a last though not very important contribution to the general difficulties, this long-ailing man left no will.

In a letter to Deyverdun written in December Gibbon outlines his embarrassments and uncertainties which it will take time to disperse.

> 'Be sure, my dear Friend', he says, 'that the idea of living with you will enter largely into my plans. Friendship, Philosophy and Inclination will always speak to me in favour of Switzerland. But will they be powerful enough to prevail against the tumult of London, against wretched obligations and the importunities of all my relations who pursue me with admirable affection, and against the projects of fortune and ambition which they persist in putting before me, I do not know myself and I am not ashamed of not knowing.'[2]

[1] *The Decline and Fall*, c. xxx, n. 86.

[2] *Meredith Read*, ii. p. 396.

Chapter 14

No. 7 BENTINCK STREET

1773

INDEPENDENCE is a magic thing even when it is saddled with embarrassments. After the first hurry of the new situation—conferences at Child's coffee-house, Doctors' Commons, letters of administration, negotiating for 'a daughter of the Poet Mallet to divert poor Mrs. Gibbon during the gloom of winter'—a new Gibbon emerges and grows apace, no longer introspective but confident of future achievement, good-humoured and decisive in the midst of difficulties, unconstrained in his relations with people.

He was now in possession of landed estate at Lenborough in Bucks and at Buriton, of a share in the New River and an interest in some copper mines. The father's debts remained chiefly in the form of a considerable mortgage; but the only problem now was to combine their liquidation with the promotion of the son's interests.

> 'It is a satisfaction', Gibbon wrote to his aunt Hester, 'to reflect that I have fulfilled, perhaps exceeded, my filial duties, and it is still in my power with the remains of our fortunes to lead an agreeable and rational life.'

For the moment he was to be reigning squire of Buriton for two years to come.

At first he was not displeased with his new dignity. He would be Farmer Gibbon in spite of everything, 'got a droll little Poney and intended to renew the long-forgotten practice of equitation', raised his rents, attended Weyhill fair, sold his hops well, pitting his judgment successfully against Mrs Gibbon's. 'Farmer Gibbon of no use!'

The amateur will always trumpet his little successes in the presence of experts. The real farmer, as Gibbon well knew, was his stepmother. 'I am in no violent hurry to dispose of the Place, which under Mrs. Gibbon's management is certainly no losing Game.' [1] She for her part was not so enthusiastic and did not care about the responsibility; but foresaw 'a great deal of trouble in letting it, as I fear it is a piece of work that will discompose Mr. Gibbon'.[2]

By the middle of 1772 Gibbon was 'tired of sticking to the earth by so many Roots'. He wanted his money out of it, and was eager to hear proposals 'for taking Miss Nancy Beriton into private keeping before I throw her upon the town'. Not for him was 'the History of a great Bullock bred upon the farm which is to bring in 28 pounds by Whitsontide', or deciphering scrawled bills 'for Cuten of Timber and Cleaven it for mending the Dong cart'.

Business took him frequently to town 'at my old lodgings opposite the Duke of Cumberland's in Pall Mall'; pleasure claimed her share of his time when he got there. 'Writings not Ridottos', he had been obliged to assure the gossips, detained him. But a taste for the Soho or Haymarket masquerades is soon declared. A domino bought in April 1772, 'trimmed blue pink and silver, £5.15.6 and work 5/–' was no vain symbol, though not to be taken too seriously in itself. Variety of companionship, old friends and new clubs, and ready

[1] *Prothero*, i. 138, 1st October 1771, wrongly dated 6th by the editor.

[2] Mrs Gibbon to James Scott, 3rd March 1772; Brit. Mus. 11907, dd. 25 (2). She had been enquiring for a house at Bath in the previous March: *ibid.* iii. 3.

access to books were irresistible calls. By the end of the year, largely by Holroyd's help, Buriton was let. Mrs Gibbon, a little difficult when the actual uprooting came, was to settle in Bath and her stepson was excitedly balancing the claims of several town houses.

Had the attachment between Gibbon and his father's widow been less warm and genuine, here might have lain the parting of their ways. Nothing of the sort happened.

> 'I know you will be glad', Mrs Gibbon wrote to James Scott a few months after her husband's death, 'to hear that Mr. Gibbon is most excessively kind and good to me. I think there never was a more worthy man, in the transactions that has called upon him to show an exactness both of Duty and honor. There are few I believe that would have the same notions he has.'

Gibbon justified this not only in his care for her in the first days of widowhood but in his constant regard for her well-being. She for her part never flagged in a maternal concern for her stepson, which might indeed have grown into an irksome control had they continued to live together. In the early days of his freedom he felt obliged to repel courteously but firmly an inclination to read him a lecture on extravagance. But an association, based on occasional visits and letters which Mrs Gibbon looked forward to with unabated eagerness, could defy decay. Nor was Gibbon tempted to neglect her amid his new friends, especially those at Sheffield Place. On the contrary she was welcomed in that delightful circle, while in her turn she in Bath formed friendships with Holroyd's father and sister.

An agreeable feature of the new life was the quick ripening of intimacy both with Holroyd and his wife. Considerable obligations were repaid with a lively and generous affection. James Scott and Stanier Porten had given their share of help, and Gibbon himself was far from being incompetent in business; but very soon Holroyd, with all his knowledge and zeal in estate-management, was invoked. Not often can help have been given so whole-heartedly. He becomes at once 'the active little man', 'the faithfull friend and Minister', 'the invaluable counsellor', 'the Oracle' whose responses never failed either Gibbon or his stepmother. 'I am so happy, so exquisitely happy', Gibbon writes in October 1772, 'at feeling so many mountains taken off my shoulders.' His friend carried or shared the burden off and on for twenty-four years.

Gibbon was now free to visit Sheffield Place often, whether for business or pleasure, and Mrs Holroyd and her children soon became 'la chère famille', 'la Sainte Famille' even. One of the links in this circle was soon broken only to strengthen the rest. There was a little boy, John William Holroyd, between whom and Gibbon a spirited attachment was growing. 'My great enemy Datch', Gibbon writes playfully, and again 'My profound respects to Mr. Datch'. But in July 1772 he saw in the papers news which he hoped vainly might be untrue—'the death of our poor little amiable friend Master Holroyd whom I loved not only for his parents' sake but for his own'. Gibbon was ready to put everything else aside if he could afford the least comfort or satisfaction to the man in the world he loved and esteemed the most. The Holroyds welcomed his sympathy, and in the following month he accompanied them on a short tour, entertaining them at Buriton on the way. His liking for and interest in Mrs Holroyd grew unaffectedly and is expressed constantly in his letters, sometimes playfully—*j'embrasse Madame autant qu'il m'est permis*—at other times with solicitous concern when she was in poor health or when he thought she needed a jaunt to town, and at all times after his settlement in town he was eager and imperious in desiring them to make Bentinck Street their inn. If he was not there, no matter; Mrs Ford and the parrot would welcome them. As for the daughter, the irrepressible Maria Josepha—the gentle Louisa was not yet born—it was very likely she, who still at a tender age first called the little man 'Gib'.

The monument of Gibbon's friendship, as well as the record of his daily life from now onwards, are seen in his flowering as a writer of letters which, in spite of his confessed dilatoriness, are so abundant.[1] These alone would be enough to establish him as a master of racy English, commanding every tone of expression, from playful notes and nonce-language and unaffected chat to the studied eloquence of great occasions. For this range of style the letters may be compared with Cicero's, as well as for a fondness for cryptic jokes and allusions. Consciously or unconsciously Gibbon had not read the great Latin writer in his youth for nothing. Ciceronian also was the quality which Lord Sheffield discerned, when he remarked with truth that 'when he touches on matters of private business, even subjects of the driest nature become interesting from his mode of treating them'.[2] The mark Gibbon made in society as a conversationalist will be considered later; on the evidence of his letters, with their unfailing humour and resource of phrase, he was incapable of being dull.

Early in 1773 Gibbon was established at 7 Bentinck Street, then on the fringes of the town, 'my own new clean comfortable dear house which I like better every week I pass in it'. The only fly that spring was the fine weather in which his importunate conscience occasionally drove him out of doors.

This was to be his home for ten years, to be the work-

[1] Of the 647 letters in Prothero's two volumes, the majority of which are addressed to Holroyd or Mrs Gibbon, only 85 belong to the first part of Gibbon's life, which ended with his father's death.

[2] *Misc. Wks.* i. 431. Do I flatter Cicero too much and those learned commentators and lecturers who made his transactions with Atticus so enthralling?

shop of the first half of his History, to witness his acceptance as a social figure, and the rise and end of his political fortunes. The choosing and furnishing of it had given him the liveliest pleasure and the most detailed concern. In conference with his upholsterer mahogany was to be proscribed in his library.

> 'The paper of the Room will be a fine shag flock paper, light blue with a gold border, the Book-cases painted white, ornamented with a light frize; neither Doric nor Dentulated (that was yours) Adamic. The Dog was to have sent me drawings tonight to enclose to you, but has disapointed me.'

Blue was very likely a favourite colour.[1]

There were three menservants and the 'virgins in the garret'. Two at least of the men, his coachman, Edward Budd, and Caplin, his butler and valet, were brought up from Hampshire; from Buriton also came Mrs Phoebe Ford, who governed his household for some nine years until age and Mr Caplin undermined her position. The crisis is of more interest than merely as being the intrigue of a bachelor's *entourage*.

Phoebe Ford was a cousin of Dr. Johnson, being the youngest of three daughters of his uncle Cornelius Ford. She had come to the Gibbon family with Mrs Gibbon. 'Mrs. Phebys room' [2] was a standing designation at Buriton and shows that she was more than a servant. The rest of her story is told in a letter which she wrote to the Lexicographer 17th May 1780.

After establishing her identity she says: 'I am at present Howsekeeper with Mr. Gibbon, author of the Roman Hisstory and with his Mother in law before she Marryed and in this Fammely this eight and thirty years'. She would have been very happy in this service 'but for my Master's servant who was a poor Labourer's son'.

[1] His room at Buriton had been painted blue, and there are bills for blue slippers and crockery. *Notes and Queries*, 13th Ser., i. 144.

[2] *Magd. Coll. Papers.*

He had been footman at Buriton, but 'my present Masster took him and put him out of Livery and a great Gentleman he is, I have more difficulty to please him than his sewperior'. He had insulted her before the other servants and she had consequently lost their respect. She had always lived in an upper station and been treated with proper regard. Now she also suspected that Mr Caplin had not done her 'manney good offisses with my Master, as his behaviour has become very different'. He used to go over the books with her once or twice a month, but now he did not see her once in six months and all orders came from Mr Caplin, who was very overbearing. Caplin would be glad to see her go and so would she, but was too old to look for another place. She complained of weak legs. She had not saved much as her wages were low and she had put out her money to two gentlemen, one of whom had gone to 'Anntigoe' and she feared the money sunk.

We do not know whether Johnson intervened. The incident was not likely to improve the relations between him and Gibbon. He apparently did not know before this letter that his cousin was the infidel historian's housekeeper.[1] Gibbon, we may assume, would have been told by Phoebe of her relationship with the great man of letters. It is improbable that he would have told Johnson that a cousin of his was a servant in Bentinck Street. It would be 'a delicate matter'. Phoebe Ford's story, therefore, has in all probability nothing to do with the relations of Gibbon and Johnson. But Gibbon must be exonerated from the imputation of having treated Johnson's cousin shabbily.

Phoebe Ford remained with Gibbon till November 1781, when he pensioned her off with her wages for life. Caplin, he tells Holroyd, would be glad to be prime minister, which shows that he still considered the old

[1] At any rate if he knew, Mrs Ford did not know that he did.

lady in that office. By his will of July 1788 he left her an annuity of £25; in that of October 1791 it was reduced to £20. Mr A. L. Reade remarks that Mrs Ford had no reason to complain of the lowness of her wages.[1]

Doubtless Mrs Ford and Mr Caplin must have discussed a certain possibility which would eclipse their rivalry. Would their master add to his well-appointed home the object that was most obviously wanting? The gossip certainly went round above stairs. 'Ah my Lady my Lady', Gibbon writes to Mrs Holroyd, 'what rumours have you diffused in the regions of Bath relating *to Sappho* and your Slave.' It was pleasant to toy with the idea, it was amusing to flutter Miss Porten, Mrs Gibbon and Mrs Holroyd. It is hardly to be thought that he was in earnest over Sappho, and very likely her uncle, Mr Rose Fuller, did no great harm when he put down his foot against her going to Boodle's great masquerade. Some months later a more serious proposal was on foot about which Gibbon had better speak for himself. He is writing to Mrs Holroyd on 17th December 1774:

> 'Surely no affair was ever put into better hands than mine has been. Your skill and friendship I am not surprized at, but Mrs. Porten is a most excellent procuress, and the Lady Mother has given as proper an answer as could be expected. There is only one part of it which distresses me, *Religion*. It operates doubly, as a present obstacle and a future inconvenience. Your evasion was very able, but will not prudence as well as honour require us to be more explicit in the *suite*? Ought I to give them room to think that I should patiently conform to family prayers and Bishop Hooper's Sermons? I would not marry an Empress on those conditions. I abhor a Devotee though a friend both to decency and toleration. However my interests are under your

[1] For Phoebe Ford's story and letter see A. L. Reade, *Johnsonian Gleanings*, iv. 46-9, and correspondence in *T.L.S.*, 22nd and 29th September, 6th October 1921.

care, and If you think that no more need be said on *the awkward* subject, I shall acquiesce.

'After all, what occasion is there to enquire into my profession of faith? It is surely much more to the purpose for them to ask how I have already acted in life, whether as a good son, a good friend, whether I game, drink, etc. You know I never practised the one, and in spite of my old *Dorsetshire* character, I have left off the other. You once mentioned Miss F. I give you my honor, that I have not either with her or any other woman, any connection that could alarm a Wife. With regard to fortune Mrs. P. speaks in a very liberal manner; but above all things, I think it should not be *magnified.* If it should be necessary to hint at incumbrances, your delicacy I am sure could place them in such a light as might raise the character of the living without injuring the memory of the dead. You see how serious I am in this business. If the general idea should not startle Miss, the next consultation would be how, and where the Lover may throw himself at her feet, contemplate her charms, and *study her character.* After that we may proceed to other more minute enquiries and arrangements.'

Not a romantic outlook but an honest one. Seven years before he had written to Holroyd on his marriage,

'that tho' as a Philosopher I may prefer Celibacy, yet as a Politician I think it highly proper that the species should be propagated by the usual method; assure him even that I am convinced, that if celibacy is exposed to fewer miseries, marriage can alone promise real happiness, since domestick enjoyments are the source of every other good.'

But his cat had been out of the bag with the preceding remark, 'tell him from me, that I am at least as well pleased that he is married as if I were so myself'. He might have said the same to Jacques Necker. He was surest and happiest in his rôle of bachelor friend, and was never tempted to disturb the harmony. He might tell Mrs Holroyd that 'in this polite age, married women of Fashion (meaning Lady Pelham), and not your Miss Sappho Fullers are the object of the Man of the World', but he obviously meant less by it than by some cynical remarks on the pursuit of *mesdames* to Victor de Saussure which so scandalised Meredith Read.[1]

The negotiation, whatever it was, came to nothing. Life went on unperturbed at Bentinck Street, the master, if we may infer from later years, exacting from his servants the punctual habits and regularity of life which he had now imposed on himself. The old way of late hours and excesses was gone without regret, and to his gain rather than loss in society. Aunt Kitty, now in retirement in Newman Street, could report on him to Bath. In a mysterious message to Mrs. Gibbon she seems to have been unenthusiastic about his projected marriage.[2] Now she had no more serious news than to lament 'a fit of the Gout which gave him great concern as he had no suspicion that he should ever have it' (this first attack had come at the end of 1772 following a fall and sprained ankle in crossing St. James's Churchyard), or possibly to wonder why he was not yet in Parliament. The last thing that there was news of was the daily task in the library.

The progress of *The Decline and Fall* is only darkly and gradually unfolded in the extant letters amid the medley of business, politics and society. The first reference to there being something on hand is not found before July 1773, when Gibbon lightly tells his stepmother that he is detained in town by some things which he wants to finish, and for which his library is requisite. 'Laugh at the bookworm if you please but excuse the

[1] Read, *op. cit.* ii. 353.

[2] Brit. Mus. 11907, dd. 25 (2). Catherine Porten to Mrs Gibbon, 24th September 1774. A complaint of her brother's 'alarmed me very much as indeed you did me with your little Gibbon in the Indias. . . . As to my liking a Little Gibbon in England, I am in doubt. I like the Great one so well I want no addition and the little thing might bring disagreeable circumstances along with it that might over balance the Pleasure of it.' She regarded Gibbon and her brother Sir Stanier as 'my governors'. It is legitimate to infer that his entry into Parliament was discussed from the interest that was shown when he was elected.

nature of the animal.' A year later (June 1774) he tells her 'I am well in mind and body, busy with my Books (which may perhaps produce something next year either to tire or amuse the World)'. Not until June 1775 did he tell her explicitly what he was about:

> 'I am just at present engaged in a great Historical Work no less than a History of the Decline and fall of the Roman Empire, with the first Volume of which I may very possibly oppress the public next winter.'

Holroyd was no doubt more in his confidence; but he gets no more than hints of 'the prosecution of my great work', or 'my peculiar employment', though Gibbon, in a sketch of himself sitting 'at Boodle's in a fine Velvet coat with ruffles of My Lady's chusing etc.', adds the rider 'that the aforesaid fine Gentleman is likewise a Historian' who feels that when he writes a page he is writing to his friend and so need not write a letter.

A literary adventure which Gibbon declined belongs to this period. Lord Chesterfield had died in 1773, and James Dodsley had given his son's widow fifteen hundred guineas for the copyright of his letters to his son. The Stanhope family went to court in their efforts to prevent publication. Dodsley had applied to Gibbon to edit them, and we may well believe that he could have written a memorable introduction. Gibbon declined. Apart from his other occupations he thought it prudent to avoid making personal enemies of the family, mainly on account of Deyverdun, who was tutor to the young earl.[1]

The restless and consequently often dissipated habits of the old days in lodgings were thankfully abandoned. But Gibbon was no recluse. He sometimes gave 'the prettiest little dinners in the world'. He was a leading

[1] *Prothero*, i. 195, and Birkbeck Hill, *Eighteenth Century Letters*, xxxiv-v.

member of Boodle's, and was becoming well known in various circles.

Through Holroyd acquaintance had been made, not very eagerly at first, with Richard Owen Cambridge. But soon references to the Cantabs and the eloquent nymphs of Twickenham reveal some intimacy and appreciation of a kindly intelligent family, in whose house men of every range of distinction might be met. The Cantabs—Gibbon calls them amphibious—were fond of water-parties. On one of these occasions Gibbon fell in. Cambridge showed Fanny Burney a finical note of Gibbon's accepting an invitation to the party in which he referred to the Thames as an 'amiable creature', and remarked that the accident was 'God's revenge against conceit'.[1]

In town Gibbon was becoming known among the literary sets, and he maintained his early interest in the theatre. In January 1774 he was present to support Colman's *Man of Business*. 'We got a Verdict for our Client; his Cause was but a bad one.' The previous night he had dined at 'the Br*ee*tish Coffee-house' with Garrick, Colman, Goldsmith, 'Ossian' Macpherson, John Home, the author of *Douglas*, and others. This coffee-house in Cockspur Street was the resort of Scottish men of letters, and there was a club there to which some Englishmen also belonged. It had been founded by Alexander Wedderburn, an adventurous advocate who had left Edinburgh for the English bar and whose political migrations were less unexception able. It was an ominous acquaintance which was to ripen into a genuine though dangerous friendship.[2]

Garrick was an old standing acquaintance, and it was

[1] *Diary and Letters of Madame d'Arblay* (Dobson), ii. 222 and 225; and F. Burney, *Memoir of Dr. Burney*, ii. 341.

[2] He is probably the Wedderburn who appears in one of the militia courts-martial. *Gibbon's Journal*, p. 18.

very likely through him that Gibbon met Goldsmith and Reynolds. The solitude of the previous August in London had been enlivened with their company. Gibbon's brief friendship with Goldsmith is shadowy but intriguing. Did they compare notes on fine clothes? One anecdote survives in which Gibbon playfully misleads the doctor on an elementary fact of Greek history. But Goldsmith died on 4th April 1774, not, however, before he had tried, as will be seen, to render his new friend a valuable service.

On Goldsmith's death it is said that Gibbon took his place as Reynolds' companion. He was a frequent caller at the studio, and Northcote, at work in another room, remembered hearing him criticise Garrick's *Richard III*. He was dining with Reynolds when the famous Round Robin was drawn up asking Johnson to write Goldsmith's epitaph in English. The two friends had a common liking for the night entertainments of London, and Reynolds' engagement-book notes: '5, Mr. Gibbon; 9, Masquerade'.

Inevitably the progress of the History was retarded, although the expectation mentioned to Mrs Gibbon of publishing in 1775 was still held in the early autumn of the previous year. Cadell had been interviewed, and proposed to publish in the following March with 750 copies if Gibbon could be ready. But Parliament also was now in sight, and Gibbon could say 'there is a fine prospect opening upon me, and if next spring I should take my seat and publish my book it will be a very memorable Era in my life'.

Another year was to pass before the book was ready. Meanwhile he had entered the House of Commons, and also become a member of that society which has always been called the Club *par excellence*.

Chapter 15

THE CLUB

1774

GIBBON was proposed for the Club by Goldsmith and balloted for on 4th March 1774, the date usually given for his election together with George Steevens. Johnson, telling Steevens of his success the next day, mentions that another gentleman was rejected. The recent publication of a letter from Garrick to Steevens reveals that the gentleman blackballed was Gibbon.[1] A month later Goldsmith was dead. But it may be assumed that his candidate still had powerful supporters in Reynolds and Garrick and probably Colman. Gibbon was certainly elected within a year of this defeat, for he was present at the first recorded dinner on 7th April 1775.

It seems vain to look for his enemy. It was certainly not Boswell, who was not in London in 1774, and it could hardly have been Johnson who could have persisted in his opposition; while it is doubtful whether the rest would have elected in his absence a candidate whom he disliked.

Boswell makes it plain, with the pride of a successful candidate, that membership was an honour not lightly conferred. On occasions, at least, aspirants were reviewed at a dinner party and sent away before the meeting. One black ball rejected. But the qualifications were undefined, and when, for instance, Johnson heard

[1] Massachusetts Historical Society *Proceedings* (1918–19), lii. 148–50.

that Vesey had gentle manners he said it was enough. If Gibbon's election was not before he had attained the distinction of Parliament, it was at least a year before his literary notoriety, after which he would certainly have had no chance.

In Boswell's *Johnson* Gibbon is allowed to appear but seldom, and then not to his advantage. The hostility of Boswell's witness is avowed. Nevertheless it has not been sufficiently acknowledged that his is not a complete picture either of Gibbon's relations with Johnson, or of his place generally in the Club.[1]

Gibbon on his side is tantalisingly silent. He not only repaid Boswell by almost completely ignoring him; he has next to nothing to say of the Club. Boswell's name is significantly omitted in a list of the members given in the Autobiography, and that list occurs only in a footnote:

> 'From the mixed though polite company of Boodle's, White's and Brook's, I must honourably distinguish a weekly society which was instituted in the year 1764 and which still continues to flourish under the title of the Literary Club. . . . The names of Dr. Johnson, Mr. Burke, Mr. Garrick, Dr. Goldsmith, Sir Joshua Reynolds, Mr. Colman, Sir William Jones, Dr. Percy, Mr. Fox, Mr. Sheridan, Mr. Adam Smith, Mr. Steevens, Mr. Dunning, Sir Joseph Banks, Dr. Warton, and his brother Mr. Thomas Warton, Dr. Burney, etc., form a large and luminous constellation of British stars.'[2]

There are singularly few references to these men in Gibbon's writings. Yet he was an assiduous and conspicuous member of the Club, and his contacts there would have contributed not a little to that 'gallery of portraits and collection of anecdotes' with which in another footnote he says 'it would be assuredly in my

[1] Boswell only records eight meetings in the *Life*.

[2] *Murray*, p. 307. Boswell's name occurs in two other footnotes only in reference to his book; once as Bozzy. *Murray*, pp. 26 and 39.

power to amuse the reader'. But he adds, perhaps with allusion to Boswell's book, 'I have always condemned the practise of transforming a private memorial into a vehicle of satire and praise'. Malone says that Lord Sheffield found among Gibbon's papers 'a great number of cards closely written on both sides, filled with the characters of some of our contemporaries'. Possibly Malone was mistaken. No such documents have come to light, and it seems unlikely that Sheffield would have destroyed them.[1]

Of Johnson himself Gibbon has but little to say. In the Autobiography the Doctor is mentioned as an 'unforgiving enemy' in relation to Mallet, and obliquely as the oracle of 'my friend Sir Joshua Reynolds'. References to him in the footnotes of *The Decline and Fall* have been marshalled to prove that Gibbon was afraid of him.[2] The evidence is by no means conclusive. In the last part of the History, published after Johnson's death, there are a number of critical references to him, but only one is in any way offensive, and if *Irene* is gently ridiculed for 'the extravagance of the rant', in one place it is quoted with approval. Only in referring to Johnson's note on *Henry IV*, *Part I*, does he write of 'the notes of Dr. Johnson the workings of a bigoted though vigorous, mind, greedy of every pretence to hate and persecute those who dissent from his creed'. This is severe, but not necessarily unmerited. Those who like to balance these things may weigh what Gibbon said after Johnson's death with what Boswell wrote about Gibbon in his lifetime. But as to being afraid of provoking Johnson, Gibbon had in his lifetime thrown down the glove in a deftly irritating manner:

---

[1] Malone to Lord Charlemont, 20th February 1794; Hist. MSS. Comm. 13th Rep.; *Charlemont*, ii. 230-31.
[2] *Birkbeck Hill*, pp. 230-31.

'Dr. Johnson', he says, 'affirms that *few* English words are of British extraction. Mr. Whitaker who understands the British language has discovered more than *three thousand*.'

Johnson's name is inseparably connected with the Club, although he was less actively interested in it than he had been in some of his earlier societies. But Reynolds had founded it and remained to the last its most effective member. Second to him in constant support comes his friend Gibbon. It might almost be said to be their club, on the records of attendance. These alone dispose of any notion that Gibbon was a cipher in it. But they do not begin before 7th April 1775. From then to Johnson's death Reynolds had been present at 131 dinners and Gibbon at 80 against Johnson's 31 and Boswell's 15. Gibbon attended eight more meetings during his visit to England, 1787–8.[1]

Boswell first met Gibbon, whom he refers to as a Mr Gibbons, at the dinner of 7th April 1775,[2] the others present being Johnson, Beauclerk, Chamier, Langton, Percy, Steevens, and Reynolds. The ham was not very good and Boswell tried to enliven the company by a laboured pun on rusticating the rusty meat. Perhaps Gibbon was not amused.[3]

It is odd that in recording in the *Life* this first dinner of the Club Boswell merely describes it as a dinner at a tavern with a numerous company. Nor does he think it worth while saying that this was his first sight of Gibbon. But he gives the famous 'black bear' anecdote. Johnson was talking of bears but could not get a hearing in the hubbub of general talk. His vociferation of 'bear' ('like

[1] See Appendix III. p. 359.

[2] Boswell was not in London in 1774. He arrived 21st March 1775. Gibbon was not present at the meeting of 24th March. *Boswell Papers*, x. p. 193.

[3] Gibbon could do better. Walpole to Mason, 25 December 1779, says, 'I have had a relapse and called it only a *codicil* to my gout. Mr. Gibbon said "Very well. But I fancy it is not in consequence of your *will*".'

a word in a catch', as Beauclerk said) was heard at intervals until silence was obtained.

' "We are told", the oracle said at last, "that the black bear is innocent, but I should not like to trust myself with him." Mr. Gibbon muttered, in a low tone of voice, "I should not like to trust myself with *you*". This piece of sarcastick pleasantry was a prudent resolution, if applied to a competition of abilities.'

It has been inferred that Gibbon was generally silent in his company. His silence in Parliament is in people's minds as a kind of parallel. It is difficult to believe that that is by any means the whole truth. To Gibbon may be applied his own remark heard by Boswell 'that Mr. Fox could not be afraid of Dr. Johnson; yet he certainly was very shy of saying any thing in Dr. Johnson's presence'. These men may not have shared Boswell's reckless zeal in cornering a bull; they may not have cared to be knocked down with the butt end of a pistol that had missed fire. Boswell records no such fate for Gibbon; and he would hardly have neglected the opportunity. Eleven days after this first meeting Gibbon and Boswell with Reynolds and Johnson met again at Owen Cambridge's villa at Twickenham. The utility of history was discussed. Johnson remarked that

' "all the colouring, all the philosophy of history is conjecture". BOSWELL. "Then, Sir, you would reduce all history to no better than an almanack. . . ." Mr. Gibbon, who must at that time have been employed upon his *History*, of which he published the first volume in the following year, was present; but did not step forth in defence of that species of writing. He probably did not like to *trust* himself with JOHNSON.'

Mr Gibbon could afford to bide his time and knew how to hold his tongue, an incomprehensible art for Boswell, who perhaps unconsciously betrays that the silence of that round, uncomely, yet animated and so dangerously intelligent countenance was an effective and exasperating weapon.

But was Gibbon always so silent? That seems very doubtful. At least once there is the suspicion of deliberate suppression by Boswell when Gibbon alone of the company takes no part in a conversation which turned on such topics as Horace's villa and his journey to Brindisi, and the comparative merits of London and Paris.[1] The more so since a truer proportion seems to be observed in the record of a Club meeting six days before. For some reason Boswell has labelled the speakers with letters. Of these I, *i.e.* Infidel (sometimes printed J), has been proved to be Gibbon. I. takes a modest but easy share in the talk, and Boswell manages to draw him out shrewdly enough by comparing place-hunting with real hunting. I. remarks that not everyone is keen enough on place to break his neck or roll in the mire; whereupon Boswell scores neatly: 'I am glad there are some good, quiet moderate political hunters'. Later on I. is allowed to correct Boswell on a small point in a discussion about the Club's wine; and when Johnson intervening said that were he their dictator he would allow no wine, and added *smiling*, 'Rome was ruined by luxury', is it too much to think that the smile indicated that Rome had been ruined by the little man in velvet and ruffles in their company?[2]

Reynolds also presents Johnson and Gibbon talking together without embarrassment, if with somewhat stilted politeness, in two imaginary dialogues designed to exhibit the Doctor's captiousness more than anything else. In the first Reynolds, praising Garrick, leads Johnson into a critical vein about the great actor; but let Gibbon, in the second, venture on a depreciatory remark and the old champion is up in arms at once.

Hannah More testified to the accuracy of the portraits:

> 'I hear the deep-toned and indignant accents of our friend Johnson; I hear the affected periods of Gibbon; the natural, the

[1] *Boswell*, 9th April 1778. [2] *Op. cit.* 3rd April 1778.

easy, the friendly the elegant language, the polished sarcasm, softened with the sweet temper of Sir Joshua.' [1]

Hannah More knew Gibbon through the Garricks. She recounts a dinner at Bishop Shipley's in 1781 attended by Gibbon, Johnson and Boswell among others. Boswell got drunk and annoyed her by his attentions. Johnson reproved her for reading Pascal. Gibbon ought to have had something to say to that, but it is not recorded. Still she adds one more link to the evidence that there could not have been any obvious feud between Johnson and Gibbon, since they were constantly meeting at their friends' houses.[2]

But the most brilliant portrait of Gibbon and Johnson together is by the younger Colman and cannot be passed over, however familiar it may be. It has often lost some of its value by separation from its context.

As a boy of thirteen or fourteen about 1775 Colman was early introduced among his father's friends, and his first experiences made him a decided anti-Johnsonian. In later years he bore witness to the bullying type of conversation prevailing in his youth. The Club, he thought, was rated too high, and even educated persons were so pusillanimous as to give in to the despotism of a self-chosen few. But while the Club intimidated the town, Johnson awed the Club.

He met Johnson and Gibbon on the same day, both having been asked to dine at his father's house in Soho Square. The 'Erudite Savage' arrived an hour too early. When Colman came down to the drawing-room with his father he saw, sitting in a gilt *fauteuil* of rose-coloured satin, a large man wearing a rusty suit of

[1] Leslie and Taylor's *Reynolds*, ii. 259.

[2] A. M. B. Meakin, *Hannah More*, p. 145. Bishop Percy's diary notes a dinner with Reynolds, 11th January 1775, attended by Warton, Johnson, Dean of Derry, Burke, Franklin, Burney, Thrale, Adam Smith, Langton, Chamier, Beauclerk, and 'Mr Gibbons': Add. MSS. 32336.

brown cloth *dittos*, with black worsted stockings; his old yellow wig was of formidable dimensions. This uncouth figure did not get out of his chair for his host. 'Doctor Johnson', said the father, 'this is a little Colman.' Johnson gave the boy a slight ungracious glance and plunged into his talk. At the first pause paternal pride ventured again. 'This is my son, Doctor Johnson.' The great man's contempt was now raised to wrath and knitting his brows he exclaimed, in a voice of thunder, 'I *see* him, sir!' and fell back in his rose-coloured satin *fauteuil*. To complete his felicity Colman was placed next Johnson at dinner and took a boyish interest in his table habits. He continues:

> 'On the day I first sat down with Johnson, in his rusty brown, and his black worsteads, Gibbon was placed opposite to me in a suit of flower'd velvet, with a bag and sword.[1] Each had his measured phraseology, and Johnson's famous parallel, between Dryden and Pope, might be loosely parodied, in reference to himself and Gibbon.—Johnson's style was grand, and Gibbon's elegant; the stateliness of the former was sometimes pedantick, and the polish of the latter was occasionally finical. Johnson march'd to kettle-drums and trumpets; Gibbon moved to flutes and haut-boys; Johnson hew'd passages through the Alps, while Gibbon levell'd walks through parks and gardens. Maul'd as I had been by Johnson, Gibbon pour'd balm upon my bruises, by condescending, once or twice, in the course of the evening, to talk with me;—the great historian was light and playful, suiting his matter to the capacity of the boy;—but it was done *more suo*; still he tapp'd his snuff-box,—still he smirk'd, and smiled; and rounded his periods with the same air of good breeding, as if he were conversing with men. His mouth, mellifluous as Plato's, was a round hole, nearly in the centre of his visage.'[2]

[1] 'Gibbon's costume was not extraordinary at this time (a little overcharged, perhaps, if his *person* be consider'd) when almost every gentleman came to dinner in full dress.—Foote's clothes were, then, tawdrily splash'd with gold lace; which with his linen, were generally bedawb'd with snuff;—he was a *Beau Nasty*. . . .' (Colman's note.)

[2] G. Colman, *Random Records*, i. 96, 107, 121.

Gibbon, whose own childhood had not been happy, never fails in his relations with young people.

Early in 1777 Johnson wrote to Boswell that he was in favour of increasing the Club to thirty; 'for as we have several in it whom I do not much like to consort with, I am for reducing it to a mere miscellaneous collection of conspicuous men, without any determinate character'. Boswell adds a footnote to explain Johnson's dissatisfaction, 'on account of their differing from him as to religion and politics'.[1] The allusion, on a review of the members, must be taken to refer certainly to Gibbon and perhaps to Adam Smith. In the previous year all had not been well. Boswell noted in his diary 10th May that he was for a new Club, a *secessio plebis*. 'Smith too' (*i.e.* as well as Gibbon), he wrote to Temple, 'is now of our Club. It has lost its select merit.'

Two years later Boswell broke out in a more direct and violent strain: 'Gibbon is an ugly, affected, disgusting fellow, and poisons our literary club to me'. The sore was not healed by time. On 27th March 1781 both Boswell and Gibbon were present at the Club, but Johnson was not there. A debate arose on the question whether absent members were to be called on to pay for their share of the wine, and was carried on with a genial parody of parliamentary procedure. Sir Joseph Banks, 'chancellor of the exchequer', opened the budget. In the course of this pleasantry Boswell was excused from his share since although he was a Scotchman he had no place under government; but Adam Smith, at the instigation of Burke and Boswell, was ordered to pay because he was a Commissioner of Customs. Gibbon

[1] Occasionally there were very small attendances (Percy records 31st December 1770, Chambers and Polman besides himself, and 9th March 1772, only himself and Chamier: Add. MSS. 32336), and there was always a risk of some remarkable *tête-à-tête* to which perhaps Johnson did not like to trust himself.

stood up for Smith as a fellow infidel and was noted down as a disagreeable dog.[1]

The appearance of *The Decline and Fall* precipitated a crisis of Boswell's hysterical frenzy against what he called infidelity; a particularly unlucky word for him to use. In vain for him to think that knocking the heads of Hume and Smith together would make 'ostentatious infidelity exceedingly ridiculous'. The hideous thing went on. He was grieved with his friend Temple for praising Gibbon's book, and gave rein to his metaphorical fury: 'As fast as infidel wasps or venomous insects, whether creeping or flying, are hatched they should be crushed'. It galled him to hear Gibbon's book discussed on all hands. It was shocking that Dr. Smith, Professor of Anatomy at Oxford, and an Ayrshire man at that, should be full of its praises. Boswell agreed that the style was 'beautiful quite mellifluous', but said it was a strange thing to meet with infidelity in a history. There should have been a warning, 'Springs and traps set here'. The most extreme counter measures were justified. The ordinary rules of polite disputation might be suspended and the *person* of an infidel opponent was not to be spared.[2]

The target was too easy. But Boswell lost his sense of proportion, and it was not his adversary who was most wounded in the end. Gibbon was ugly and he was vain, especially among the ladies. But Johnson fancied the ladies too and had his share of ugliness, and we only smile when he is reported as expressing disgust at Gibbon's looks,[3] or as being amused when Mrs Thrale adapted some twaddling lines from an old geography book to fit the historian. Johnson thought them worth

[1] *Boswell Papers*, xiv. 176. It is of some significance that the only members present when Smith was elected were Reynolds, Gibbon, Beauclerk, Sir William Jones (Rae, *Life of Adam Smith*, p. 267) and Percy. (Add. MSS. 32336.)

[2] *Boswell Papers*, xi. 175.

[3] *Boswell*, 19th March 1781.

repeating to Malone.[1] Nor is it easy to see how an argument against abolishing slavery should be helped by recalling the fact that Gibbon was a *beau garçon* who included in his works 'his pleasing countenance to captivate the ladies'.[2] Gibbon was wiser than ever when to the last he held his tongue about Boswell.

Boswell and Johnson's agitation about religion was not the manifestation of serene faith. They were both sceptics against their will; but neither knew nor cared to know what were the issues raised by Gibbon's work. Hence their blind fury. Boswell in particular was incapable of cool enquiry. At Tom Warton's in 1776 he remarked that as Gibbon had changed his system several times he did not despair of seeing him a Methodist preacher. Johnson gloomily decided that having published his infidelity Gibbon would probably persist in it.[3] But Gibbon's changes were nothing to Boswell's. He had sampled most of the current creeds, including

[1] See Bohn edition of Croker's *Boswell* for Malone's note about Johnson repeating these verses to him at Brighton. Mrs Thrale wrote the verses in her copy of *The Decline and Fall*. She said they were translated from some Latin verses at the end of Cluverius. But see an anonymous letter, *T.L.S.*, 13th January 1921.

This was sinking very low. Here is another example of the incompetent malevolence which was drawn out by Gibbon. Polwhele, *Traditions and Recollections*, i. 354, quotes an epigram in Latin and English. This is the English:

> To sinners wonderfully civil
> Gibbon declares there is no devil,
> Ah, trust him not! for if we look
> Upon his portrait in his book,
> The boldest infidel would swear
> He sees the very devil there.

This is feeble enough, apart from the fact that Gibbon never made any such declaration. The lines are in fact stolen from a French quatrain on Bekker, an Amsterdam divine who in 1699 tried to prove, in a work to which his portrait was prefixed, that Satan was confined to hell and could molest man no more. See *N.Q.*, 3rd Ser. ix. 84.

[2] *No Abolition of Slavery, or The Universal Empire of Love, Addressed to Miss* . . . , 1791 (it was an act of mercy to leave out the lady's name to whom these disreputable verses were dedicated.)

[3] *Boswell Papers*, xi. 177.

Catholicism, and had ended up with High Anglicanism tempered with occasional visits to the Quakers. His dominating religious interest was a torturing apprehension of total extinction. Hell was comparatively of little account.[1]

This single fear was the motive of his immediate antagonism to the ideas of Hume, Smith and Gibbon or any others who ventured to disturb any part of a position whose terrain he would have been at a loss to describe, and which he could only defend by methods which may be compared to massing boiling oil in the face of a machine-gun attack. But this is not enough to explain his intense antipathy to Gibbon. With other infidels or disturbers of the peace, notably David Hume, Boswell was on good if not affectionate terms. Rousseau and Voltaire were great men to him; yet nothing came amiss if it might belittle Gibbon.

There is nothing surprising in the clash of these confronting vanities. Both men competed too much in the same fields of conceit. If Gibbon over-cultivated his appearance, Boswell did not shrink from making absurd exhibitions of himself. Both were full of social pride and yet were arrivists in London. Here, however, the advantage lay with Gibbon and increased as the years went on. Boswell too, so often an exile in Edinburgh, may well have been jealous of the place which the little infidel maintained in the Club. Both had literary ambitions but Boswell's were not to be satisfied for many years to come. Both had travelled and had seen something of the wider intellectual life of the Continent. But Boswell's acquaintance with Voltaire may have been an embarrassment to him at the Turk's Head, while Gibbon, who had nothing to lose with Johnson, was free to compare the narrow round of casuistry which

[1] *Boswell Papers*, xii., Introduction. See also *The Hypochondriack*, No. XIV., November 1778, M. Bailey's edition, i. 199 (California, 1928).

makes up so much of Johnson's topics with the unprejudiced air of Ferney and the restless enquiries of the Parisian salons. Even if he said nothing, Boswell must have guessed what was passing in his head.

All the evidence shows that Gibbon enjoyed the Club and was on good terms with the other members. Writing from Paris in 1777 he asked Garrick to assure Sir Joshua that he had not lost his relish for *manly* conversation and the society of the brown table. His friendships with these two men were close and lasting. At Garrick's funeral in 1779 he rode in the third coach assigned to the Club with Colman, Chamier and Banks. When Reynolds died in 1792, the same year as Lord North, Gibbon exclaimed, 'Two of the men and two of the houses in London on whom I most relied for the comforts of society'. He was on intimate terms with Beauclerk and Lady Di, 'one of the most accomplished women in the world'. With Burke he had little in common, but they were not unfriendly. Boswell in vain hoped to see the Dean of Derry enter the lists against the infamous chapters; instead he included Gibbon in his pleasant lines on the art of growing old. Gibbon knew Sir William Jones well and saluted him magnificently in several of his notes.[1] Adam Smith is saluted too as a sage and a friend, and the latter term was anything but an empty one.[2]

Of the members elected later Ossory, Palmerston, John Dunning, his cousin Eliot, Spencer and Lucan were all either old or new friends.

The notification of election still used by the Club is

[1] *The Decline and Fall*, c. xliv. nn. 144, 168; also c. xxvi. n. 20, c. l. n. 41, c. lii. n. 71, c. lvii. n. 42; also letter from Jones to Gibbon, *Misc. Wks.* ii. 252.

[2] *Ibid.* c. xxiv. n. 15; also c. xl. n. 148, c. lxx. n. 92. Writing to Gibbon in 1788 on the completion of his History, Smith ends 'most affectionately yours': *Misc. Wks.* ii. 429. Smith is very likely the 'Adam' mentioned once or twice in Gibbon's letters.

said to have been drawn up by Gibbon, who at least once acted as secretary.

> 'Sir, I have the pleasure to inform you that you had last night the honour to be elected a member of the Club.
>
> 'I have the honour to be,
>
> 'Sir, your obedient humble servant.' [1]

Gibbon admittedly preferred small gatherings. There is evidence that he could be silent in other company than Johnson's. But something must be allowed for progression towards seniority both in a club and in the world. For in his later years Gibbon was ready enough to talk, and Maria Holroyd noted that he could not bear to play second fiddle. Malone, who had seen Gibbon at the Club often enough, remarks on his fund of anecdote and erudition, and says he 'had acquired such a facility and elegance of talk that I had always great pleasure in listening to him'. Praise from Malone is valuable.[2] Another critic writing soon after Gibbon's death mentions an unaccountable fascination which made him agreeable and impressive in spite of an ungraceful articulation and pedantic manner.[3] Guizot, drawing on French tradition, says that Gibbon's tone was decisive, not from any desire to dominate but out of self-confidence. His vanity indeed was of the ingratiating kind; he was anxious to succeed by pleasing.[4] Gibbon regarded talk as a relaxation. But his memory was so ready that he could on occasions debate with skill. Yet he had no taste for the browbeating by which the younger Colman says the talkers of the previous generation had established an undeserved ascendancy.

[1] He informed Malone of his election. R. B. Adam, *Johnsonian Library*, iii. p. 108. For the formula see M. E. G. Duff, *The Club, 1764–1905*. Birkbeck Hill's version, got from Tennyson, differs. It omits the ending with the apparent quippical contrast 'You had the honour . . I have the honour'.

[2] Hist. MSS. Comm. 13th Rep.; *Charlemont*, ii. 230.

[3] *Gent. Mag.* lxiv. 178.

[4] Guizot's introduction to his edition of *The Decline and Fall.*

Apart from the Club, Gibbon was not particularly drawn to literary society. He told Holroyd that authors and managers were good company to know but not to live with. Perhaps that was youthful insolence. But Wraxall says that he avoided such things as Mrs Montague's parties.

He belonged to Boodle's, Brooks's and White's clubs. In 1774 the novelty in St. James's was the Chess Club, founded by admirers of the French player Philidor. Gibbon, with his friends Wedderburn and Fox, was among the earliest members.[1] He also became a Mason. On the 19th December of the same year he was initiated and advanced to the third degree at the Lodge of Friendship, No. 3, at the Star and Garter, New Bond Street, and on the following 8th March he attained the sublime degree of a Master Mason.[2]

1 P. W. Sergeant, *A Century of British Chess*.

2 Add. MSS. 34887. The certificate is signed by Lord Wentworth.

Chapter 16

THE MEMBER FOR LISKEARD

1774

GIBBON had news for his stepmother in September 1774 to which he could add nothing in the same letter 'but what would be flat and insipid'. 'Mr. Eliot has in the most liberal manner assured me a seat in Parliament, an event which changes the colour of my whole future life.'

The offer came unexpectedly but had not been altogether unhoped for. Parliament was indeed an almost necessary qualification for the complete man-about-town. What in the end were Boodle's and Atwood's if a man could not go down with his friends to the House?

A growing frequency of references to Edward Eliot, the Cornish 'Lord of Boroughs', may conceal some aspiration beyond mere cousinly goodwill. At last in September 1773, when Gibbon was on a visit to Port Eliot, after describing his cousin's fair situation he takes Holroyd into his confidence.

> 'One possession he has indeed most truly desirable; but I much fear that the Danae of St. Germains has no particular inclination for me, and that the interested Strumpet will yield only to a Golden Shower. My situation is the more perplexing as I cannot with any degree of delicacy make the first advance.'

Nearly a year passed and Gibbon was more concerned in advising Holroyd not to stand for a county seat since he was still a *novus homo* in Sussex and would have to face the enmity of all the animals—bears, hogs, asses and rhinoceroses—who by the courtesy of England are called Gentlemen, than in building castles for himself in Cornish boroughs. But once more Eliot was in town, and once more he did not belie the reputation he seems to have had for slow and cautious movement. The result was a dramatic tale for Gibbon to write for Holroyd.

> 'It is surely infinite condescension for a Senator to bestow his attention on the affairs of a Juryman.[1] A Senator? Yes, sir, at last *Quod nemo promittere Divum auderet, volvenda dies en! attulit ultro.* About ten days ago Eliot spent an hour with me, talked sensibly of his will, and his children, and requested that I would be Executor to the one and Guardian to the other. I consented to accept an office which indeed I consider as an essential duty of social life. We parted. Yesterday morning about half an hour after seven, as I was destroying an army of Barbarians, I heard a double rap at the door, and my Cornish friend was soon introduced. After some idle conversation he told me, that if I was desirous of being in Parliament, he had an *independent* seat very much at my service. You may suppose my answer, but my satisfaction was a little damped when he added that the expence of election would amount to about £2400, and that he thought it reasonable that we should share it between us. I paused, and recovering myself, hinted something of Paternal extravagance and filial narrowness of circumstances and want of ready money, and that I must beg a short delay to consider whether I could with prudence accept of his intended favour, on which I set the highest value. His answer was obliging, that he should be very much mortified if a few hundred pounds should prevent it, and that he had been afraid to offend me by offering it on less equal terms. His behaviour gave me courage to propose an expedient, which was instantly accepted with cordiality and eagerness, that when his second son John (who is now thirteen) came of age I would restore to him my proportion of the money.'

Besides his sense of the dramatic Gibbon was no mean hand at a negotiation.

[1] Gibbon had been giving Holroyd his views on a case in which the latter was concerned. See especially his comments on juries in *Prothero*, i. 221.

He did not know for the moment whether his seat would be Liskeard or St. Germans, and the existing Parliament had some six months more of legal existence. But the dissolution came unexpectedly at the end of September 1774, and in a fortnight, without needing to stir out of London, Gibbon was elected member for the borough of Liskeard. He distributed brief announcements of his triumph, each with the important postscript: 'Franks do not take place till the 20th'.

The old ladies, his faithful chorus, chanted their satisfaction in the background.

> 'I take the first opportunity', wrote Kitty to Dolly Gib,[1] 'to rejoice with you upon the prospect we have of Our Friend making a figure in Parliament. I own I flatter myself as I am sure you do . . . why it was not done sooner and several other things upon that subject, I defer till I have the pleasure of seeing you.'

Do these words conceal the fact that Aunt Kitty has opened the proposals to nephew Edward Eliot which delicacy has prevented Gibbon from attempting?

In a few weeks Gibbon had taken his seat. At the debate on the Address he had been tempted to speak but was well satisfied later not to have sacrificed his parliamentary virginity prematurely. Early in the next year he was writing, 'If my confidence was equal to my eloquence and my eloquence to my knowledge, perhaps I might make no very intolerable speaker. At all events, I fancy I shall try to expose myself.' But a week later there was such an inundation of speakers that 'neither Lord George Germaine nor myself could find room for a single word'. A curious combination in silence. Again in the same month of February—'I am still a Mute; it is more tremendous than I imagined; the great

[1] So Lord Sheffield endorsed one of her letters. Miss Porten to Mrs Gibbon, 24th September and 1st November 1774, in Brit. Mus. 11907, dd. 25 (2).

speakers fill me with despair, the bad ones with terror'. Final resignation that would last his time in the House is foreshadowed in a brief note soon after: 'Still dumb; but see, hear, laugh sometimes, am oftener serious, but upon the whole very well amused'.

In the same strain he had already told Mrs Gibbon that although the House might never prove of any real benefit to him he found it at least a very agreeable coffee-house. 'We are plunging every day', he adds equably, 'deeper into the great business of America.'

For a man with such an easy mind and for those days of impromptu politics, Gibbon took pains to bring himself abreast of events; which we should think the more creditable if we could agree more with the conclusions reached. Some play has been made with the fact that the great historian was on what most people would now agree to be the wrong side of the House in the dispute with America. This is not fair. He must be judged on equal terms with his fellows as a man and not as a historian, unless we expect our Regius Professors to have more than ordinary political sagacity. In one aspect of the matter he is no more than an instance of the fate which may overtake the most intelligent and disinterested men when they lend a too respectful ear to the experts in a strange field.

Before his entry into Parliament Gibbon's interest in affairs does not rise beyond retailing, in the manner of his age, scraps of political gossip to his country friends. He confesses that his anxiety about an old Manor took away much of his attention from a New Continent. The prospect at this time (February 1774) was disturbing enough. Intelligence of the Boston Tea Party had lately come in, and the Privy Council had voted that the petition of Massachusetts for the recall of Governor Hutchinson was 'groundless, vexatious and scandalous'. These events had stirred Gibbon's old Lausanne friend

Godfrey Clarke 'into military Fury; but he is an old Tory and you (Holroyd) are a Native of the Bog. I alone am an Englishman, a Philosopher and a Whig.'

But in the first months of his political life Gibbon was delivered into the tutelage of two men who could be least trusted to give him a wise or impartial view. One was Israel Mauduit, a pamphleteering woollen-draper. Gibbon would spend four hours at a time with Mauduit and adds an ingenuous comment on their *tête-à-têtes*: 'He squeaks out a great deal of sense and knowledge, though after all I mean to think, perhaps to speak, for myself'. Mauduit had artfully brought the new member acquainted with Governor Hutchinson himself, and Hutchinson was an assiduous propagandist from whom Gibbon had 'as much probability of arriving at a just conclusion as a Roman Senator who took his idea of the Sicilian character from a private conversation with Verres'.[1]

In the following letter, so illustrative of the vague and piecemeal way in which news came to hand, Gibbon repeats one of his lessons to his patron:

'Dear Sir,

'I am happy to hear from various quarters that you have at length reached Bath in good health, spirits and a disposition to take the amusements which the Law of Moses may prescribe to you. John I am sure, William I hope, are happy and well, but I hear that Mrs. Eliot already begins to turn her eyes again toward Cornwall. With regard to yourself I must beg the favour of a line to inform me of your intended motions. If you do not mean to proceed farther westward I will certainly contrive to run down to Bath for a week rather than miss the opportunity, but if inclination or business leads you to the Capital, my literary engagements will persuade me to defer till the Autumn my annual Visit to Mrs. Gibbon and to content myself for the present with saluting my rustic Cousin from a distance.

[1] G. O. Trevelyan, *The American Revolution*, i. 236.

'You have seen by the papers the unpleasant news from America; unpleasant as a single drop of blood may be considered as the Signal of civil war. For otherwise it was not an engagement, much less a defeat. The King's troops were ordered to destroy a magazine at Concord. They marched, did their business and returned, but they were frequently fired at from behind stone walls and from the windows in the Villages. It was to those houses that they were obliged to set fire. Ensign Gould (of Northamptonshire) had been left with twelve men to guard a bridge and was taken prisoner. The next day the Provincial Congress sent a Vessel without her freight express to England; no letters were put on board but their own, nor did the crew know their destination till they were on the banks of Newfoundland. So that Government has not any authentic account. The Master says that the day after the engagement the Country rose and that he left Boston invested by 1500 Tents with Canon and under the command of Colonel Ward who was at the head of a Provincial Regiment in the last war, but unless Fanaticism gets the better of self-preservation they must soon disperse as it is the season for sowing their Indian corn, the chief sustenance of New England. Such at least is the opinion of Governor Hutchinson from whom I have these particulars.

'I am

'Dear Sir

'most sincerely Yours

'E. GIBBON

'LONDON, *May the* 31*rst* 1775.'[1]

A month later the pupil had learnt from Governor Hutchinson that General Gage had plenty of provisions, fresh and salted flour, fish, vegetables, etc.: '*hopes* he is not in danger of being forced——'

Priding himself that he had sucked these sedulous tutors very dry, Gibbon emerged

'more and more convinced that we have both the right and the power, and that, though the effort may be accompanied with some melancholy circumstances, we are now arrived at the

[1] From the original MS. at Port Eliot.

> decisive moment of persevering or of losing for ever both our Trade and Empire.'

By such lights he became a zealous though silent friend to the Cause of Government, which, *in this instance*, he thought the Cause of England.

As time went on and North's government blundered more deeply in the toils, Gibbon began to have suspicions about the expediency if not the justification of their policy. 'We have a warm Parliament but an indolent cabinet.' 'I sometimes doubt Lord North.' But at the same time he was becoming bound to his government by ties which he found difficult to ignore. Early in 1775 the new member was to meet the First Lord of the Treasury at Twickenham, and was expecting to be invited to his lordship's own house. A friendship began. 'If they turned out Lord N. to-morrow, they would still leave him one of the best Companions in the Kingdom.' Another friend was Alexander Wedderburn the Solicitor-General. This 'artful and able man', of whom Junius said that Treachery herself would not trust him, has one of the most unenviable reputations among political intriguers. But Gibbon never failed to see in him an agreeable companion and a helpful friend. Nor should it be forgotten that both Mrs Gibbon and Holroyd were undoubting supporters of the Government's policy.

There is at least some probability that the Government were taking notice of a new member whose potentialities could with reason be valued very highly. Before Gibbon is condemned for sacrificing his judgment to opportunism, we must reflect how easy it is for a man to deceive himself when the forces of flattery and friendship, of obligation (for even if Gibbon's seat was truly *independent* there was little doubt what was expected of him) and of artful suggestion direct his steps towards the division lobbies. Gibbon the politician may have been weak; there is no evidence that he was dishonest with himself any more than with others. The embarrassments into which he ultimately fell belong to a later chapter. Meanwhile with vigour of mind increased if anything 'in the winter hurry of society and parliament', he approached the day when he should 'oppress thc public' with the first volume of his book.

Chapter 17

'LO, A TRULY CLASSIC WORK!'

1776

'THE press is just set to work', Holroyd was informed in June 1775, 'and I shall be very busy the whole *summer in correcting* and composing.' Nothing would draw Gibbon from his books and London—when he was tired of the Roman Empire he could laugh away the evening at Foote's Theatre—until the end of August when he went down to Sheffield Place, taking with him Aunt Kitty, for she too had been welcomed into the family there. Another break occurred in October, upon the news that Mrs Gibbon had an attack of smallpox. Her stepson left everything at once, starting at half-past three and travelling the first evening 'till the Moon failed'. At Bath he waited unannounced for forty-eight hours for fear of alarming the patient. Back again in town 'and so comfortably in mine own dear Library and mine own dear Parlour', he continued his work into the winter and not till January could he announce the finishing of the impression. His preface was dated 1st February from Bentinck Street, and he announces to Holroyd that 'it is to-morrow *sevennight*, the 17th that my book will decline into the World'.

Upon Gibbon's remarking that he had begun to print the head before the tail was quite finished, Holroyd had expressed his apprehension that the work was being produced precipitately, and had apparently advised Gibbon to submit it to a friendly critic. Gibbon scouted both notions, revealing some of the secrets of composition.

> 'The *head* is now printing true, but it was wrote last year and the year before, the first Chapter has been composed *de nouveau three times*; the second *twice*, and all the others have undergone reviews, corrections etc. As to the tail, it is perfectly formed and digested (and were I so much given to self-content and haste) it is almost all written. The ecclesiastical part, for instance, is written out in fourteen sheets, which I mean to *refondre* from beginning to end. As to the friendly Critic, it is very difficult to find one who has leisure, candour, freedom, and knowledge sufficient. However, Batt and Deyverdun have read and observed. After all, the public is the best Critic. I print no more than 500 copies of the first Edition; and the second (as it happens frequently to my betters) may receive many improvements.' [1]

The tone of Gibbon's letters bears out the assertion of the Autobiography that 'during this awful interval I was neither elated by the ambition of fame nor depressed by the apprehension of contempt'. Working imperturbably towards his goal he was conscious of and satisfied with his merits. All his references to the book betray a quiet complacency—'we proceed triumphantly with the Roman Empire'—and he had already established himself as 'the Gibbon' to his friends.

The long expected day came at last. '*The History of the Decline and Fall of the Roman Empire, by Edward Gibbon Esqr, Volume the First*' appeared on the 17th February 1776.[2] This first of six thick quartos, costing a guinea unbound, sold, in Cadell's phrase, like a threepenny pamphlet on current affairs. In a fortnight not a single copy remained; a second edition of fifteen

[1] To Holroyd, 1st August 1775. *Prothero*, i. 264; *Misc. Wks*. ii. 141.

[2] Gibbon tells Deyverdun, 16th February. Elsewhere 17th February is given. H. M. Beatty (Bury's edition of *The Decline and Fall*, vii. 349) points out that the 17th was a Saturday and perhaps at the last moment was abandoned in favour of the previous day. 17th February is the date given in the diary in the Pierpont Morgan library.

hundred was undertaken for June, and a third was prophesied by the end of the year.[1]

It is in a letter to Deyverdun that we can catch the high mid-summer of Gibbon's elation, which has its complement in the autumnal glow which warms the narrative in the Autobiography. Deyverdun is to know that the History has had the most complete and flattering success. But the jubilant author must first prepare the scene circumstantially with an account of his early diffidence yielding to his publisher's rising enthusiasm. The original agreement with Cadell had been to sound the public taste with five hundred copies.[2] Upon Strahan and Cadell's importunate representations he had consented to a thousand, although haunted with the fear that the younger members of his numerous family might be condemned to languish ingloriously in a warehouse.

But 'the ancient history of your learned friend has succeeded like the Novel of the day', and Gibbon confides to Deyverdun, as one old bachelor to another, that he is infinitely pleased with the praises of fashionable women, especially if they are young and pretty. Yet their approval is not the weightiest. 'Hear what Robertson says; lend your ear now to the good David', and Gibbon transcribes a part of that classic letter from Hume of which he says in his Autobiography that it overpaid the labour of ten years.

> 'As I ran through your Volume of History with great Avidity and Impatience, I cannot forbear discovering something of the same Impatience in returning you thanks for your agreeable Present, and expressing the Satisfaction which the Performance has given me. Whether I consider the Dignity of your stile, the Depth of your Matter, or the Extensiveness of your Learning, I must regard the Work as equally the Object of

[1] The second edition appeared on 3rd June and the third in April 1777.
[2] 750 according to *Prothero*, i. 205, referred to above, p. 220.

Esteem. . . . I know it will give you Pleasure (as it did me) to find that all the Men of Letters in this Place concur in their Admiration of your Work, and in their anxious Desire of your continuing it.'

Moreover, how fortunate that these two great writers, Hume and Robertson, were Scotchmen! For Gibbon continues:

'Our good English groaned for a long while past under the superiority that these historians had acquired, and as national prejudice is maintained at very little expense they hastened to hoist with acclamations their unworthy compatriot to the niche of these great men.'

Another point on which Gibbon congratulates himself is his honest neutrality in politics. It was the custom then, far more than now, for a new work to be scrutinised for party bias even if it dealt with remote centuries. But

'an under-minister much attached to the prerogatives of the Crown complimented me for having inculcated the healthiest maxims. Mr. Walpole and Lord Camden on the other hand both declared partisans of liberty and even of republicanism are persuaded that I am not far from their ideas.'

Next with rather smirking irony he forecasts trouble to come:

'Now let us look at the reverse of the medal and pay attention to the means which heaven has been pleased to use for the humiliation of my pride. Would you imagine, my dear Sir, that injustice would be carried to the point of attacking the purity of my faith. The outcry of the Bishops and of a great number of ladies respectable equally for their age and their enlightenment has been raised against me. They dare to assert that the last two chapters of my pretended history are nothing but a satire on the Christian religion, a satire the more dangerous as it is disguised under a veil of moderation and impartiality and that the emissary of Satan after having entertained his reader for a long time with a very agreeable story leads him insensibly into his infernal trap.

You perceive, Sir, the horrible nature of such conduct and you are well aware that I shall only present a respectful silence to the clamour of my enemies.'

Finally the translation. Deyverdun was to cause Gibbon to be read and burned in the rest of Europe. The sheets had been sent to Germany as they came from the press, and Deyverdun must have had the whole for some time. Was the translation finished? How did Deyverdun propose that it should be published? Various fears, some only too well founded, assailed the impatient author, accidents on the way and the translator's indolence or other preoccupations. The Duc de Choiseul had told Walpole of his intention to have the book translated. Gibbon had tried to discourage this by assuring people that Deyverdun's translation was already printing at Leipsic. It would be annoying to be anticipated either by some clever fellow in Paris or by a Dutch bookseller's hack.[1]

'I have always despised the gloomy philosophy which would have us insensible to fame', Gibbon wrote to Suard at the end of this memorable year. It was as well. The outburst of praise might have turned a less alert vanity. A great book has perhaps seldom been praised immediately by those most fitted to judge it with such unanimity and such frequent identity even of language, accompanied, it must be admitted, by a wary avoidance of the real issues. Robertson prudently had not read the last two chapters. 'Such depth—such perspicuity—such language, force, variety and what not!' were typical words from Camden, eagerly transmitted by Garrick, whose delight—'whenever I am truly pleased I must communicate my joy'—makes a breathless little note not less impressive than more judicious tributes.

[1] Passages from Gibbon's letter of 7th May 1776 to Deyverdun have been translated from the French MS. Another version of the whole letter is in *Meredith Read*, ii, p. 386.

It was from the North that the most generous and discerning praise came, from Robertson, Adam Ferguson, Wallace, Professor Campbell of Aberdeen, and above all from Hume, who had begun to despair of good literature's coming from England. Magnificent as was his letter to Gibbon, part of which has already been quoted, not less gratifying may have been his unforced expressions of regard and interest in a letter to Strahan which came into Gibbon's hands. Hume with others expressed the liveliest hopes that Gibbon would continue his work. He himself was to read no more. His health was failing rapidly. As he passed through London on a journey to Bath, Gibbon saw him for the last time, 'his body feeble, his mind firm', and in August 'that truly great man'[1] died the calm death of a sceptic.

But to a man who had his eyes on more worlds than one, there must have been peculiar satisfaction in Horace Walpole's congratulations. They had not been unsought for. In those days the opinions of such men were more influential than the reviews, and the gift of an advance copy might be of mutual value. Walpole's reaction was certainly perfect.[2]

'You have unexpectedly given the world a classic history' was his neat summing up of the situation. He praised the book with discernment, recommended it to his lady friends and wished for the author's closer acquaintance. He assured Gibbon that he was not flattering him and that Gibbon would always hear that Walpole said the same of him to everybody. That may be so, and Walpole certainly did write to Mason, 'Lo, there is just appeared a truly classic work', but he also

[1] Gibbon in a letter to Adam Ferguson. Rae's *Adam Smith*, p. 287.

[2] Walpole wrote to Gibbon twice before the day of publication, once in an undated note which Toynbee places before 6th February, and again on the 14th.

said of Gibbon whom he had known slightly for some time,

> 'he is the son of a foolish alderman, is a member of Parliament and called a whimsical because he votes variously as his opinion leads him. I know him a little, never suspected the extent of his talents, he is perfectly modest.'

That probably expresses the surprise of the town in general at the achievement of this silent and rather uncertain little politician.[1]

On 12th May, five days after the exultant letter to Deyverdun, Gibbon went down to dine and spend the night at Strawberry Hill and Walpole read an unpublished chapter from his *Essay on Modern Gardening* to him.[2] Gibbon very likely was already registering his judgment of the author as an 'ingenious trifler'.[3] Nevertheless his host's attention was flattering and Gibbon became a constant caller at Arlington Street. Walpole on his side was more fitted than most people in society to appreciate not only the humorous aspect of Mr Gibbon, as he almost invariably calls him, but his historical achievement as well. Moreover he made use of him not only as retailer of political gossip but as a scout in Johnson's territory, which he himself steadily refused to enter. In 1781 Gibbon reported to Walpole that someone had asked Johnson if he was not afraid that Mason would resent the liberties he had taken with Gray in his *Lives of the Poets*. 'No, no, sir', Johnson had said. 'Mr. Mason does not like rough handling.' Walpole sent this on to Mason, remarking, 'I hope in the Muses' name that you will let him see which had most reason to fear rough handling. The Saucy Caliban!'

[1] On 22nd February 1775 Gibbon had voted against the government for Wilkes' motion to rescind the previous Parliament's measures concerning the Middlesex election: *Prothero*, i. 251, n. 2, and 255. It is not known, I think, on what other occasions Gibbon may have voted against government at this time.

[2] Gibbon's diary in Pierpont Morgan library.

[3] *Misc. Wks.* v. 571.

The great letter-writer gives us one or two glimpses of Gibbon in London society in this triumphant summer. He describes how at Beauclerk's he

> 'found Lord Pembroke, Lord Palmerston, Garrick, Burke, the Dean of Derry, Lord Robert Spencer, and Mr. Gibbon; but they talked so loud (not the two last) and made such a noise, and Lord Palmerston made so much more noise with trying to talk, that it was impossible to know what they said.'

It wanted a few more years, and two more quartos, before Gibbon could take the fireplace, as Malone describes, plant his back to it, and taking out his snuff-box begin to pour forth a fund of anecdote and of erudition of various kinds.[1] To begin with, at any rate, a better snuff-box was required, and Walpole did at least one substantial service for Gibbon, and incidentally for posterity too, in helping to supply one.

The historian's snuff-box is one of his inseparable attributes. As early as his days in Turin he had sketched himself with it, and later caricaturists and memoirists seldom leave it out. The time had now come for such a man to have a box worthy of him. Within two months of the appearance of *The Decline and Fall*, Walpole was asking Mme du Deffand to procure a box for M. Gibbon, of whom she had heard favourably from Mme Necker. The matter received the active attention of the old lady and her friends. Box after box was examined only to be rejected, and it was not until July that one was despatched and, to Mme du Deffand's satisfaction, approved of by Walpole. This is the massive gold box embossed on the lid with cupids attending an altar, which is now in the British Museum.[2]

[1] Malone to Lord Charlemont, 20/2/1794. Hist. MSS. Com. 13th Rep.; *Charlemont*, ii. 230.

[2] Toynbee, *Lettres de la marquise du Deffand à Horace Walpole*, iii. 203-268 *passim*. Gibbon paid £37 : 5 : 6 for the box; Gibbon's MS. diary for 1776 in the Pierpont Morgan library.

Chapter 18

PARIS REVISITED

1777

If anything were wanting to complete Gibbon's satisfaction, the want was filled—for there are singularly few loose threads in his story—by the presence in London of the Neckers, to see him in the first bloom of his glory. Necker came over in May on some financial business, bringing with him his wife and daughter Germaine. Gibbon was in immediate and constant attendance.

> 'I live with her,' he told Holroyd, 'just as I used to do twenty years ago, laugh at her Paris varnish, and oblige her to become a simple reasonable Suissesse. The man, who might read English husbands lessons of proper and dutiful behaviour, is a sensible good-natured creature.'

Mme Necker saw Garrick act eleven times, often one may guess in Gibbon's company, and struck up a lively acquaintance with the great actor. Hannah More records a party at the Garricks' when she and Mr Gibbon were the only English guests amid a crowd of *beaux esprits, femmes savantes* and academicians.[1] After she returned to France Mme Necker wrote to Garrick full of enthusiasm for Shakespeare and his own acting. In his reply Garrick called it the most flattering, charming, bewitching letter that ever came to his hand. It was to be put in the famous mulberry-wood box. He adds a vivid little sketch of their friend:

---

[1] A. M. B. Meakin, *Hannah More*, p. 71.

'Mr. Gibbon, our learned friend and excellent writer, happened to be with me when I received the bewitching letter. In the pride and grateful overflowings of my heart, I could not resist the temptation of showing it to him—he read—stared at me—was silent, then gave it me, with these emphatical words emphatically spoken—*This is the very best letter that ever was written*, upon which, *à la mode d'Angleterre* the writer was remembered with true devotion and full libations.' [1]

The connexion with Mme Necker, thus resumed after eleven years of apparently complete silence, was never to be broken again. Her husband was soon included in the friendship and her astonishing daughter too, who was to try her spells on her mother's old lover. The family returned to France taking with them Gibbon's most solemn assurances of following in less than two months.

The visit was deferred for nearly a year. The autumn and winter passed with Parliament, visits, dinners, suppers, and an hour or two stolen with difficulty for *The Decline*. Stimulated by praise, Gibbon had lost no time in going on to fulfil his promise to carry his history to the end of the Empire in the West, and, with the optimism of authors, was soon prophesying another volume. He wrote the first chapter of the second volume, except the notes, between 4th June and 4th August.[2]

Meanwhile there was a small disappointment. 'No news of Deyverdun or his French translation. What a lazy dog!' Gibbon invited Suard, a French writer whom he had met in Paris in 1763 and who had translated some of Robertson's works. But Suard declined with the flattering suggestion that Gibbon was the one best qualified to translate his own works. Mme Necker had been of the same opinion.[3] That was more than Gibbon

[1] Mme Necker to Garrick, 5th October, Garrick to Mme Necker, 10th November 1776. *Correspondence of David Garrick*, ii. 625.

[2] MS. diary in the Pierpont Morgan library.

[3] Mme du Deffand to Walpole, 8 avril 1776.

could undertake. In December he received a small volume, the first seven chapters only, but 'admirably well done by M. de Septchênes (Sevenoaks) . . . who sent me a very pleasant dose of flattery on the occasion'. The packet received by post cost Gibbon two and a half guineas, and he instructed the young man how to avoid this expense on the next occasion by directing his letters to Sir Stanier Porten, Under Secretary of State.

Guineas were beginning to be important. Success indeed was more likely than not to add to his embarrassments. The first hint comes with his election in May to Almack's, an event ominous for more than one reason.

> 'The style of living though *somewhat* expensive is exceedingly pleasant and notwithstanding the rage of play I have found more entertaining and even rational society here than in any other Club to which I belong.'

It was the rational society which was to prove more dangerous than the sight of Fox and his friends equipped with eye-shades and leather aprons plunging for tens of thousands of pounds. In two years Almack's was to be taken up and transformed by Brooks, whose new club in St. James's Street was the too attractive home of the Opposition.[1]

The summer had witnessed the outbreak of active hostilities with the colonists. Gibbon viewed the prospect with misgiving. He feared, only too justifiably, that 'our Leaders have not a genius which can act at a distance of 3000 miles' and would have liked to see Holroyd in the place of the fatal George Germaine, who, in spite of having been very soundly adjudged by court-martial to be unfitted to serve His Majesty in any capacity whatever, was now misdirecting his Sovereign's

[1] In fairness to Gibbon's subsequent conduct it must be remembered that Brooks's was not a party club. Men of all parties and of none belonged.

forces from the highest position. But Gibbon hob-nobbed with him and retailed his opinions to his correspondents. One little sentence is pregnant with omen: 'Lord G. G. who is playing at whist says there is not any news though great hopes'. We are relieved when we hear that Gibbon is off to eat a turtle with Garrick at Hampton.

Like his leaders Gibbon was unable to realise the dangers and horrors of war at so great a distance. He dismissed the guards drafted to America tepidly as 'poor dear creatures', and just as a few years before he had contrasted the troubles of the New World with those of his old Manor, so now he complacently expressed his own preoccupations in metaphors drawn from the topic of the day. In November he reported to Mrs Gibbon that he was very well and 'unhurt amidst as hot a cannonading as can be pointed against Washington'. The attack was not unforewarned. Within a month of his publication he knew that the clergy were showing their teeth. Dr. Beilby Porteous was said to be sharpening his goose quill. By October fire was opened by an anonymous pamphleteer, and soon afterwards the heavy artillery of Dr. Watson and another adversary were brought into the field.

Meanwhile Gibbon was resolute in his first decision to stand the attack in silence. The various clouds which we discern so clearly were not yet sufficient to dim the sunshine, and we may follow him to Paris, where during a stay of six months he reached and enjoyed to the full the climax of this first period of glory.

A number of incidents delayed this journey; one was an incursion into a new field. In the early part of 1777 variety and relief from historical studies were found in attending Hunter the great surgeon's lectures, and some on chemistry by Higgins. These lessons, together with a taste for books on Natural History, 'contributed to multiply my ideas and images, and the Anatomist or Chemist may sometimes track me in their own snow'.

Attendance at Hunter's lectures on anatomy for two hours in the afternoon 'opened a new and very entertaining scene within myself' and lasted from February into April. Gibbon deferred setting out for Paris until they were over. Adam Smith used to go with him. A young student recalled seeing them there together and heard much of the conversation between Gibbon and Hunter:

> 'for Mr. Gibbon, at the end of every lecture, used to leave his seat to thank the doctor for the pleasure and instruction which he had received. The mild, courteous, polite, and affable manners which Mr. Gibbon on these occasions manifested, were very different from those which may be supposed to have animated the mind of Junius.'[1]

Hunter repaid his questioner with the present of a commentary on Thucydides's account of the plague, a quarto of six hundred pages published in Venice in 1603.[2]

The proposed trip to Paris was an occasion to call forth Mrs Gibbon's maternal solicitude. It was necessary to combat her two ingenious objections. Either her stepson would be imprisoned, if not put to death, by the priests, or he would sully his *moral* character by making love to Necker's wife. In a long letter he solemnly disposed of her ideas, even at the expense of ungallantly stressing the ravages time had made on his old flame's beauty. As for the priests they were harmless. Could she imagine a British subject falling

[1] John Taylor, *Records of My Life*, ii. 262. Taylor was a grandson of the Chevalier Taylor who had been among the many called in to treat Gibbon in his childhood. On the preceding page Taylor mentions that his old friend Mr Boaden, 'a gentleman well known and justly respected in the literary world', had tried to show Lord Sheffield that Gibbon was Junius. 'His lordship returned a very polite answer . . . and intimated that he knew Gibbon was not Junius.'

[2] *The Decline and Fall*, c. xliii. n. 90.

into their hands? David Hume (the name the most abhorred by the Godly) had been oppressed only by civilities. The rising author expected no less for himself. Even Holroyd had raised objections and got himself called Sir Wilful for his pains.

In May he was off, promising to write from Calais, or perhaps from Philadelphia, for there were American privateers in the Channel. But safely landed he felt his mind expand with the unbounded prospect of the Continent. Who does not? From thence onward he enjoyed six months of felicity unclouded by any thoughts of America or his own sticky acres. He prepared himself carefully for the figure he meant to cut as a man of the world and as a man of letters, but did not consider he was being extravagant at the rate of sixty pounds a month. He arrayed himself in silk and silver lace, had two footmen in handsome liveries behind his coach (the 'dear inseparable Caplin' was there too), and lived in an apartment hung with damask, at the Hôtel de Modène, rue Jacob, in the Faubourg St. Germain.

A typical day began with a morning in the King's Library;[1] then dinner with a duke; the comedy was seen from a princess's *loge grillée*, after which he must decide whether to sup with Mme du Deffand, Mme Necker or the Sardinian Ambassadress. Even more than on his first visit, he found Society easy, polite and entertaining, and the acquisition of valuable and memorable acquaintances a daily occurrence. He naturally scorned the Colisée, the Vauxhall and the Boulevards, the forerunners of haunts which are still Paris to most of his countrymen. Particularly gratifying was the complete harmony of the animal. His stomach proved itself a citizen of the world, and he regularly ate everything put before him, to the admiration of his hosts, and drank 'a dish of strong coffee after each meal'.

[1] Now absorbed in the Bibliothèque Nationale.

That is the way to be a success. The eupeptic historian proceeded to digest all the society that came his way, with great ease and aplomb. Mme du Deffand reported on him very favourably to Walpole, taking to him herself and describing the grace and adaptability which was winning him a great success.[1] The Duc de Choiseul, minister of Foreign Affairs, sought out his acquaintance; he met the eccentric Emperor Joseph II at the Neckers'; was presented at Court; and *by accident* dined with Benjamin Franklin.

The septuagenarian American emissary was also being fêted in Paris, and according to one of his biographers, 'breathed incense every day'. He certainly gives in his letters a very different version from Gibbon's of the attitude of the French towards the question of intervention in the American quarrel. Cobbett gives a curious account, taken from an old newspaper, of the meeting of these two men, not in Paris but on the road. On arriving at an inn Franklin was informed that Gibbon was there too and sent in to request the pleasure of passing the evening together. A card came back to the effect that, notwithstanding Mr Gibbon's regard for Dr. Franklin as a man and a philosopher, he could not reconcile it with his duty to his king to have any conversation with a revolted subject! Franklin replied that in spite of Mr Gibbon's refusal he had such a respect for the character of Mr Gibbon as a gentleman and a historian, that when in the course of his writing the history of the *decline and fall* of empires, the *decline and fall* of the British Empire should come to be his subject, as he expected it soon would, Dr. Franklin would be happy to furnish him with ample materials which were in his possession.

The story may be *ben trovato*. Cobbett did not pretend to say. He found the expressions strictly in character,

[1] Toynbee, *Mme du Deffand*, iii. *passim*.

Bon pour quatre Cent —
Livres.

L400. E Gibbon.

le 1 Juin. 1785.

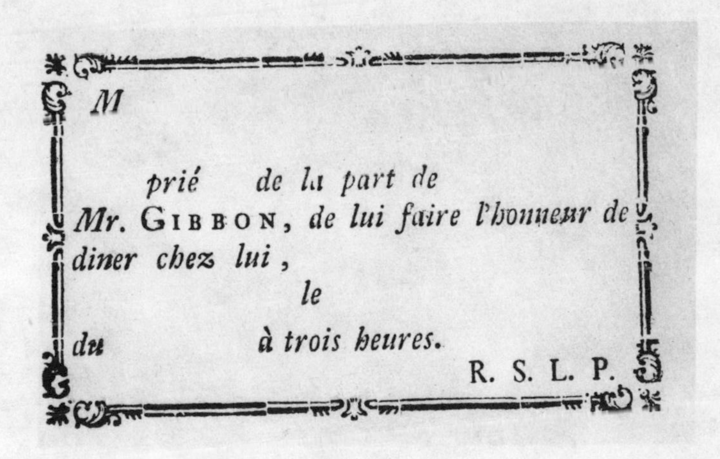

M

prié de la part de
Mr. GIBBON, *de lui faire l'honneur de*
diner chez lui,
le
du à trois heures.
R. S. L. P.

(a) GIBBON'S AUTOGRAPH

(b) GIBBON'S INVITATION CARD

and remarks, 'in Gibbon we see the faithful subject, and the man of candour and honour; in Franklin the treacherous and malicious "old Zanga of Boston".' [1]

One of the regretted omissions of Gibbon's first visit was mended when he sought Buffon's acquaintance. But the only record of their meeting is in a footnote to one of the Memoirs.[2] In the text Gibbon was then remarking that he would soon be entering that last period which Fontenelle considered the most agreeable of his long life. The note adds, 'See Buffon, p. 413. In private conversation that great and amiable man added the weight of his own experience.'

One other encounter with a scholar is of peculiar importance. In his Autobiography Gibbon prints an extract from an anonymous French writer which describes an encounter between himself and the Abbé de Mably at M. de Foncemagne's. A discussion arose on the relative merits of republicanism and monarchy. Mably pressed the case for the former with instances from Livy and Plutarch, and had expected to find the Englishman agreeing with him. But Gibbon took up the defence of monarchy with spirit, and with his apt memory and readiness soon dominated the conversation. The abbé lost his temper. Gibbon remained cool and pressed his adversary all the more successfully. The discussion was growing heated when their host broke it up by rising from the table, and by the time they reached the drawing-room no one was inclined to resume it.[3]

[1] Cobbett's *Works*, vii. 241, and Parton, *Benjamin Franklin*, ii. 209.

[2] Memoir E, *Murray*, p. 348 n.

[3] *Misc. Wks.* i. 227. Sheffield has incorporated in the text what Gibbon had put in a note: *Murray*, p. 314. The anecdote above is from *Supplément à la manière d'écrire l'histoire*, p. 125, by Gudin de la Brennellerie, a pamphlet in answer to Mably's *Manière d'écrire l'histoire*, in which he had avenged the scene at de Foncemagne's by making disparaging remarks on Gibbon's work. Mably was extremely jealous of contemporary writers. Gibbon bore him no malice, and praises him more than once in notes to *The Decline and Fall* and elsewhere. See *Murray* cited above, and *B. Hill*, p. 317.

The 'fatal month of October' drew near with Gibbon's zest for Parisian life unabated. He might regret that he had chosen the summer when people were leaving Paris. But he had been invited to the country houses round Paris. He had formed a friendship with Mme du Deffand which she was more eager to keep up than he; he was observed to be distinctly *épris* with Mme de Cambis, who, though not young, practised with success a coquetry which was *sèche, froide et piquante*, and he was on intimate terms with Mme de Genlis, who in time was to pay him a despicable turn.[1] As for the priests, he gloried in having sat down to supper between two archbishops. A dubious triumph perhaps, because probably they had not read his history and had possibly had their part in seeing that the authorised French translation did not go so far as the dangerous chapters.

It is to the time of his departure probably that the story belongs of little Germaine Necker, who offered to marry M. Gibbon because then he would never need to leave them.[2]

Her mother gave the visitor a handsome report in a letter to Garrick:

> 'Le voilà votre Tacite, votre Tite Lire! We have not spoilt him in spite of all our efforts. If he had sounded the feeling of this country, he might tell you that our most beautiful and aristocratic ladies first wished to know him out of curiosity and then could not part from him for real liking. Mr. Hume was the vogue amongst us because his manners and good nature contrasted somewhat with his reputation which was never lost to sight. But Mr. Gibbon, after the first moments, has stolen all the homage that one wished to pay to his book. He takes nothing away with him here, for it is he that has given every-

[1] Mme du Deffand complained to Walpole that Gibbon had ceased to write to her. In 1779 Gibbon tells Deyverdun, in an unpublished letter, that he owes letters to Mme de Cambis, Mme de Genlis and the Princesse de Beauvau.

[2] Blennerhasset, *Madame de Staël*, i. 101.

thing; however he returns with the esteem, friendship and sad regrets of all good people." [1]

Gibbon was not ungrateful and repaid his friends in his own magnificent way. After describing the Paris of the fourth century he says:

> 'If Julian could now revisit the capital of France, he might converse with men of science and genius, capable of understanding and of instructing a disciple of the Greeks; he might excuse the lively and graceful follies of a nation whose martial spirit has never been enervated by the indulgence of luxury; and he must applaud the perfection of that inestimable art which softens and refines and embellishes the intercourse of social life.' [2]

Bentinck Street and the problems of existence were reached on the 3rd of November. It would be several years before he was to enjoy such unalloyed happiness again, if ever. The first disagreeable incident, however, was the revolt of his overworked citizen of the world, which had diffused through his system a very British complaint. He supported the attack for a fortnight with good-humour and announced:

> 'the Gout has behaved in a very honourable manner; after a compleat conquest . . . the generous Enemy has disdained to abuse his victory or torment any longer an unresisting victim.'

[1] *Garrick's Correspondence*, ii. 626. The letter is in French. Mme du Deffand told Walpole, 21st September, 'Il se conduit fort bien et sans avoir, je crois, autant d'esprit, que feu Mr. Hume, il ne tombe pas dans les mêmes ridicules'.
[2] *The Decline and Fall*, c. xix. *ad fin.*

Chapter 19

A VINDICATION

1779

THE surprise which Gibbon expressed at the reception of his first volume need not be ironical. It was an age of free enquiry, and in spite of his own experience, he continued to hold that the ferment of controversy had subsided and the most pious Christians of the day were ignorant or careless of their own belief.[1] His old friend George Lewis Scott, the mathematician, who read the proofs, had observed that the author would be 'thought to have written with all due moderation and decency with respect to received (at least once received) opinions'.[2] Gibbon's psychology may have been at fault; yet who could fail to see in the arrangement of that volume, ending with the fifteenth and sixteenth chapters, a carefully laid train leading to a violent if not dangerous explosion?

It was a commonplace of outraged readers that he had led them unforewarned through flowery paths to this deadly feast. It was equally common knowledge that many eager readers let the first fourteen chapters alone. A dreadful situation. Davis puts this charge in the forefront of his pamphlet. But he does not develop this argument, nor was it the sting which drove Gibbon at last to reply.

When Gibbon was accused by Davis circumstantially

[1] *The Decline and Fall,* c. xlvii. (6-29) and also c. lviii. (7-188).
[2] *Misc. Wks.* ii. 141.

of wilfully misrepresenting and even falsifying his authorities, he was bound to defend his honour both as a gentleman and as a serious investigator.[1] There was no difficulty in that. The details do not interest us now. Yet the *Vindication* can still be read as an example of deadly polemic. Gibbon's prose was never more forceful. He strengthened his position by saluting Dr. Watson as an adversary whose mind and manners commanded respect, and having dealt firmly but moderately with two other pamphleteers, he announced that he had replied once and for all. The *Vindication* was printed in octavo to prevent people binding it up with the history.

Davis wrote a counter reply. Others rushed into the fray. Abstention from controversy is not a thing that comes easy to the writing-tribe. But with rare wisdom Gibbon never went back on his word. Indeed what was there to reply to? His enemies 'furious and feeble' could not parry a stroke which had already dealt a decisive wound. They could only lash out spitefully as they lay on the ground.[2] Phrases such as 'Gibbon's implacable hostility to Christianity' beg a large question. That is not so important as that this loose accusation obscures the Historian's real achievement. He remains a useful bogy even for many who stand on ground he won for them.

What infuriated the pious, even if they did not at once realise the full measure of it, was that Gibbon had broken down for good the frontiers between sacred and secular history. By the simple device of explaining the rise of Christianity through five secondary causes added to the Divine Will, he eliminated God from the field of

[1] H. E. Davis, *An Examination*, etc., 1778.

[2] The Many against Gibbon have been exhaustively catalogued and summarised in masterly manner by Shelby T. McCloy in his *Gibbon and his Antagonism to Christianity*, New York and London, 1933.

all historical research for ever. His critics could only change or multiply the secondary causes. Henceforth 'It was God's will' was going to solve problems for no one outside a Sunday school. The ground may have been prepared by Middleton, Hume and Voltaire. The final drive was Gibbon's own, a very brilliant piece of tactics. It was a signal advance in historical science.

In the subsequent volumes Gibbon pursued his task of secularising the history of the Church. He destroyed the phantom of primitive purity, and showed on the contrary that no evil feature of human nature was absent. 'Ambition is a weed of quick and early vegetation in the vineyard of Christ.' [1]

If Christianity has ever been a system founded on superstition and privilege, which puts influence above truth and defends nonsense with cruelty, intrigues with inexhaustible duplicity and buys power with gold and blood, which bullies and cringes by turns, preaches peace and enjoys war, demands the blind obedience of the reason, and approves a cynical disparity in morals between profession and act, then indeed Gibbon may be said to be its implacable enemy and veracious historian.

But the Christianity of the Historian's England was not anything so lurid, and he could look on with amusement while 'the forms of orthodoxy, the articles of faith, are subscribed with a sigh, or a smile, by the modern clergy',[2] whose peace and security, he observed with equal contentment, were most favoured by religious indifference.[3] It suited himself as well as anyone. A gentleman in England had no need to go shouting 'Écrasez l'infame', and Gibbon was betrayed into a most unusual display of temper and bad manners, and indeed undignified temporising, when the upstart Dr.

[1] *The Decline and Fall,* c. lxix. (8-211).
[2] *Op. cit.* c. liv. (7-61). [3] *Op. cit.* c. lxix. (8-190).

Priestley tried to involve him in a public debate on the corruptions of Christianity.

But, again, if an observer in our own day reviews the inroads made by the churches themselves into that centre of the sacred field which Gibbon had scrupulously avoided—an avoidance which had but demonstrated its vulnerability—or if he observes ecclesiastics proving their latter-day change of heart by scourging their predecessors, he may well wonder wherein the quarrel with Gibbon lies. Such men as Voltaire, Hume and Gibbon should be recognised among the Fathers of the modern churches.[1] That is not to say, however, that they would welcome an affiliation order.

But gratitude is seldom a theological virtue, since those who are indebted to divine guidance cannot express much obligation to men. Besides Gibbon has not got a very good tone. To be a scientific historian is one thing; to go about his work with such inimitable wit and gaiety of attack is another. He does not fit in with those earnest workmen who claim to be rebuilding while they are still blowing up the foundations. Fighting parsons have felt his indirect methods to be somewhat unmanly. No doubt there is some truth in the observation that Gibbon's irony was designed to disarm prosecution. But one cannot suppose that he could have expressed himself very differently. *Le style c'est l'homme même.* Witness the characteristic signs in his early letters. Nevertheless his attack is not so unvaryingly oblique as might be imagined from some of his critics, friendly or hostile. The solemn sneer is by no means his only weapon, and there is no lack of forthright decisive strokes.

Gibbon was well aware of another risk. 'It should

[1] Cf. Gibbon's own remark, 'I am sorry to observe that the three writers of the last age, by whom the rights of toleration have been so nobly defended, Bayle, Leibnitz and Locke, are all laymen and philosophers' (*op. cit.* c. liv. n. 39).

seem that the zeal of our ancestors boiled higher' (he was contrasting 'miscreant' with the literal 'mécréant' of the French crusaders), 'and that they branded every unbeliever as a rascal. A similar prejudice still lurks in the minds of many who think themselves Christians.' [1] He must have known that he had already exposed himself by his improprieties, though the full force of his enemies' resentment on this score took some time in gathering.

If any are still scandalised by the historian's sallies, they will scarcely be helped by learning that a great part of them are drawn from the Fathers of the Church whose dirt Tillemont had raked together.[2] Nor will they be conciliated by Gibbon's taking cover with poor Sterne behind a bishop.[3] Gibbon's plea of *nihil humani alienum* for including in his history what people preferred to ignore was sound enough,[4] and the present age can only smile at his having needed to enter it. But he spoilt his case to some extent by his uncritical zest for scandal and his monotonous gibes about the frailty of nuns. It may be that the sack of cities has been a welcome break in conventual routine. But the joke soon becomes inartistic, and its removal from one sentence would certainly improve the great description of the pillage of Constantinople.[5]

These improprieties are almost entirely confined to his History. But the contrast of the historian's letters has been remarked on with needless surprise. For it is not difficult to see that his correspondence is pervaded with sexual metaphor. Taken with the persistent harping on feminine frailty of *The Decline and Fall*, this seems to form a literary compensation for a grievance which Gibbon had never got over, in spite of his attaining to

[1] *The Decline and Fall*, c. lviii. n. 83.
[2] *Op. cit.* c. xxvii. n. 51.
[3] *Op. cit.* c. lvi. n. 14.
[4] *Murray*, p. 337.
[5] *The Decline and Fall*, c. lxviii. (8-173).

friendships with women of the kind which he admitted were best suited to his nature, and about which no scandalous tongue could ever wag.

The expurgator is inevitably an altruist, and there is commonly a false ring about his indignation. When the worst is said, no one really wishes Gibbon had written otherwise. Bowdler's edition was never a success and aroused immediate protest. The condemned passages contain too much wit and too much learning; they are too deadly an exposure of the hypocrisy of centuries. Gibbon's fun is only the morality of the Fathers turned inside out.

In the turmoil which his pleasantries aroused, his more serious observations on sex have been overlooked, though one of them drew down contemporary censure. It would on the whole be applauded to-day. He stands up for the princess Honoria, who had 'yielded to the impulse of nature', and says that guilt and shame are the absurd language of imperious man.[1] He also balances his tales of Theodora by questioning whether the female mind is totally depraved by the loss of chastity.[2]

One might see too almost an irony on some modern aspirations, when he gives an appreciative glance at 'the gentle and amorous people' of Tahiti.[3] But Gibbon understood his Europe too well to suppose that a general licence could be given 'to the most amiable of our weaknesses'.[4] While recognising the need for divorce, he did not suppose that all our matrimonial troubles would be ended if it was conceded without restraint. The true happiness of marriage and fidelity are never sneered at, and he recognised that Christianity had done something to raise the dignity of marriage.[5]

[1] *Op. cit.* c. xxxv. (4-229).
[2] *Op. cit.* c. xl. (5-45).
[3] *Op. cit.* c. lxvi. n. 29.
[4] *Op. cit.* c. xiv. (2-143).
[5] *Op. cit.* c. xliv. *passim.*

More attention may be paid to the assertion that Gibbon was devoid of religious feeling and incapable of appreciating the poetry of Christianity. The argument is partly irrelevant, or not very creditable if it is thought or hoped that a deeper sentiment might have blunted the edge of Gibbon's intellect. There is also a lurking anachronism. Gibbon was spared the worst of the Gothic revival. And it is not fair to judge him, any more than his most pious contemporaries, by the enthusiasms of a later age. Yet it cannot be denied that Gibbon's deficient comprehension of religious experience renders his account unsatisfying. Something of the Middletonian school with its rough and ready theory of imposture hangs about him. Moreover his preoccupation with the backsliding of the clergy involves an insufficient attention to the changes in the people's morals. Modern insight into religious psychology and the comparative study of religions have revealed aspects of which Gibbon hardly dreamed. Scholars have in fact removed much of the remaining mystery in the rise of Christianity.

To accuse a person of lacking religious feeling or even beliefs is deceptively easy, since serious proof or rebuttal can have little part in the game. It may be said with confidence that Gibbon did not subscribe to any of the articles of the Creed except the first. On occasions he would affirm with sincere emphasis the conventional existence of God. It was a convenient working symbol for the inexplicable. Beyond that he knew with Aristotle that the Deity had received such attributes as man from time to time felt inclined to allow Him, and he himself protested that terms like the wrath and anger of God were qualities very foreign to the perfect Being.[1] In another passage that anticipates modern sentiment,

[1] *The Decline and Fall*, c. xxvii. (3-369), and c. lvii. n. 27, and Add. MSS. 34882 f. 49.

he remarks that the church of St. Euphemia, where the council of Chalcedon met, stood on a hill near the Bosphorus, 'whence the boundless prospect of the land and sea might have raised the mind of a sectary to the contemplation of the God of the universe'.[1]

He understood, better than some modern divines, that there must be an element of the irrational in every religion if it is to make a deep and lasting impression.[2] But his sympathies were with the Reformers, and he hailed Erasmus as the father of rational theology,[3] and when he says 'theology may perhaps be superseded by the full light of religion and reason', the vague aspiration (which might come out of a modern sermon) seems to anticipate some sort of ethical church in which 'the pure and simple maxims of the Gospel' no doubt would play their part. Gibbon shows none of the animosity to Jesus common in modern times, but he takes no great interest in him, and seldom mentions him except to draw reproachful attention to the discrepancy between his mild and humble virtues and the intolerance of his followers.[4]

It might not have been so necessary to consider the quality of the historian's views had not both friends and enemies, for their several ends, started the notion that Gibbon in the end became something of a believer.

Too much has been made of an artful letter to Hester Gibbon, containing the remark that religion was the 'best guide of youth and the best support of old age'. It all depends on the religion of course. But a man is not on his oath when he writes to his aunt. A speck of dust must neither be magnified into a stumbling-block nor into a rock of witness. When Catherine Porten died in 1786, Gibbon could say no more than 'I will

[1] *Op. cit.* c. xlvii. (6-27).
[2] *Op. cit.* c. viii. (1-336).
[3] *Op. cit.* c. liv. n. 38. The whole of this chapter is of the greatest importance for Gibbon's views on Protestantism.
[4] *Op. cit.* c. l.

agree with my lady that the immortality of the soul is on some occasions a very comfortable doctrine', and in 1793 after Lady Sheffield's death he told her husband that if there was a future state, her 'mild virtues' must surely be rewarded. At another time he argued with his friend that there could not be errors in annihilation, since one would know nothing about it.[1]

Nor should much weight be given to le doyen Bridel's evidence. Bridel, who often dined with Gibbon, remarks that he never spoke against religion at table. Very true, no doubt. But when it is said that Gibbon wished he had never written against Revelation and that he died 'avec des sentiments religieux', we require a more impartial witness than this friendly pastor. And there were certainly others who did not agree with Bridel.[2]

Gibbon's utterances may have taken colour from the piety of the friends who surrounded him in his last years. He was always susceptible to the personal equation. He may even have imagined that he would have written his famous chapters differently had he known the pain they were to give.[3] It may be so. As life advances one should learn to respect sincerity in one's opponents. There is a legitimate difference between the combative spirit of a man's books and his bearing in society. Apollo is not always shooting. But the difference should be respected on both sides, and it is difficult not to smile when at the close of his seventieth chapter Gibbon says 'nor am I willing in these last moments to offend even the Pope and clergy of Rome'. There is at any rate no

[1] Add. MSS. 34882, f. 49. Gibbon's objection to Christian or philosophical doctrines of immortality was that they did not allow that 'a union of sensual and intellectual enjoyment is requisite to complete the happiness of the double animal'. Mahomet knew better. *Op. cit.* c. l. Modern spiritualists seem to have felt the same difficulty.

[2] B. de Lalonde, *Le Léman ou voyage pittoresque*, etc. (Paris, 1842), pp. 277 *sqq*.

[3] *Murray*, p. 316.

evidence that he ever moved from the intellectual position to which he had advanced in early manhood.

Johnson, and Bowdler after him, prophesied a short day for infidel writers. But it is Gibbon who remains, while the apologists have risen and fallen in a chain of slaughter, somewhat like the keepers of the Arician grove. Paley, who was applauded by Boswell at Gibbon's expense, has at last been trodden firmly under heel by Dr. Inge.[1] He survived longer than most, thanks to the University of Cambridge; otherwise his is a typical fate.

The secret of Gibbon's permanence in this field of history lies not merely in the victories he won, but in those he may still win. Superstition, institutionalism and intolerance, the especial objects of his attack, are not dead, but his weapons have not rusted. His broad and pregnant generalisations are as provocative as ever. 'In the profession of Christianity the variety of national characters may be clearly distinguished.'[2] Never more true than at the present day. 'The successors of St. Peter appear to have followed rather than guided the impulse of manners and prejudice.'[3] He might have included the reformed churches too, which even more obviously follow with tentative footsteps the moral grazing of their flocks; for 'private reason always prevents or outstrips public wisdom'.[4] If it has been admitted above that Gibbon pays too little attention to the changes in popular morals effected by Christianity, a corrective of searching power may be supplied in the aphorism, 'much more is to be ascribed to the humanity than to the religion of the people'.[5]

[1] W. R. Inge, *Protestantism*, p. 52. The writer has exposed the weakness of nearly every form of Protestantism with great mastery. J. M. Robertson (*Gibbon*, p. 68) has some amusing remarks on the quarrels of Gibbon's commentators, especially on the way Milman and Bohn's anonymous clergyman rallied to their wicked compatriot against the attacks of foreign critics.

[2] *The Decline and Fall*, c. liv. (7-46).

[3] *Op. cit.* c. lix. (7-269).

[4] *Op. cit.* c. xxv. n. 44.

[5] *Op. cit.* c. l. n. 105.

The superficial weakness of this remark lies in Gibbon's own demonstration that religion itself is but one of the works of man. But he means to contrast the broad and irresistible progress of the general conscience with the claims of self-constituted authorities to have checked or impelled it. He reaches forward indeed to the modern conception that systems like Christianity are not so much salves applied from without, as the moulds, for good or evil, of forces working within the human spirit, which vary infinitely with the variations of time, place and racial instinct.

Chapter 20

A LORD OF TRADE

1779

THE harmony of a successful historian's life was marred by two mutually conflicting themes; his lack of faith in the Government more and more forcibly expressed, and the growing insistence of the truth that unless Government found him a place, he could not continue to live in London, not, at least, in the style to which he scarcely knew an alternative.

Gibbon's enthusiasm for the Government's policy had never been markedly spontaneous, but on the outbreak of regular hostilities with the colonists in 1776, he seems to have assimilated a little of the ministerial optimism which fell in well with his own elated mood. Rumour came home from Paris of a pitched battle between him and the Duke of Richmond, Fox's leader in the other House. Gibbon put in a disclaimer, although he confessed that the extravagance of both French and English supporters of the Americans sometimes inspired him with extraordinary vigour. But he proceeds to kick away his own weak stool. He found it much easier to defend the justice than the policy of the Government's actions. 'But there are certain cases where whatever is repugnant to sound policy ceases to be just.'

By the end of the year his expressions were more trenchant. The glow kindled by Howe's success at Philadelphia had been extinguished by Burgoyne's surrender at Saratoga. 'Are you still fierce?' Gibbon asked Holroyd, and reported a universal desire for peace in which he obviously shared. He threatened revolt.

> 'I shall scarcely give my consent to exhaust still further the finest country in the world in the prosecution of a war from whence no reasonable man entertains any hope of success. It is better to be humbled than ruined.'

Nor did he confine his opinions to Holroyd's confidence. Walpole wrote in his journal in November:

> 'Mr. Gibbon told me soon afterwards that he was convinced that if it had not been for shame, there were not twenty men in the House but were ready to vote for peace. I did not think it very decent in so sensible a man to support the war and make such a confession.' [1]

But Gibbon not only went on to say harsher things of the Government, he said or wrote them at Almack's, very likely within hearing of Charles Fox's passionate declamations.

Fox's was a potent spell. In him were united qualities which made him pre-eminent in the most diverse companies. 'Other men of his time had all these advantages but none of them had also the cheerful simplicity of character and the unfailing kindness which made his friendship a thing to be cherished through life and commemorated after death.' [2] The best of his powers and vitality were now being exerted to build up the opposition to Lord North's unhappy government.

Gibbon had known Fox at least as early as 1774 when they both joined the Club. Fox was then at the bottom of political and monetary fortune. He had never been a frequent or prominent member at the Turk's Head, and with the increase of his parliamentary activity he almost

[1] Walpole, *Last Journals* (ed. A. F. Steuart), ii. p. 76.
[2] E. Lascelles, *The Life of Charles James Fox*, p. 160.

ceased to attend.[1] But he was always to be found at Almack's, the brilliant centre of a brilliant though extravagant company, to which Gibbon felt himself intellectually if not financially akin, from the moment of his election. Gibbon has been accused of courting Fox. It is just as likely that Fox courted him. While he tried to unite and inspirit the listless factions of the Whigs, it was important to wear down the Government majority by detaching, one by one, members whose interests or convictions were suffering in the stress of the war. The silent Gibbon's vote was as valuable as the most loquacious member's, and Fox's easy school might well succeed to Governor Johnson's intensive tuition.

It may not be without significance that in October 1776 Gibbon is found being cheerfully entertained at Ampthill by Lord Ossory, whom, with his brother Fitzpatrick, Fox had recently won over to his side. Be that as it may, Gibbon was steadily drawn into Fox's circle. It was natural that he who could hardly say one sentence without premeditation, should admire Fox's passionate impromptus in the House, and enjoy hearing Thurlow and Wedderburn vainly cajoling each other to rise and answer him.[2] But such impartial admiration was of less avail at Almack's, where, as he writes his brief lively notes, 'Charles Fox is at my elbow declaiming on the impossibility of keeping America'. With this intoxication stimulating only his reason and better feelings, Gibbon was incited to his brief revolt against the Government.

'I shall perhaps sup with Charles etc. at Almack's' Gibbon told Holroyd on 26th January 1778, and the next day he voted with the minority on a motion asking for the despatches from the generals in America. A week later came Fox's famous motion 'that no more

[1] See Appendix III, p. 359. [2] Walpole, *Last Journals*, i. p. 584.

of the Old Corps be sent out of the Kingdom'. The motion was lost, but the opposition vote had risen in a month from 89 to 165,[1] and Gibbon had been among them. Two days later there was a vote of supply for new levies, and Gibbon voted with the majority. It looks as if he had been brought to heel. There is no record, I believe, of his voting against the Government again.

Almack's was not given up—though fewer surviving letters are directed thence—and Gibbon's tongue was not altogether silent. Perhaps the Whigs still hoped to get him. In March Holroyd hears 'this moment Beauclerk, Lord Ossory, Sheridan, Garrick, Burke, Charles Fox and Lord Cambden (no bad set you will say) have just left me'. But, pull devil, pull baker. Four months later Gibbon was living 'not unpleasantly in a round of ministerial dinners'.

Gibbon returned to North; but North was now standing on a Whig platform. Fox's motion on the Old Corps had been inspired by a fear of European war as much as by a desire to end the American. North was moved to produce conciliatory proposals which were so staggering a surrender that Fox could only say that they were identical with Burke's of three years before, but were now too late. A commercial treaty between France and the colonists, of which the Opposition were as well informed as the Government, made a new war a certainty. Gibbon thought, as men commonly think in such a national crisis, that it was better to support the ministry in being than to make chancy experiments. And chance and Fox were almost synonyms. The noble humanity of the 'Black patriot'[2] and his appeal to the principles of 1688 were fine fuel for singeing the Government. It was less certain whether they would yield the timber for a settlement with the Americans

[1] Lascelles, *op. cit.* p. 73.

[2] *Prothero,* ii. p. 4.

and their allies. Subsequent events can hardly have persuaded Gibbon that he was wrong.

The historian's own affairs were progressing towards a crisis. He was still burdened with his father's debts, and his own expenses were certainly not sinking. Perhaps he could count on £700-£800 in a good year. He was spending over £1000. A few hundred pounds from his History was only a transitory gratification, and towards the end of 1778 the position was becoming very awkward.

After years of suspense the sale of Lenborough, which had promised so much, finally broke down. Instead of using part of the £20,000 hoped for to pay off an ancient debt, Gibbon was forced by the bankers, Clive and Gosling, to sell his New River share—'a delicious morsel'. Of £7500 got thus he only saw £500. At the same time the Buriton estate caused him unexpected trouble and expenses. These were serious losses, but the crisis was precipitated by Mrs Gibbon's announced intention of leaving Bath.

A long conciliatory reply from her stepson reveals at last the root of her difficulties. Life at Belvedere was too expensive, and it was so because Mrs Gibbon was not receiving the full interest on a bond to her late relative James Scott for £1980. The facts are veiled on both sides with a becoming delicacy of phrase. But it is clear that Gibbon had been trading on his 'Mama's' good nature while he cut a figure in town.

He would not admit that he was being extravagant, or had incurred any *considerable* debts since his father's death. But economy must be understood to be a relative matter.

'As long as I am in Parliament, a house in Bentinck Street, a coach, such a proportion of servants, clothes, living etc., are almost necessaries.'

But other countries were less expensive:

'France, Switzerland or perhaps Scotland, may afford an humble Philosophical retreat to a man of letters, nor should I suffer any accidental change of fortune, any fall in the World to affect my spirits or ruffle my tranquillity.'

It was an effective and not altogether unjustifiable threat. Gibbon's friends and relations were always more anxious to see him rise in the world of politics than he was himself. They must pay for this pleasure. As it was, Mrs Gibbon agreed to wait patiently for the development of an alternative darkly hinted at, and then outlined less vaguely. He was closely connected with the Attorney-General, as Wedderburn now was. There was a prospect of a joint progress in which the lawyer's friend might reach 'a seat at one of the boards with an additional income of £1000 a year.' Such a turn of fortune might be expected about Easter 1779.

In July patience was rewarded by Gibbon's appointment to a seat at the Board of Trade and Plantations. The salary, £750 only, was enough to remove pressing difficulties. Gibbon immediately undertook to pay his stepmother an additional £100 a year (£300 in all) which would represent five per cent on his bond. The appointment was suggestively timely. It had been a close thing.

'Every morning', he wrote, 'I expected the event of the evening and every evening the return of the morning. Till the business was absolutely finished a hundred accidents might have dashed the cup from my lips.'

One last awkward corner was successfully turned. His appointment under government would necessitate a by-election. But Mr Eliot was now in opposition, and as

Gibbon remarked of a later and less happy occasion, the electors of Liskeard were commonly of the same opinion as Mr Eliot. A persuasive letter was necessary.

'DEAR SIR,

'Yesterday I received a very interesting communication from my friend the Attorney General whose kind and honourable behaviour to me, I must always remember with gratitude. He informed me that in consequence of an arrangement he had just made with Lord North a place at the board of trade was reserved for me, and that as soon as I signified my acceptance of it, he understood that the business would immediately be settled. My answer was sincere and explicit. I told him that I was far from approving all the past measures of administration even some of those in which I myself had silently concurred; that I saw with the rest of the World many essential defects in the character of the Ministers and was sorry that in so alarming a Crisis the Country had not the assistance of several able and honest Men who are now in Opposition. But—that I had not formed with any of those Members of Opposition any connections or engagements which could restrain my parliamentary conduct; that I did not discover among them such a superiority either of measures or abilities as could make it a duty for me to attach myself to their cause; and that I perfectly agreed with Charles Fox himself in thinking that at a time which required our utmost unanimity, Opposition could not tend to any good purpose and might be productive of much serious mischief. That in this view of public affairs, I saw no reason which ought to prevent me from accepting an office under Government and that I was ready to embrace so advantageous and honourable an offer. But that he must be sensible that it was impossible for me to give a decisive answer till I had consulted the person to whose generous friendship I was indebted for my seat in Parliament, and to whom I must be obliged for my resurrection as well as for my creation. That from my knowledge of your dislike to the present System it was not in my power to determine whether you might not feel some reluctance to replace me in a situation in which I could never oppose and must *generally* support the measures of Government. But that the experience of your friendship inspired me however with a lively hope that you would not refuse on this interesting occasion to renew and confirm the obligation you had already conferred upon me, and that perhaps you might not esteem the addition (if it can be called the addition) of a mute of any great moment to the numerous and regular forces of administration. That my conduct must depend entirely on your resolution; but that your resolution, whatever it might be, would not find room in my breast for any other sentiments, than those of the warmest gratitude and regard.

Perhaps, Dear Sir, you will ask why I have troubled you with this formal Epistle instead of calling on you in Spring Garden and talking over the business in a friendly and familiar way. The reason which prevented me arises from something which still remains to be said and which it would have been painful to me to say or for you to hear—Your answer will decide whether I may continue to live in England or whether I must speedily withdraw myself into a kind of Philosophical exile in Switzerland. My father left his affairs in a very embarrassed and even distressed condition. My efforts, perhaps not very skilful ones to dispose of a part of my landed property have been hitherto unsuccessful and the times do not grow more favourable to them; and the plan of my expences however moderate in itself deserves the name of extravagance since it exceeds the measure of my real income. The addition of the salary which is now offered will make my situation perfectly easy; but I hope you will do me the justice to believe that my mind would not be so, unless I were sincerely persuaded that I could accept the offer with honour and integrity.

'I am
'Dear Sir
'with affectionate regard
'most faithfully Yours
'E. GIBBON

'BENTINCK STREET
'*June the 20th* 1779.'[1]

The appeal was successful, and the new Lord of Trade entered his new office, which, though not a sinecure, did not make too great a claim on his time. The remainder

[1] From the original MS. at Port Eliot. It differs considerably from the draft text in *Misc. Wks.* i. 236.

of the year passed cheerfully. The second volume of *The Decline and Fall* progressed so well that its appearance was prophesied for the following year, and since Cadell strenuously urged the curiosity of the public, the author had sat during May to Sir Joshua and the portrait was to be engraved by Hall as a frontispiece.

Gibbon disclaimed being 'the Champion of any party', but he rendered his benefactors service by composing his *Mémoire Justificatif*, a document addressed to Europe on the impropriety of France's interfering in a domestic quarrel. Trevelyan has said that 'no more ably composed and entirely readable state paper was ever issued'.[1] Its topic makes it of some interest at the present day.

That Gibbon wrote this document after his appointment is proved by a letter to Lord Weymouth, Secretary of State, enclosing the first draft. It was published in October.[2]

'My Lord,

'I have endeavoured to execute the very honourable task which your Lordship and the Lord Chancellor wished me to undertake, and I now submit to your judgement my first, imperfect, Essay, in this kind of Composition. I am apprehensive that to many other defects it may add the fault of being too long; yet I am not conscious that it is more diffuse than the style of these public declarations almost inevitably requires. It far exceeds the measure of the French Declaration; but it must be considered that facts and arguments will take up more room than mere empty declamation. However if the paper which I have the honour of transmitting to your Lordship should be thought to require or to deserve any alterations, I shall esteem it as a very particular favour, if I may be permitted to attend your Lordship, and the Chancellor to receive your farther instructions. If I have been totally unsuccessful in the execution of your Commands, I flatter myself that the attempt will be

[1] *American Revolution*, iii. 263. [2] *Prothero*, i. 371 and n.

accepted as a slight but sincere proof of my zeal for his Majesty's service and Government.

'I have the honour to be, with the highest respect,
'Your Lordship's
'Most obedient and most humble servant,
'E. GIBBON

'BENTINCK STREET
'*August the* 10*th*, 1779.'[1]

The shafts of the wits were not to be avoided. Verses attributed to Fox circulated at Brooks's (late Almack's) in which George III was alleged to have bought Gibbon's silence for fear that he would write the history of the decline and fall of the British Empire. The verses are neat and stinging, but not malicious. Posterity has taken more seriously the story of Fox's inscription in a copy of *The Decline and Fall* among his effects when he was sold up.[2] It sold for three guineas, more in honour to this inscription on the first leaf than to the work:

'I received this from the author (on such a day).—

'N.B. I heard him declare at Brooks's the day after the Rescript of Spain was notified that nothing could save this country but *six heads* (of certain Ministers whom he named) upon the table. In fourteen days after this anathema he became a *Lord of Trade* and has ever since talked *out* of the House as he has voted *in* it, the advocate and champion of those Ministers. Charles Fox.'

No one appears to have seen this inscription, and it may be questioned how far it is consistent with Fox's character, of whom Gibbon himself said in later years, 'perhaps no human being was ever more perfectly exempt from the taint of malevolence, vanity, or false-

[1] From the original at Longleat.

[2] G. Hardinge to Walpole, n.d. Nichols's *Literary Illustrations*, iii. 213. Anthony Storer says the book was withdrawn from the sale in spite of Fox's wishes. No record of the book's having been seen since the sale appears to exist.

hood'. Eliot's son in 1796 told Wilberforce that Gibbon asserted that he had said 'till both North's and Fox's heads' were on the table.[1] Who can say if it is the true version or a wriggle?

Another attack which may have been more exasperating at the time has nearly been forgotten. During the year Macpherson, one of the old associates of the British Coffee House, published *A Short History of the Opposition*. It was poor stuff, and those who attributed it to Gibbon were exposing their own intelligence to ridicule. Nevertheless, Gibbon found it necessary to tell his stepmother that he had not written it and knew nothing of its production. The rumour persisted however, and in the same year appeared an acrimonious answer to which was prefixed 'an address to Messrs. Wedderburn, Gibbon and Macpherson'.

After handling Wedderburn very roughly for a turncoat the writer opens with a peculiarly aggravating turn: 'To you Mr. Gibbon I had a great deal to say but I have forgot it'. Nevertheless the author rushes into a round of abuse, not without side glances at North. Gibbon is accused of apostasy from God, his country and his political friends. He would have betrayed the secrets of the Opposition if they had been simple enough to trust him. Now he abuses them, while throwing out oblique censures on Administration. Lord North had hired him as a faithful servant. But North was merely a registry office, unable either to fix the wages or assign the offices of his employees. Later the writer comes back to his victim again.

'If Mr. Gibbon had succeeded as an *author* or had been trusted by the party on whom he obtruded himself, what would the American Secretary[2] do for an Atlas to support the burden of the state, while his lordship is innocently amusing himself with

[1] R. L. and S. Wilberforce, *Life of Wilberforce*, ii. 179.

[2] Lord George Germaine.

his two bosom *friends* Sir John Irwin and General Cunningham.'[1]

The rancour of a party pamphleteer is hardly evidence of anything but itself. Such abuse was part of the price Gibbon had to pay for maintaining himself in Bentinck Street with his coach and liveries, and his stepmother at Belvedere.

The peace of mind thus attained was not to remain completely untroubled. The Government's position was becoming increasingly precarious in the House and in the country. A general election was in sight, and the effects of an unsuccessful war, bad trade and rising taxation were bound to alter the composition of the next House. The strength and spirits of the Opposition were already rising. An attack was launched which might almost seem to be singling out Mr Gibbon.

Burke introduced his plans for an 'economical Reformation'. Useless offices and sinecures were to be abolished, though the reformer is said to have excepted the Clerkship of the Pells from the scheme because he intended his son to have it. At any rate in March 1780 a motion was carried by a narrow majority to abolish the Board of Trade and Plantations.

Gibbon accepted the vote with tranquillity and impartially admired the enemy's eloquence with its not unpleasing references to himself. Burke recognised the part that the board had played as an asylum of literary men, and paid an ironic compliment to the 'historian's labours, the wise and salutary results of deep religious researches'. But Gibbon was confident that the decision would be reversed in the Lords, or that some other provision would be made for him. In fact, the proposed

[1] *Observations on a pamphlet entitled 'A Short History of the Opposition' etc.* 1779.

reform was dropped and the Lords Commissioners drew their salaries for another two years.

The approaching dissolution was another matter. Although Eliot had allowed his cousin to be re-elected on his appointment, he intimated that he would not support him again. Gibbon replying in August ventured on an appeal against what he termed a sentence of banishment from his native country. Eliot had kept him in suspense, but Gibbon did not claim that an earlier announcement of this decision would have enabled him to secure another seat. On leaving Liskeard, the £1200 which Gibbon was to refund when Eliot's son came of age would fall immediately due, and Gibbon warned his cousin that owing to the failure to sell Lenborough he would have to ask for some indulgence.

Eliot stood firm declaring that he too must be *independent* in his choices. Since his cousin had attached himself to Government he could trust them not to leave so valuable a man 'sur le pavé.'[1] Gibbon expostulated with smooth irony. He defended his conduct on the truth of one single assertion, that he had never renounced any principle, deserted any connexion or violated any promise. He had uniformly asserted the justice of the American war. He had supported the Government except in the crisis of Burgoyne's surrender. He had agreed with Eliot in thinking that when the substance of power was lost the name of independence might be granted to the Americans. But both parties had rejected the idea almost equally. He reminds Eliot that there was no disgrace in sitting at the Board of Trade, where Eliot himself had sat through several successive governments, and Eliot had none of those domestic reasons which might be alleged in his own favour.

Gibbon was satisfied with this vent to his feelings, and

[1] Add. MSS. 34886, f. 111.

both sides agreed that there was no use in prolonging the discussion. The cousins remained on the friendliest terms for the remainder of the historian's life.

This letter was written in September, a week after the dissolution of Parliament, and the day before Gibbon had informed Holroyd that he had still hopes of continuing to breathe the pestiferous air of St. Stephen's Chapel. On William Eden's advice he had made a detailed statement of his situation to Lord North and others, and made it clear that he could only contemplate an almost gratuitous seat. He was informed that if he was not immediately elected, he would be brought in at one of the re-elections caused by those who had been chosen for more than one constituency.

Parliament was necessary if Gibbon was to retain his place, and his place was necessary if he was to remain in England. But now he was expressing his weariness and indifference to the life, and throwing out hints of the sweet vision of Helvetic retirement. He watched philosophically the impatience of some strong competitors who pushed between him and the door. It would seem that his friends' desire to keep him in the House was stronger than his own, and some references in letters convey the hint that he was still regarded as having some political future. He was finally returned for Lymington on 25th June 1781, in the room of Mr Dummer deceased.

To a feverish crisis of the previous year belongs the story of an encounter with Pitt, to which a good deal of importance has been attributed. It cannot be true in the form in which it has come down to us.

In June 1780 'the flames of London, which were kindled by a mischievous madman, admonished all thinking men of the danger of an appeal to the people'.

Holroyd took a leading part in quelling Lord George Gordon, and the Northumberland Militia with which he was connected was quartered in Lincoln's Inn. Thirty-eight years after the event Sir James Bland Burges described a dinner party given for the officers, to which among others Gibbon was invited. He gives what seems an authentic enough account of the way in which Gibbon dominated the conversation, allowing no interchange of ideas, but bewildering everyone with a flow of anecdote and epigram on a confusing variety of topics. Then, of course, the rapping on the famous box, the signal that applause was due. But a deep-toned clear voice broke in with a challenge. The disconcerted raconteur found himself attacked and pressed so hard by a tall thin ungainly young man called Mr Pitt, that at last he rose and left the room. Burges found him outside looking for his hat: efforts to bring him back were fruitless, and he went away although Holroyd also came out to Burges's assistance.[1]

The late J. M. Robertson was the first to challenge this story.[2] He suspected it was a doublet on the story of the Abbé de Mably and Gibbon, conveniently turned round. A somewhat similar picture is given of Buffon by Marmontel, who says the great naturalist hated to be contradicted by younger men and would politely leave the room.[3] These stories in fact are all cast in a mould whose popularity never flags for those who enjoy seeing the expert caught out. Nor can it be denied that elderly authorities are apt to resent contradiction.[4] But Gibbon was only forty-three at this time and was admittedly an accomplished man of the world who must be

[1] Sir James Bland Burges, *Letters and Correspondence*, pp. 59-61. The passage is quoted at length in *Prothero*, ii. 28.

[2] J. M. Robertson, *Gibbon*, pp. 108-10.

[3] Marmontel, *Mémoires*, ii. 14.

[4] There is perhaps also a suggestion of Bentley's 'Walker, my hat!' in Burges's conclusion of the story.

ready for all kinds of encounters. Robertson is no doubt right in emphasising the improbability *a priori* of Gibbon's behaving so childishly and in a way that is inconsistent with all that we know of him. Yet a man may lose his self-control once in a way.

But there is a more decided flaw in the story which Robertson has overlooked. He calls attention to Gibbon's statement in 1782 that he had no connexion with Pitt—that does not necessarily exclude this alleged encounter—and to the cordial praise which he bestows on the young statesman more than once. But he seems to have forgotten that Sheffield explicitly states that in 1793 Gibbon went to dine with Lord Loughborough to meet various men, 'and particularly Mr. Pitt with whom he was not acquainted'.

If the incident alleged by Burges were true, Sheffield could hardly have forgotten it, and he could hardly have had the face to assert that Gibbon and Pitt did not meet till 1793, when there must have been many contemporaries who might bring up an incident which was only sixteen years old, and was not likely to have gone unreported. Burges's story written some thirty-eight years later cannot be regarded as a strong authority, and Robertson gives another example to show that his regard for truth was not of the strictest.

Nevertheless Burges must be granted his dinner party and his picture of Gibbon the conversationalist, which is by no means inconsistent with other accounts. Time and malice have obscured the real events of the evening. If nothing untoward happened, Sheffield and Gibbon may have forgotten that Pitt was there.

In November of this year the active Holroyd was rewarded with a barony in the peerage of Ireland and took the name of Sheffield. Gibbon was in the secret, and when the honour was imminent, wrote to Mrs Holroyd with mingled delight and humour:

'Do you not feel some titillations of vanity? Yet I will do you the justice to believe that they are as faint as can find place in a female (you will retort, or a male) heart, on such an auspicious event. When it is revealed to the Hon. Miss, I should recommend the loss of some ounces of noble blood.'

While his political fortunes were in suspense, Gibbon was at last, in his own phrase, delivered of twins in February 1781.

The second and third volumes carried his History to the end of the Empire in the West, and Gibbon's first promise to his public was fulfilled. A sensation such as had followed the first volume was not to be expected. The edition went more slowly; there were some complaints that the story was too prolix, a criticism to which Gibbon to some extent agreed, but on the whole his vanity was dexterous enough to interpret the different reception favourably. If people were not reading with the immediate avidity of five years before, they were buying the volumes to consume at their leisure during the summer in the country.

He had lent Walpole the second volume some months before its appearance. But this time the device did not prove successful. Gibbon was trapped into betraying his annoyance at Walpole's coolness. Walpole perhaps makes too good a story.

'You will be diverted to hear', he wrote to Mason in January 1781, 'that Mr. Gibbon has quarrelled with me. He lent me his second volume in the middle of November. I returned it with a most civil panegyric. He came for more incense; I gave it, but alas!, with too much sincerity; I added, "Mr. Gibbon, I am sorry *you* should have pitched on so disgusting a subject as the Constantinopolitan History. There is so much of the Arians and Eunomians and semi-Pelagians; and there is such a strange contrast between Roman and Gothic manners, and so little harmony between a Consul Sabinus and a Ricimer, Duke of the

> Palace, that though you have written the story as well as it could be written, I fear few will have patience to read it." He coloured; all his round features squeezed themselves into sharp angles; he screwed up his button-mouth and rapping his snuff-box, said, "It had never been put together before"—*so well*, he meant to add—but gulped it. He meant *so well* certainly, for Tillemont, whom he quotes in every page, has done the very thing. I well knew his vanity, even about his ridiculous face and person, but thought he had too much sense to avow it so palpably.'

Even if Gibbon himself later admitted that he had dived too deep in the mud of the Arian controversy, he might well have expected Walpole to be a more discerning critic than this. Indeed if 'the ingenious trifler' gives his actual words, the author's annoyance is comprehensible.

The quarrel, if it can be so called, begun in November, lasted into the next year. Mason received the news of its termination.

> 'The lost sheep is found; but I have more joy in one just person than in ninety and nine sinners that do not repent; in short the renegade Gibbon is returned to me after ten or eleven weeks, and pleads having been five of them at Bath. I immediately forgave even his return.'

Fortunately for us the friendship was resumed. We might have lost that exquisitely comic glimpse of December 1781.

> 'I was diverted last night at Lady Lucan's', Walpole tells Lady Ossory; 'the moment I entered, she set me down to Whist with Lady Bute—and who do you think were the other partners? The Archbishopess of Canterbury and Mr. Gibbon!'

Chapter 21

'JE PARS'

1783

THE remainder of Gibbon's political career is quickly told. Nine months after his re-entry into Parliament Lord North's government came to an end, and Gibbon was expecting his fate with resolution. The Lords of Trade did not fall with the Government, but their fate was settled by the revived progress of Burke's reforms, and in May 1782 Gibbon received a circular letter from Lord Shelburne to the effect that the Board of Trade was to be suppressed, and his Majesty had no further occasion for his services. He had held his office a little less than three years.

With the loss of office Gibbon's seat in Parliament had become useless. He continued to sit, fascinated by the political marches and countermarches out of which he could hope to get nothing. The economy reforms had reduced the resources of patronage, while the number of aspirants was doubled.

The new prime minister, the Marquis of Rockingham, died in July; and Gibbon prophesied truly enough that if Lord Shelburne succeeded him, the Rockingham Whigs would quarrel with him before Christmas.

> 'At all events I foresee much tumult and strong opposition from which I should be very glad to extricate myself, by quitting the H. of C. with honour and without loss.'

Gibbon was right. Fox resigned when Shelburne

became prime minister, and in the autumn the battle of the three parties was developing.[1] 'From honour, gratitude and principle' Gibbon announced his loyalty to Lord North, and early in February 1783 a first victory over the Government was gained. The issue was not long in doubt. Lord Shelburne resigned, and the incredible was realised when Fox, whose political life 'had been mainly directed to the extinction of Lord North', was sworn in side by side with him, the two Secretaries of State under the leadership of the Duke of Portland. Those who grow warm over Gibbon's minute vacillations should first digest this coalition.

Gibbon tells his fortune in one sentence: 'My vote was counted in the day of battle, but I was overlooked in the division of the spoil'.[2] There was not indeed much to hope for. Promises were made of a seat at the board of customs or excise. But the chance was vague; incumbents often proved tough. Such an appointment would have entailed leaving the House, no intolerable matter, but also a constant attention to tedious business which would have seriously retarded the historian's work. Yet Gibbon could not bring himself to say that he would refuse the offer. His affairs were still precarious and he had his stepmother to consider. Another post, more attractive but also more exacting, and at the same time of most uncertain tenure, was the secretaryship to the embassy in Paris. In the end Anthony Storer was appointed and Gibbon never knew that it was through Fox's intervention—Sheffield interpreted it as an act of friendship—that his claims were rejected.

A scrap of paper has survived in which Gibbon drily

[1] *I.e.* Shelburne's, Lord North's, and the Rockingham Whigs with Fox.

[2] Wedderburn now Lord Loughborough, and his cousin William Eden later Lord Auckland, with whom also Gibbon was friendly, took a considerable part behind the scenes in negotiating the coalition.

tabulated the conflicting motives of history and the world:

FOR	AGAINST
1. The credit of being distinguished and stopped by Government when I was leaving England.	1. The renouncing a rational and agreable scheme on the point of execution.
2. The salary of £1200 a year.	2. The disappointing a friend at Lausanne who expects me with impatience.
3. The society of Paris.	3. Losing at least £1000 and incurring many expences.
4. The desire of obliging a friend in England.	4. Giving up the leisure and liberty for prosecuting my history.
5. The hope of a future provision for life.	5. The engaging without experience perhaps without talents in a scene of business which I never liked.
	6. Giving myself a Master at least a principal of an unknown perhaps an unamiable character.
	7. The perpetual danger of the recall of the Ambassador or the change of ministry.[1]

Gibbon never showed himself more equable in temper or more sincerely pleased with his way of life, than in the months when it was becoming increasingly doomed. While Lord North's government declined daily, the Lord of Trade's interest appears more engaged by Caplin's promotion to prime minister on Mrs Ford's resigning her key basket. The administration was strengthened by sending the housemaid to White's to be made a good cook for private ordinary days.

Having fulfilled his first promise with the fall of the Western Empire, he took nearly a year's holiday in

[1] Add. MSS. 34882, f. 256.

which he returned 'by a natural impulse' to Greek literature, reading Homer, the historians, Attic drama and 'many interesting dialogues of the Socratic school'. After this relaxation an equally natural impulse led him back to the satisfaction of the daily task, and before he left England in 1783 he had almost finished his fourth volume.

Three months of the summer of 1781 had been spent at Brighton—Miss Elliot's Lodging, Cliff House.[1]

> 'The air gives health spirits and a ravenous appetite. I walk sufficiently morning and evening, lounge in the middle of the day on the Steyne, booksellers' shops, etc. and by the help of a pair of horses can make more distant excursions. The society is good and easy. . . .'

Good and easy society he found everywhere; whether dining, quite intrigued, with Loughborough and Mrs Abington, or being teased by the ladies of Bath and wondering whether it was proper to escort Mrs Hayley to Lady Miller's literary *salon*—a very Victorian age really—or spending sober evenings with the bookseller Elmsley, a valued friend, or discussing poor Lady Di with Burke and Sir Joshua in a window at Richmond.

In the autumn of 1782 he hired a villa at Hampton Court from 'Single Speech' Hamilton.

> 'Every morning I walk a mile or more before breakfast, read and write *quantum sufficit*, mount my chaise and visit in the neighbourhood, accept some invitations and escape others, use the Lucans as my daily bread, dine pleasantly at home or sociably abroad, reserve for study an hour or two in the evening, lye in town regularly once a week, etc. etc. etc.'

The experiment succeeded so well that in 1783 he had secured the house by May and was proposing 'every week to steal away like a Citizen from Saturday to Monday'.

[1] *Magd. Coll. Papers.*

This could not last. Gibbon's signal devotion to North when he was carried down to the House in flannels and crutches to sit there till eight in the morning before the coalition could get their slender majority, was not going to be rewarded in a hurry, if at all. It was all very well to joke about becoming dancing-master in the Prince of Wales's new £100,000 establishment.[1] Something must be obtained, and even Sheffield's active and ardent spirit admitted that there was perplexity in his friend's situation. Yet he may have been surprised, and was certainly annoyed when he found that very soon he would be asked to come 'Bentinckising' no more.

In May Gibbon wrote a long exploratory letter to Deyverdun reciting his political rise and fall, and throwing out with circumspection a reminder of their project, formed so long ago, of living together. Deyverdun's reply, equally long and judicious, surpassed all expectation. Not only had he not ceased to hope, but he had the means now of carrying out their plan. He had inherited his aunt's house La Grotte. It was too big for himself and he had divided it and sublet part of it. That would be available for Gibbon in the autumn.

Deyverdun is a shadowy although constant figure in Gibbon's life. Only in the letters that were now exchanged is his voice heard with any clearness, and it is certainly the voice of an eager yet prudent friend full of understanding and solicitude. Where Sheffield and others were still scheming to retain Gibbon in a life to which he was so unsuited, Deyverdun could say that he had always viewed the adventure with suspicion and regret. When Gibbon wrote rather weakly, 'Si je ne consultois que mon cœur et ma raison, je romperois sur le champ cette indigne chaîne', Deyverdun replied sharply, 'Eh! que voulez-vous consulter, si ce n'est votre cœur et votre raison?'

[1] *Auckland Correspondence*, i. p. 531.

The five letters indeed which were now exchanged are a serene eclogue in which the two friends anticipate their long-deferred union, Gibbon eagerly accepting the delights, which Deyverdun depicts not without warnings of what the passage of time has effected and the contrast between London and the pastoral simplicity of the Pays de Vaud. It would be a kind of marriage, the contract of which they were settling agreeably, with all the caution which two wary old bachelors could bring to such an adventure, without detriment to their genuine affection.

At last on the 1st of July 1783 Gibbon wrote:

> 'Après avoir pris ma résolution, l'honneur, et ce qui vaut encore mieux, l'amitié, me défendent de vous laisser un moment dans l'incertitude. JE PARS. Je vous en donne ma parole, et comme je suis bien aise de me fortifier d'un nouveau lien, je vous prie très sérieusement de ne pas m'en dispenser. Ma possession sans doute ne vaut pas celle de Julie; mais vous serez plus inéxorable que St. Preux.'

It remained to break the news at home. It was largely Lord Sheffield's 'manly and vehement friendship' that had held Gibbon so long in 'the narrow and dirty circle of English politics'. Fearing a loss of temper on both sides the fugitive wrote a long letter revealing at last his IRREVOCABLE resolution; not however without the hedging suggestion that in four years' time, with a recovery in his fortunes, he might return to a permanent and independent establishment in England. Sheffield might complain to Eden that Gibbon had baffled all arrangements but had to admit that 'of all circumstances the most provoking is that he is right'.[1] He loyally undertook yet another burden, the disposal of his friend's seat.

Gibbon was much more apprehensive of wounding his stepmother's tender attachment, and months after

[1] Lord Sheffield to William Eden, 7th August 1783, *op. cit.* i. p. 56.

he was settled in Lausanne could tell her that conveying his decision to her was one of the most painful struggles of his life. She set herself indeed in flat opposition. The more she considered his plan the less she liked it, and made two unpalatable proposals somewhat bluntly:

> 'As the gout grows more frequent I think it might be a good reason of your giving up all very expensive society, and if you would give me a room in your house, I should live the retir'd Life I long for. Two hundred a year would pay your house and coach and with the remainder I should be very rich and happy.'[1]

It had been prudent to be committed with Deyverdun beforehand. The motherly offer must be gently refused, though perhaps it was neither very kind, nor quite true, for Gibbon to reply that two hundred a year would scarcely keep a coach. There was no farewell visit to Bath. Mrs Gibbon did not feel she could bear it. But she did not relax her anxiety, and in one last touch of solicitude remarked that she heard that his new home was in 'the most beautiful situation imaginable . . . but the inside of the House may not be so comfortably prepared as you are used to (for Mr. Deyverdun is a Philosopher)'.

Two months quickly passed in preparations. A selected working library was shipped to Rouen. The lease of Bentinck Street was resigned. Other things were stored in Downing Street. Lady Sheffield might use the musical clock there, but was asked not to take it to Sheffield Place. The beloved house was left on the 1st of September, a date humbly attested by Mary Pitt's washing bill with the instruction 'to be sent home Thursday Lord Sheffield's Downing Street Westminster'.[2]

Gibbon had already taken farewell of the Holroyds in Sussex and remembered the day as one of the most

[1] Brit. Mus. 11907, dd. 25 (2). [2] *Magd. Coll. Papers.*

affecting of his life. Sheffelina was his dear friend, his sister. An almost tearful situation had been relieved by Maria's pertinent asking whether he intended to be buried in Switzerland or England. The last days in England were spent drearily alone in Downing Street. No confirmatory letter had been received from Deyverdun. He might be dead; anything might have happened. At last, after waiting in vain for the Flanders mail to bring him his sailing orders, Gibbon decided to venture. He left on the 15th of September, sailed from Dover on the 17th and was driven into Boulogne instead of Calais. On board with him were two Americans, Henry Laurens, President of Congress, who had been in the Tower since 1779, and Benjamin Thompson of Massachusetts, an odd character known later as Count Rumford.

From Boulogne Gibbon travelled smoothly across France, conversing with Homer and Lord Clarendon, often with Caplin[1] and Muff, his dog; and 'sometimes with the French postillions—of the above-mentioned animals the least rational'. On the 27th of September 1783 he drove into Lausanne after an absence of nineteen years and five months.

Deyverdun was alive and expectant. But the lazy fellow had failed to discover that he could not get possession of Gibbon's part of the house until the following spring. Since his own part was too small, the two friends hired an apartment for the winter, at the end of the rue du Bourg, with access to their garden. It was not a good beginning, but Gibbon, who knew his Deyverdun, put up with the disappointment as a sage should.

[1] After a trial of Swiss life 'the dear inseparable Caplin' went home; a blow to Gibbon especially since consideration for his servant had entered into his hesitation before deciding to leave England.

Chapter 22

'FANNY LAUSANNE'

1783–1787

'JULIAN inviolably preserved for Athens that tender regard which seldom fails to arise in a liberal mind from the recollection of the place where it has discovered and exercised its growing powers.'[1] Gibbon clearly reveals his own long-cherished aspiration in these words, and now that he had come back to his own Athens, he only discovered new causes of gratitude. The one regret was that he had not returned three, five or even ten years earlier.

It had not been a moment too soon. In a few months the ill-assorted Coalition came apart. His successful rival, Storer, lost his place, and Gibbon could reflect how desperate would have been his own outlook in the same plight. Now he followed the political shifts with increasing detachment; Pitt and Fox were becoming less to him than Caesar and Pompey, and the country could be ruled by boys for all he cared. He could forgive Lord North's slight in letting him leave the country without a word, and with recollections of his pleasant companionship turn to framing the mellow compliment with which he offered him the last three volumes. For a while he could not bring himself to say he would refuse a post if it came his way, and he thought he would like to be minister at Berne. But in a while he was resigned to the fact that there was no eagerness to recall

[1] *The Decline and Fall*, c. xix. (2-395).

him to mend his country's fortunes. 'Nor', he was destined to write, 'is there perhaps a more exquisite gratification than to revisit, in a conspicuous dignity, the humble and laborious scenes of our youth.'[1]

In the prettiest and most obliging letters since those of Paul of Tarsus, he delighted to twit his friends on their mistaken prophecies. Far from being lost in a dull provincial round, he found Lausanne a more cosmopolitan city than it had been twenty years or more ago. Of the 40,000 English reputed to be travelling on the Continent a large proportion divided the year between Switzerland and the South. Gibbon can produce a string of fashionable names at any moment. The adorable Lady Elizabeth Foster would come to consult Tissot, and Gibbon spent some golden hours at her bedside.

But there were more important people to stroll on his Terrace; M. Mercier, author of the *Tableau de Paris*, the Abbé Raynal, whose *Histoire des Indes* was on the Index, and a host of minor princes and royal bastards. Against such visitors of every degree Lausanne wished to parade the grand Gibbon, and he was a public character expected to see and be seen.

How would his fortunes support the position? In a normal year—the expenses of moving had been heavy—he expected to reduce expenditure by three or four hundred pounds, spending six or seven against over a thousand a year in London. It was not that Lausanne was so much cheaper; but the things that drained away the money inexorably in London did not exist there. It is the common and perpetual experience of the English abroad. On the other side he was not by any means free of worry. He had expected to get £1100 for his seat in Parliament. But the end of the Coalition made its value very precarious, and he would be lucky to get

[1] *The Decline and Fall*, c. lviii. (7-181).

£500. Then, although shortly after his departure Sheffield succeeded at last in selling Lenborough, Gibbon was woefully disappointed in the price, and impatient for the money, for he had some long bills and had also taken up some French annuities. On the other hand he was confident that in two years he would be returning with a manuscript worth at least £3000. There were as well his expectations on the old ladies' lives.

His references to this have been brought up against him, and one might certainly wish that they were not so frequent. Gibbon cannot be blamed for mentioning these possibilities to his chancellor. There was no need for him to pretend to an affection for Aunt Hester, and he no doubt inherited his father's notion that she had been too well endowed by his grandfather. Moreover, the Saint had been so un-auntlike as to try to borrow from her nephew, while, though on polite terms with the little infidel, she had refused to enter his house. Mrs Gibbon's case was different. She was almost uncomfortably fond of him, and Gibbon proved his affection for her in more than one way. If he traded on her good nature for some years over the bond, he made amends by his care of her interests later. To say that he desired her end would be a gross slander, but he might have left Holroyd to make any calculations on it for himself. And since she did in fact survive her stepson, the laugh of the world has been against him.

La Grotte is said to have stood on the site of a vault or crypt belonging originally to the Franciscan convent of which the church, S. François, survives. It was a large rambling house, dating in part from the sixteenth century, with high sloping roofs, and stood at the head of the old steep road to Ouchy, a little behind the position of the modern post-office. The grounds, all part of the old conventual domain, extended from the Ouchy road to the rue du Petit Chêne.

> 'A Terrace, one hundred yards long, extends beyond the front of the House, and leads to a close impenetrable shrubbery; and from thence the circuit of a long and various walk, carries me round a meadow and vineyard. The intervals afford abundant supply of fruit and every sort of vegetables; and if you add that this villa . . . touches the best and most sociable part of the town, you will agree with me, that few persons, either princes or philosophers, enjoy a more desirable residence.'

Deyverdun had offered his friend an apartment of eleven rooms, far more space than he could desire or need. A different partition was made when they took possession early in 1784. Gibbon had a bedroom and dressing-room, a store-room and a library about the same size as that in Bentinck Street, 'with this difference however, that instead of looking on a paved court twelve feet square, I command a boundless prospect of vale, mountain and water'. Deyverdun's kingdom was not so large. The rest of the house was held in common. 'We have a very handsome winter apartment of four rooms; and on the ground floor, two cool saloons for the summer, with a sufficiency, or rather superfluity, of offices, etc.'

Neither friend entered the other's rooms unannounced, and the mornings were generally spent alone. Gibbon rose at seven and was at work about eight. The two men dined together at two, an early hour, but the latest for which Gibbon could wait. The rest of the day passed in various amusements. If they were alone they read a book together, talked and played chess or billiards. Deyverdun smoked; his friend was true to snuff. Eleven o'clock generally saw the end of the day, and Gibbon went to bed thinking of his friends sweating in St. Stephen's Chapel.

They got on excellently, but found that two bachelors who had lived long independently had to be mutually forbearing. 'When the mask of form and ceremony is laid aside, every moment in a family life has not the sweetness of the honeymoon.' But Deyverdun's 'heart and head were excellent' and Gibbon could now exercise his 'propensity for happiness' with ease. It had been something of a *tour de force* in London, as he confesses to Sheffield.

Deyverdun was an assiduous gardener, and under his guidance Gibbon, whose considerable eye for landscape had nevertheless seldom seen the trees for the woods, began to

> 'dwell with pleasure on the shape and colour of the leaves, the various hues of the blossoms, and the successive progress of vegetation. These pleasures are not without cares; and there is a white Acacia just under the windows of my library which in my opinion was too closely pruned last Autumn, and whose recovery is the daily subject of anxiety and conversation!'

It is almost the voice of Cowper.

He had never spent so much time in the open air nor probably walked so much, paying visits on foot through the mountainous streets, wrapped in a fur cloak as the winter advanced. He had not been so well for years, and had an extraordinary appetite. He ate a good breakfast, and was observed to dine and sup copiously with large cups of coffee after each meal. The most exact punctuality was required of guests 'sans quoi l'on était accueilli de fort mauvaise grâce'.[1]

At first a pleasing contrast was recognised between the simple style of Swiss living and the English dinner with its prolonged sitting over the bottles. But Deyverdun was an epicure and under his direction a course of good living was set which was destined to carry away

[1] Bailly de Lalonde, *Le Léman ou voyage pittoresque*, etc., i. 277 *sqq*. Le doyen Bridel's recollections.

himself first in 'a series of apoplectic fits', and to undermine his friend's constitution more insidiously.

In the spring of 1785 the old enemy, believed to have been left behind in a damper climate, descended with unexampled vigour. Gibbon was chained to his library and his great chair. But no work was done for three months. Madeira was exchanged for milk, and even at parties Gibbon sat down to his simple basin, not without enjoying the pathetic distinction. His Swiss friends were anxious and assiduous in their attentions, and Gibbon could not but contrast the old days of lonely indisposition in London, when to get Peter Elmsley to come and see him was as much as he could hope for.

With his ailments and his bulk there became noticeable that protuberance which Gibbon so oddly fancied for years had passed unobserved. It now excited some concern among his new friends. Perhaps they ventured on interfering where his older friends knew it was hopeless.

> 'Between ourselves', Jean Huber wrote to Salomon de Sévery, 'Mathieu has told me that M. Gibbon has undoubtedly a hydrocele which tapping would remove at once for six months, with a chance of its returning, but that he is so much afraid of tapping that it is impossible to speak to him about it. Would it not be possible to persuade him through his valet?'[1]

'Health is the first consideration' was a favourite dictum of Gibbon. But the only part of his body that he treated respectfully was his sight. Far back in his militia days he had consulted a doctor on the first symptoms of what his friends were now noticing with concern, and at some time he ruptured himself. Yet

[1] *M. et Mme de Sévery*, ii. 5. The letter is undated, but Huber died in 1786. Mme de Sévery told the writer Mathieu had the reputation of an eager surgeon.

he would persistently assert, what he hoped rather than knew to be true, that he was in excellent health.

The company of distinguished people was flattering and stimulating: 'yet I am still more content with the humble natives, than with *most* of these *illustrious names*'. Midway came the Neckers who were neighbours for a while at Beaulieu.[1] Necker now fallen from greatness purchased the estate of Coppet. Their daughter was now eighteen, one of the great heiresses of Europe—'wild, vain but good-natured, and with a much larger provision of wit than beauty'. Mme Necker was in failing health and when she left for the south of France in 1784 Gibbon did not expect to see her again.

But a new and very close friendship grew up in these years with Salomon de Charrière de Sévery, and his wife whom Gibbon had known slightly in her girlhood as Catherine de Chandieu. They belonged to that highest circle of the rue du Bourg which Gibbon had scarcely penetrated in his roving days. Now they offered him a welcome union of easy intelligence and unaffected simplicity. The day's work done, Gibbon preferred to unbend over shilling whist or not too vigorous conversation. In arranging their informal entertainments notes would come across from 'Jardinier Georges et Philosophe Gibbon'. They were also known in one of these circles as 'La Pluie' and 'Neptune'.[2] The family still preserve many of these playful effusions. 'M. Gibbon fermera aujourd'hui sa boutique à sept heures et le rest du jour sera tout pour Zaïre' must belong to the last days of intensive labour on his History.

Gibbon was also drawn into a more precious side of local society. The *Samedis* of Mme de Charrière-

[1] A country house then on the outskirts of Lausanne. The house still stands near the Place d'Armes.

[2] *M. et Mme de Sévery,* vol. i.

Bavois shone among these little societies for which the Lausannois had an undying zest. Candidates must present some *jeu d'esprit* in prose or verse and the Abbesse invested them with a white cloak and swore them to fidelity, chastity and poverty! The evenings passed in charades, plays and detached discussions of a kind which, it is said, lets us understand why in the Pays de Vaud the Revolution caused more wine than blood to flow. Gibbon praised these *Samedis*, but young Benjamin Constant when bored with Brunswick compared 'le climat' to them.[1]

Lausanne society was predominantly feminine. Gibbon avowed that the French and Swiss women were superior to the men. There is nothing surprising if his ready susceptibilities were aroused. There were half a dozen ladies, he confides to Lady Sheffield, who would please in one useful or ornamental way and another, and could all their qualities be united in one person, he should pay his addresses and dare to be refused. Maria Holroyd need not have sneered that Mr Gibbon never seemed to consider the possibility of rejection. It may be believed that an Eve would have been ready to fill the one obvious gap in the paradise of La Grotte. But when it came to the point, each Adam seemed anxious that the other should make the necessary sacrifice. One strong attraction there was which lasted for more than a year. Maria like everyone else knew of it. She clearly was unaware of the scandalous accretions to the story.

Jeanne Pauline Polier de Bottens was a daughter of the minister who had examined Gibbon on his return

[1] H. Perrochon, *Une Femme d'esprit Mme de Charrière-Bavois, passim*; for Gibbon and the *Samedis*, *vide* p. 20. For a reading from his works at one of these meetings, *vide* Achard, *Rosalie de Constant*, ii. 60. Mme de Charrière Bavois must not be confused with Mme de Charrière, Boswell's Zélide, who had but a slight acquaintance with the historian, and preferred Geneva to Lausanne as more serious. In one of her tales she writes caustically of 'l'amour à la Gibbon'.

to Protestanism. At that time she was a little child. She had married Benjamin de Crousaz de Mézery and was left a widow in 1775 at the age of twenty-four. Three years later she had eloped with Lord Galloway; but the match had been frustrated by the young nobleman's tutor. This event seems symbolic of a sickly romanticism which pervades her voluminous works. The widow turned her energies to composing novels in the vein of current German sentimentality. Her portrait shows a pretty woman with piercing vivacious eyes, undoubtedly attractive and far more piquante than her books. Gibbon compared her to Lady Elizabeth Foster and she is meant for the ideal mistress-wife in his list.[1]

It was natural and charming that she should take the two literary gentlemen of La Grotte into her confidence about her work. *Caroline de Lichtfeld* is unreadable to-day. But Maria Holroyd thought it the best of its kind far away, and said that it owed much to Gibbon's finishing touches. Gibbon at least was pleased to say that he and Deyverdun had been judges and patrons. Deyverdun seems to have gone further, and by showing the manuscript about, to have forced the lady into publication. The book appeared in 1786 and in the same year the authoress became Mme de Montolieu. Gibbon told the Sheffields of both achievements, adding that he had been in some danger. He did not dissemble that. It is incredible that he had anything else to conceal.

The story that Gibbon knelt to make a declaration to this lady, and being unable to rise unaided had to wait while she rang for a footman, originates from Mme de Genlis. By calling her Mme de Crousaz, Mme de Genlis places her tale before 1786. She was well acquainted with both Gibbon and the lady and may have felt it was time to do them an ill turn, for Gibbon

[1] *Prothero,* ii. 119.

had neglected to answer her letters years ago[1] and Mme de Montolieu had taken her in when she arrived from France in 1793 destitute.[2]

Anyone might judge the value of the story by comparing another told by Madame de Genlis almost in the same breath. When the Abbé Chauvelin made unwelcome love to Mme de Nantouillet, she rang for her footman, who placed the abbé, a small deformed man, on the mantelpiece. Just then opportunely a visitor was announced.[3]

This is altogether too much of a good thing. The untimely lover being put in his place is perhaps a stock theme of eighteenth-century gallantry. The caricature of Voltaire prostrate before Mlle Clairon may well have aided Mme de Genlis' genius. Mme de Montolieu's emphatic denials of any occurrence might not necessarily be convincing.[4] But it would hardly be worth while to labour the impossibility of the story to those who appreciate Gibbon's circumspect character, nor to follow up the variations including a number of different ladies about whom it has often been told. The name of one of them, Lady Elizabeth Foster, an obvious bait for English tatlers, leads us to the origin of this scandal.

Gibbon did in fact kneel to a lady, and tells us the story himself.[5] He naturally gives no hint that he had any difficulty in rising again. He may well have had, for it was in 1792 when he was very fat and infirm. Six years before he had been by his own standards more active.

He knelt to the Duchess of Devonshire—Lady Eliza-

[1] *Misc. Wks.* ii. 304.

[2] Achard, *op. cit.* ii. 161. She also claimed to have helped with *Caroline de Lichtfeld.*

[3] Cousin d'Avalon, *Genlisiana* (Paris, 1820), pp. 132-5.

[4] *Revue Suisse*, 1839, pp. 603 *sqq.*

[5] Gibbons to W. de Sévery, 12 Oct. 1792, translated in *Meredith Read*, ii. p. 497

beth was there—and received the accolade as proxy for his young friend Wilhelm de Sévery whom the duchess was receiving into her own order of chivalry. It was but one of those rather anaemic parlour diversions which seemed to breed so naturally then in the Swiss air and gave people something to chat and laugh about. But the incident strikes at the other story in two ways. It is a very obvious source, and Mme de Genlis no doubt picked it up for her own purpose when she arrived a refugee a year later. Secondly, if the first incident were true it would be very unlikely that Gibbon would care either to remind people of it by a parallel, or to risk another ignominious resurrection.

The only value of the story is to illustrate with what weapons and with what persistency it has been thought profitable to ridicule Gibbon. From Mme de Genlis too comes that other story of Mme du Deffand in her blindness running her hands over Gibbon's protuberant face, and then protesting that a trick in the worst taste had been played on her.

At the end of two years Gibbon could protest that his passion for his wife, or mistress (Fanny Lausanne), was not palled by satiety or possession.

> 'I have seen her in all seasons and humours and though she is not without faults, they are infinitely overbalanced by her good qualities. Her face is not handsome, but her person, and everything about her, has admirable grace and beauty: she is of a very chearful, sociable temper; without much learning she is endowed with taste and good sense; and though not rich, the simplicity of her education makes her a very good economist; she is forbid by her parents to wear any expensive finery; and though her limbs are not much calculated for walking, she has not yet asked me to keep her a Coach.'

From time to time promises were thrown out of a return to England with his completed manuscript:

> 'But let no man who builds a house, or writes a book, presume

> to say when he will have finished. When he imagines that he is drawing near to his journey's end, Alps rise on Alps and he continually finds something to add and something to correct.'

The autumn of 1786 had been named, and then June or July of the next year, as the date of his return. But in the beginning of 1787 the historian realised that unless he doubled his diligence another year would pass away. So he undertook 'a bold and meritorious resolution'. The evenings were added to the mornings' work, cards and society were renounced. He refused 'the most agreeable evenings' or perhaps appeared only at a late supper, doubtless to be greeted with enthusiasm as a martyr to learning.

On 2nd June 1787 he tells Lord Sheffield, 'My great building is, as it were, compleated, and some slight ornaments, the painting and glazing of the last finished rooms, may be dispatched without inconvenience in the autumnal residence of Sheffield Place', and on the 21st July he writes to say that his departure has been postponed—'the march of heavy bodies, such as armies and historians, can seldom be foreseen or fixed to a precise day'—but he promised to be in London on or before the 9th of August.

He does not give an inkling of the emotion felt on a night of the previous month, an emotion which did not cease to vibrate within himself until it reached expression in what must be one of those passages of pure poetry; for anyone who can read it even now without a thrill is to be gravely pitied.

The famous summer-house has long since disappeared along with the acacias from which Byron plucked a memento. Sightseers took the original away bit by bit and even the restored parts went as well. It was allowed to fall into decay, and at last even doubt arose about the exact site, so that it has been confused with a part of La Grotte itself that opened on the terrace. But it lay, as seems certain, some hundred yards from the house near the rue du Petit Chêne, and anyone who cares to look out on the unchanging lake and mountains from a small platform on that side of the post-office, can have the satisfaction of knowing he is not far from the spot.

'I have presumed to mark the moment of conception,' Gibbon wrote in his Autobiography; 'I shall now commemorate the hour of my final deliverance. It was on the day, or rather the night, of the 27th of June 1787, between the hours of eleven and twelve, that I wrote the last lines of the last page in a summer-house in my garden. After laying down my pen I took several turns in a *berceau* or covered walk of Acacias, which commands a prospect of the country, the lake and the mountains. The air was temperate, the sky was serene, the silver orb of the moon was reflected from the waters, and all Nature was silent. I will not dissemble the first emotions of joy on the recovery of my freedom, and perhaps the establishment of my fame. But my pride was soon humbled, and a sober melancholy was spread over my mind by the idea that I had taken my everlasting leave of an old and agreeable companion, and that, whatsoever might be the future date of my history, the life of the historian must be short and precarious.'

* * *

'Adelphi Hotel, *August the 8th*, 1787

'Intelligence extraordinary.—This day (August the 7th) the celebrated E. G. arrived in the Adelphi with a numerous retinue (one Servant). We hear that he has brought over from Lausanne the remainder of his history for immediate publication.' [1]

[1] Gibbon to Lord Sheffield, *Prothero*, ii. p. 157.

Chapter 23

THE HOUR OF TRIUMPH

1787–1788

THE business of the final touches and the proofs consumed the autumn, partly in lodgings in London, partly at Sheffield Place. Publication was at first expected in April and then fixed for the 8th May 1788, the historian's birthday. An agreement of 16th August with Andrew Strahan and Thomas Cadell secured to Gibbon £4000 for his three volumes; £500 to be paid on executing the deed, £1750 within four months of publication and £1750 within twelve months.

Pleased with his friend's company, Lord Sheffield perhaps accepted his own valuation of his health. Triumph was near and spirits were high. Mrs Gibbon was informed that the historian had never seemed so well nor ate so well, though certainly he was more enormous. A detailed report to Deyverdun is more ominous.

'He amuses himself with the notion that he is not grown fatter, but he appears to me greatly increased in bulk. I was forced to threaten him yesterday that if he would not do as he was bid, we should be obliged to lay him on his back that like the turtle he may not be able to get up. Considering the little exercise he uses, I think he indulges too much with oysters, milk etc. at supper. Two breakfasts are never omitted and at dinner he seems to me to devour much more than he used to do. But he is most provoking on the subject of future residence. He has no view but towards Switzerland.' [1]

[1] Letter of 4th November 1787, from the MS. in the possession of Mme Grenier-Brandebourg.

In November Gibbon returned to London, attended one meeting of the Club, now relieved for ever of Johnson's presence,[1] visited Sir Joshua and was proposed by him to be Professor of Antient History in the Royal Academy in the place of the late Dr. Franklin.[2]

He was preparing to visit Bath, when the gout which he believed to have drowned in Switzerland at the bottom of a cup of milk, descended on him and kept him prisoner in London till December. Christmas was spent at Bath with Sheffield and his elder daughter to support him. Gibbon, who was probably still far from well, appears to have been bored, and the trio planned a premature escape. Early in January they returned to Sheffield Place, where Gibbon could recuperate at his ease and await his final triumph.

During these months Gibbon appears through a fresh pair of eyes. After not a little coaxing he had persuaded M. and Mme de Sévery to allow their son to follow him to England. He was to learn English there and see something of society, and it would not come amiss that someone from Lausanne should be there to see the grand Gibbon introducing his three youngest children to the world. Wilhelm landed at Dover in October and was sent first to a family at Uckfield to learn English in preparation for accompanying his friend into the world. In his letters home and in his brief diary we have the most closely knit record of Gibbon's day-to-day contacts in society. He is tantalisingly silent on

[1] Possibly that of 26th November at which Reynolds showed Boswell a letter he had written to the Prince of Wales to get Dr. Warton appointed to St. Cross. It was a tricky business, and Boswell considered Reynolds had done it 'exquisitely well'. Reynolds had shown the letter only to Lord Aylesbury and Gibbon. *Boswell Papers*, xvii. 57.

[2] F. W. Hilles, *Letters of Reynolds*, p. 181, letter to Bennet Langton, 23rd November 1787. Gibbon's letter of acceptance preserved at the Royal Academy is dated 4th April 1788. The professors of history and literature gave no lectures. Gibbon was much annoyed later to find that he had to pay a fee of 25 guineas for this empty honour.

some points, and yet the picture gains from being unstudied and not a shadowing of the great historian.[1]

At Sheffield Place we see Gibbon spending two hours in talk with Lady Sheffield every morning and in the evenings making Wilhelm and the girls read a French play, *Zaïre* once more, that familiar old drama at which Suzanne Curchod had been caught out pretending to cry. When Gibbon was away he cautioned Sheffield about letting Wilhelm get into bad company at Lewes —'a set of drunken dragoons'[2]—and when he returned Wilhelm notes 'une charmante journée', and thereafter mentions long conversations with him.

In March it was time to move on London. Gibbon and the Sheffields were at Downing Street, the young man in rooms. The whole family went to Drury Lane to see Mrs Siddons and Kemble in *Jane Shore*. They all floated down to Woolwich and back again on the tide to see the *Prince*, 98 guns, which was to be launched in June. Gibbon took his charge with him on visits to North and Loughborough, to Sir Joshua's studio where Sheffield was sitting, and to dine with him, to evenings with the Miss Berrys, to theatricals at the Duchess of Richmond's, to hear Texier, to the Academy Banquet, with Lord Ossory to see some fireworks, to a review at Wimbledon and to dine with Sir Willoughby Aston, an old militiaman. Wilhelm was fairly launched in London society and no doubt Gibbon was present at many of the parties and balls.

Sheffield gave dinners, at one of which were Fox, Burke and North; at another, in honour of Calonne the fallen French Director-General of Finance, were North and his son, Stormont, Loughborough and others.

[1] *M. et Mme de Sévery*, ii. 73-97, for his letters. M. de Sévery very kindly allowed me to make use of the diary, which remains unpublished.

[2] Nevertheless de Sévery went to the ball at Lewes and supped with Sir John Shelley.

Dinner began at six and they sat till eleven; an ordeal for a young man however august the company. Yet it is no mean compliment that this youth testifies to Gibbon's success and spirits as he dined out night after night. 'Il a le talent de se renouveler, il est toujours amusant.' Once at least he was rewarded with some unexpected comedy; it was at a dinner at which the Chevalier d'Eon was present, all the other guests being men. The Chevalier who managed his fan like a sword persisted in addressing the historian as Gibson.

The story of Gibbon's encounter with one of the royal dukes rests on good contemporary authority, though there is more than one version. Perhaps the best is as follows. Gibbon was at one of the Duchess of Cumberland's evenings—Wilhelm certainly mentions playing pharaon there—when someone told the Duke that he ought to say a word to the great historian. 'So,' said he, greeting his guest, 'I suppose you are at the old trade again—scribble scribble scribble!' Nothing is recorded of Gibbon's round-eyed astonishment. He could hardly complain. He had said some hard things of royalty.[1]

Some of Wilhelm's sightseeing was entrusted to other friends. But Gibbon took him to see the pictures and the Queen's Library at Buckingham Palace—fifty thousand volumes. 'You used to think I had many books,' said Gibbon, 'but you see the King has far more.' 'Yes,' replied the excellent young man. 'He has

[1] Miss Sayer to Mme Huber in 1789, *Auckland Correspondence*, ii. 280-81. The Rev. Henry Best in his *Personal and Literary Memorials*, 1829, p. 68, says it was Gloucester. He says Gibbon had presented his first volume to him. This looks like a confusion with the presentation to the Duke of York in 1763. The clergyman goes on with a very spiteful commentary on the scene in which he ingenuously lauds the Duke for his behaviour. There is another version. Lady Katherine North attributes the remark to the King, who, instead of his stock question 'Do you walk, do you get out?' (once uttered to Burke who had just resigned office!), said to the historian 'How do you do, Mr. Gibbon? Always scribble scribble, I suppose.' The authority at any rate is better than Best's. *The Glenbervie Journals*, p. 195.

more than you but has he read them?' One almost hears the box rapped with satisfaction.

Gibbon also came under Boswell's eye once more.[1] He attended seven more meetings of the Club during this year and met the old enemy at least twice at Sir Joshua's. At the meeting of 22nd January Boswell notes that Fox attended after an absence of some years. Others present besides Gibbon were Bunbury, Malone, Steevens, Warton and Langton. On the 19th February Boswell presided over Gibbon, Malone, Steevens, Banks, Lucan and Macartney, and later Windham. But he went home about ten sober and well.

On Friday 11th April Boswell dined at Sir Joshua's with Monboddo, Malone, Gibbon, Langton and others. Talk ran on the old dispute about ancients and moderns. Brocklesby said that in a thousand years Burke would be more admired than Demosthenes. Malone and Boswell tried to draw Monboddo, who was 'wildly dogmatical' on the side of the ancients. Boswell argued that *a priori* all things that did not involve a contradiction were equally probable; therefore belief in them must depend on evidence. He was trying to draw Gibbon, who, however, sat snug and would not venture.

Three days later Boswell was called in at the last moment to take Sheridan's place and met Burke and his wife, Dr. Parr, Gibbon, Sir Gilbert Elliot, Windham and others. The great Dr. Parr announced that he was about to write on Johnson and had found forty points of similarity between him and Plutarch. Upon Burke's saying Plutarch was the only ancient writer who could be read with pleasure in a translation, Gibbon suggested Melmoth's version of Pliny's Letters, which he considered better than the original. Burke agreed. After dinner the Burkes with Windham, Jack Lee, Gibbon and Boswell went upstairs to tea with Miss Reynolds.

[1] *Boswell Papers*, xvii. 67, 68, 92 and 94-5.

Gibbon made Burke give the story of the Coalition's fall. Boswell felt that he was laughing, although outwardly serious.

Along with all these social successes and the prestige enjoyed at the Club comes a brief but memorable acquaintance. One of the greatest of all scholars had championed one of his conclusions, and in the *Letters to Archdeacon Travis* Gibbon himself recognised 'the most acute and accurate piece of criticism since the days of Bentley'. Porson was asked to call, and we have from his memory very likely the most exact report of Gibbon's spoken words:

> 'Mr. Porson,' he said, 'I feel truly indebted to you for the Letters to Travis, though I must think that occasionally, while praising me, you have mingled a little acid with the sweet. If ever you should take the trouble to read my History over again, I should be much obliged and honoured by any remarks on it which might suggest themselves to you.'

Porson, it is said, was much flattered with this interview and loved to talk of it. He thought *The Decline and Fall* beyond all comparison the greatest literary production of the eighteenth century and was in the habit of repeating long passages from it. This is worth remembering beside his more widely quoted criticisms of Gibbon's style and bias.[1]

But what of the day of days when the double festival, the publication and the author's fifty-first birthday, 'was celebrated by a chearful litterary dinner at Cadell's house and I seemed to blush while they read an elegant compliment from Mr. Hayley'? Alas! a young man whose mind ran on dancing at Lady Mary Duncan's, or trips to Greenwich with Lady Clarges, puts the matter in a different perspective.

> 'Jeudy 8. Écrit tout le matin, rangé mes affaires dans ma chambre, puis allé diné chez le libraire de Mr. Gibbon, Mr.

[1] *Porsoniana* in *Rogers's Table Talk*, p. 324.

Cadell, puis allé de là à l'opéra dans la loge de Mad. Boone, revenu à la maison.'

The grand climax was over. A magnificent epilogue remained; that 13th June when four hundred people were waiting outside Westminster Hall at seven in the morning, and tickets were changing hands at fifty guineas for a chance of hearing Sheridan on the Begums of Oudh. He spoke from midday till nearly five, and remarked in the course of his speech, 'nothing equal in criminality was to be traced either in ancient or modern history, in the correct periods of Tacitus or the luminous page of Gibbon'. Thus saluted in his own presence and in the presence of the flower of the nation, Gibbon may well have been vain, and Sheridan may have tried to tone him down afterwards by saying he meant 'voluminous'. But there is no real doubt that Sheridan did pay this tremendous compliment.[1]

After that there was little to do but pack and go. A new carriage had been bought, and sets of Wedgwood chosen—busts of Voltaire and Rousseau were to be got if they matched!—and de Sévery's dogs were sent on in a basket.[2] Gibbon had dined with Warren Hastings and the Prince of Wales, 'both by special desire'. The last days were spent at Sheffield Place, where many people were invited to see the historian. Sir Joseph Banks and his family spent several days there with him, and Nichols the anecdotist.

The Sheffields and others had to acknowledge the inevitable. Their friend was now firmly wedded to 'Fanny Lausanne'. He was as attached as a child to his garden and summer-house and had brought over a plan to show his friends. He talked of *his* lake and *his* view and his compatriots the Swiss. In a letter to Mme de Sévery written in the height of his success he tells her

[1] Fraser Rae, *Sheridan*, ii. 69.

[2] Embarqué mes chers chiens le soir dans leur panier. W. de Sévery's MS.

EDWARD GIBBON

From a Wedgwood Plaque

he is always thinking of their dinners in the *plaque*,[1] their games of *tricet* in the green salon and his covered walk of acacias. Someone asked him how many people there were in Lausanne. He said there might be nine or ten thousand; but the essential thing was a society of two hundred persons as good as one could desire. On the eve of their journey Wilhelm noted that he was buoyed up 'par l'idée de revoir son *home* car c'est ainsi qu'il l'appelle toujours'.

Poor Mrs Gibbon, growing stouter and feebler, alone was unreconciled. She snatched at an idle rumour which if true might lead to a breaking of the chain.

> 'I will not say another word about the leave you seem to be taking of this Island but that wherever you go and wherever you are, my dearest and kindest wishes will ever attend you.... A Lady friend of mine who attended the trials tells me Mr. Sheridan made you blush. She also tells me you are going to be married for she says your curiosity is so great that having pursued it thro' every state of human knowledge you have nothing else to be instructed in, and she is sure the leisure you promise yourself will be employed in seeking and finding the Land of Matrimony and I wish she was your partner....'[2]

How curiously gossips will transpose a man's mind and impulse into their own key.

On the 19th July Gibbon and de Sévery, with Lord and Lady Sheffield, went to stay with Lord North at Tunbridge Wells. The travellers left for Dover on the 21st, taking leave 'avec beaucoup de peine'. Lausanne was reached on the 30th and Gibbon announced, 'I am as well arranged, as if I had never stirred from this place'. But Deyverdun's health was obviously failing.

[1] A room heated from the back of the stove of an adjoining room.

[2] Brit. Mus. 11907, dd. 25 (2). Letter of July 1788 in answer to Gibbon's of 29th June and replied to by him 18th July; *Prothero*, ii. 174 and 175.

Chapter 24

THE LUMINOUS HISTORIAN

By universal assent *The Decline and Fall* had set Gibbon 'at the very head of the whole literary tribe at present existing in Europe'.[1] Robertson voluntarily renounced any claims to primacy. 'Before you began your historic career, I used to pride myself in being at least the most industrious historian of the age; but now, alas! I can pretend no longer even to that praise.'

The deliberate ambition of Gibbon's youth had been surpassed. He had once looked up to Robertson and Hume as almost inaccessible peaks. Now he stood above them and had been acclaimed by both. There was certainly some excuse for being vain.

It was said that Gibbon came to believe at last that he was the Roman Empire. The jest veils a true compliment, so completely was he immersed, yet not lost, in his subject. Moreover, and it is the triumph of imaginative art, he carries his reader into it with him. It may not be easy to fix the sources of such an impression. It depends in part on simple devices. Gibbon always speaks from Rome or Constantinople and defines 'beyond the Alps, the Rhine, the Danube, etc.', accordingly.[2] He makes no exceptions. The British in India are described as 'a company of Christian merchants

[1] For Adam Smith's letter see *Misc. Wks.* ii. 429, and Robertson's, *ibid.* ii. 416 and 424.
[2] Postscript to the preface of the fourth volume.

of a remote island in the Northern ocean'.[1] The reader insensibly surrenders; he surrenders still more to the pervading dream of antiquity in which the author moves.

'Our early studies', Gibbon says, 'allow us to sympathise in the feelings of a Roman.'[2] The most sceptical of men has no doubt either of the supremacy of the classical authors or of his own complete intimacy with their spirit. It was no sentimental enthusiasm.

Nor could it have been merely vanity that sent him with undefeated energy down what Bywater, I think, calls the dusty corridors of learning. They were very dusty and encumbered in those days. This knowledge he reconstructed in a solid world of space and time, in which he moves to and fro at his ease, but always with a sense of inexorable progress towards its end. By numberless touches the whole story seems to be his intimate concern. He tells us the limits of his personal acquaintance with the Bishop of Hippo. He takes a courteous leave of Ammianus, 'the last subject of Rome who composed a profane history in the Latin language', and warns us that henceforward he must advance amid fragmentary and prejudiced authorities, 'with doubtful and timorous steps'.[3]

The calamities of human affairs may recur, though not always with a Tacitus to depict them. A feature indeed of such times is the inconceivability of a Tacitus existing in them at all. The peaks of civilisation, on the other hand, are those ages in which political freedom, all the manly virtues and literary excellence occur together as though with some essential connexion. The periods which Gibbon chose had in the main for him only the negative value of contrast with that ideal. Whenever he pauses to survey the road he has traversed, there is

[1] *The Decline and Fall*, c. lxv. (8-66). [2] *Op. cit.* c. lxxi. n. 3.
[3] *Op. cit.* c. xxvi. (3-346) and nn. 91 and 114.

only one method of valuation. After the growth of superstition in the fourth century has called forth all his wit, he adds:

> 'If it be possible to measure the interval between the philosophic writings of Cicero and the sacred legend of Theodoret, between the character of Cato and that of Simeon, we may appreciate the memorable revolution which was accomplished in the Roman empire within a period of five hundred years.' [1]

By pinning his faith to one standard, Gibbon becomes at times as much involved in the consequent notion of degeneration as some modern optimists have been in the idea of progress. He sometimes forgets that brave men have lived since Agamemnon, and his picture of the decay of military virtue in the provinces does not explain the success of the barbarians. Sometimes he tries to have it both ways, as when he accuses Christianity of inculcating pusillanimity, and at the same time never fails to record a fighting bishop. Nevertheless his claim to have recounted the triumph of barbarism and religion is not to be denied. He showed that they were inseparably connected with each other and with the passing of the ancient world, and he opened a debate which shows no sign of terminating.

A disregard for Gibbon's values has led to an unfair severity towards some parts of his work. It is true that he treats the Byzantine period summarily and at times unjustly. Nevertheless it is improbable that he would find any reason to revise his judgment or alter his proportions. In his view, the decline of Constantinople was almost coeval with her foundation.[2] He was well aware of the city's function as 'the most important barrier of the West'.[3] He does not dispute 'the long prosperity of the Byzantine Caesars',[4] and in his 53rd chapter he gives an admirable sketch of Byzantine civilisation, especially in

[1] *The Decline and Fall,* c. xxxvii. (4-322).
[2] *Op. cit.* c. lxiv. (8-28).
[3] *Op. cit.* c. lviii. (7-185).
[4] *Op. cit.* c. lxviii. (8-168).

its contrast with the contemporary condition of Europe. It was a stagnant pool, however. The value of an age lies with Gibbon in what it bequeaths, and the greatest legacy must be literature, art and science. But the later historians who have done such immensely important work on the Byzantine world do not pretend to induce us to read the literature. Even the modern interest in Byzantine art is lukewarm. We gaze at the mosaics, but 'there is no speculation in those eyes'.

But the Roman Empire in its turn is Gibbon. Everything is subdued to his thought and style. Even the vicious Tertullian appears in an English dress indistinguishable from his introducer's. Walpole perceived this truth when he compared the homogeneous texture of *The Decline and Fall* to the smoothness of a Flemish picture. Later critics have been more concerned to complain that Gibbon reduces all ages and varieties of humanity to a periwigged uniformity. I do not know whether this criticism is improved or not by the reflexion that Hellenism in our day has been made to run about in house colours and shorts.

Gibbon was in fact well aware of the predicament which no historian can escape:

> 'Tout homme de génie qui écrit l'histoire y répand, peut-être sans s'en apercevoir, le caractère de son esprit. À travers leur variété infinie de passion et situation, ses personnages semblent n'avoir qu'une façon de penser et de sentir; et cette façon est celle de l'auteur.' [1]

The historian who is conscious of this inevitability will be the more guarded against earning a place among those many historians who put us in mind of the admirable saying of the great Condé to Cardinal de Retz: 'Ces coquins nous font parler et agir comme ils auroient fait eux-mêmes à notre place'.[2]

[1] 'La Monarchie des Mèdes', *Misc. Wks.* iii. 126.
[2] *The Decline and Fall*, c. xiv. n. 4 (2-107).

But opposite to the whirlpools of imaginative reconstruction stands the barren wall of self-stultification which arises out of too much knowledge. The more minutely the historian of our day examines the past, the more aware must he be of other worlds than his own; and the more diffident he becomes of committing himself. Froude has eloquently described the impassable barrier which stands between us and even our fellow countrymen of the Middle Ages.

Gibbon avoided these dangers by keeping to fundamental probabilities. He believed in the stability of human nature and in 'the sure operation of its fierce and unrestrained passions'.[1] Such guides could not retrieve a story whose records were lost, but they could destroy one the evidence of which was inconsistent with themselves. Of the eulogistic records of a Persian dynasty he writes with a force that anticipates so much of the burden of *The Decline and Fall*:

> 'Je pense bien que ces rois ne sont pas uniquement occupés des lois, des sciences, et des beaux-arts . . . si cette histoire s'étoit conservée, on y liroit comme dans toutes les autres, les vices des grands, et les malheurs des peuples; on y verroit ce triomphe perpétuel de la violence et de l'intrigue sur la justice, qu'elles outragent en la violant, et qu'elles outragent cent fois davantage en se servant impunément de son nom sacré.' [2]

This broad psychology is part of the strength of Gibbon's work. If it is unadventurous it is unassailable. It has the merit of design. Gibbon assuredly was not incapable of the fine analysis of character. His Journal proves as much; but in the long journey of his History he could not linger over subtleties of that kind.

Those who know the old engravings of dramatic scenes and of actors (the upturned eyes and streaming hair) will be insensibly reminded of them as they read

[1] *The Decline and Fall*, c. xxvi. (3-320) and c. x. (1-373).
[2] 'La Monarchie des Mèdes', *Misc. Wks.* iii. 85.

The Decline and Fall. The characters rush on and off stage tumultuously. They intercede and upbraid, they tremble, they blush—even Baronius blushes in a footnote—and they weep. Akin to this are the epithets which Gibbon uses so summarily to praise or to damn. One after another the personages are artful, credulous, intrepid, timorous, equitable or haughty, etc. Here it is the epic rather than the dramatic manner, and Gibbon has received it from Homer through Pope. These methods have their weaknesses as well as their merits. A great amount of learning and thought may be staked on a single word. There can be no reservations or redress, and the vivacity of the narrative may sometimes appear specious.

But history was in Gibbon's view essentially personal and dramatic. He believed in the man and the hour. When in the flight from Mecca to Medina, Mahomet encountered the emissaries of the Koreish, 'the lance of an Arab might have changed the history of the world'.[1] 'In human life the most important scenes will depend on the character of a single actor',[2] and 'an acrimonious humour falling on a single fibre of one man may prevent or suspend the misery of nations'.[3] This is rather highflown, but it bears a lesson for an age which deals overmuch in impersonal inevitabilities, and has even seen an attempt to reduce history to a graph. It is an outlook which will always win human attention.

'Some tincture of philosophy and criticism', Gibbon remarks, is demanded of a work that is to instruct or amuse an enlightened age.[4] It is no contradiction of this to say that another and still greater element of durability in *The Decline and Fall* is the author's

[1] *The Decline and Fall*, c. l. (6-242).
[2] *Op. cit.* c. lxv. (8-72).
[3] *Op. cit.* c. lxiv. (8-32).
[4] *Op. cit.* c. lxiv. n. 41. It is apropos of Johnson's choice of one Knolles as 'the first of historians'.

abstention from theorising. He has nothing to prove. The detachment which was the politician's weakness is the historian's strength. With the exception of the 15th and 16th chapters his analysis of causes is perfunctory. When at the close of his third volume he has brought the Western Empire to an end, he feels obliged to reflect upon the causes. But he is content to remark that the extraordinary thing is not that the Roman Empire fell, but that it stood for so long. The last three volumes, moving so surely over a vast scene, propound and answer no questions explicitly, but their power of suggestion is inexhaustible. The structure of the narrative stands by itself. An architect builds a house; he is not called upon to say why it does not fall down. Gibbon's criticism is absorbed in his creation, which is a picture of human destiny.

This destiny is no external force. 'Man has much more to fear from the passions of his fellow creatures than from the convulsion of the elements.'[1] In this wider generalisation religion falls into its own place. There are many other superstitions and impostures to be denounced; the sentimentalities that cling about the almost divine quality of kings, the follies of militarism, and the mystifications of the law; a very personal grievance here. No ruse of modern dictatorship, no political stratagem is absent from his pages. The History is charged with reflexions that anticipate the most progressive thought of our own day and earn the judgment of 'the ultimate modern morality of his work'.[2] It is modern because, like *The Decline and Fall* itself, it is firmly planted on this earth and does not look beyond the life on it.

But Gibbon was neither a propagandist nor a preacher. Hence we still read him.

[1] *The Decline and Fall*, c. xxvi. (3-294).
[2] E. Blunden, *Edward Gibbon and his Age*, p. 33.

'History which undertakes to record the transactions of the past, for the instruction of future ages, would ill deserve that honourable office, if it condescended to plead the cause of tyrants, or to justify the maxims of persecution.'

But its lessons are negative. It does not propose what is to be done. The final conclusion seems to be that though individuals may learn from experience, 'it is seldom profitable to the successive generations of mankind'.[1]

With this reflexion, he accepted, as most of his advanced contemporaries did, the existing order of society. He chastises the vices of the great. But his banners were not likely to be found on the side of the people. Still 'all that is human must retrograde if it do not advance'.[2] On the whole he felt it to be advancing in his day. Reason was keeping her head up. The competition of the European nations was productive of good. Even war was conducted in a gentlemanly fashion. The barbarian invasions could not recur. Gibbon did not reckon with the barbarism that might arise from within. He had witnessed a surprising increase in England's prosperity, and reflects that luxury never hurt a vigorous people. In one at least of his political judgments he had been triumphantly right; he prophesied that the loss of the American colonies would not ruin England's trade. There is much to smile at here. But even we have our optimisms.

As early as 1763 Gibbon had set his ideal of a historical writer in an appreciation of Herodotus. He must be 'un observateur dont le coup d'œil pénétrant et juste ne voit que les grands objets, qui les voit de sang-froid et qui les peint avec chaleur'.[3] One of the best of Gibbon's modern critics sums up his achievement in very similar words: 'His picture is drawn with

[1] *The Decline and Fall*, c. xli. (5-123). [2] *Op. cit.* c. lxxi. (8-269).
[3] 'La Monarchie des Mèdes', *Misc. Wks.* iii. 102.

the integrity of a scholar, and coloured with the intention of an artist'.[1]

The extent and accuracy of Gibbon's scholarship has been weighed and accepted by the few men who have been his equals or even superiors. The merits and defects of his style have been similarly canvassed. Here the verdict is more subjective. It has been increasingly favourable in recent years with the passing of the grand manner from contemporary letters. We admire the bow which we do not presume to draw, and which is no longer made contemptible in the hands of vulgar suitors. Mr Young has laid a sure finger on the oratorical quality of Gibbon's prose. He achieved here what he never dared to attempt in Parliament, and seems often at the end of a period to be waiting for the applause which should break out. A complementary criticism may not be out of place, if the notes are said to be Gibbon's table talk. Here he is conversing familiarly in the library and filling in the miscellaneous information which the dignity of Clio's House would not allow.

For Gibbon's style was based on the Latin orators; but both the architecture and the decoration of his History owe much to Herodotus. Like Herodotus he chose a great and moving theme of human destiny, and like him too moved slowly towards his goal, marshalling a still more complex army of events with deliberation, and surveying at the same time the whole field of human knowledge on his way, and not disdaining to entertain his audience in many a learned and witty by-way. Like Herodotus also, he was under Homer's spell. Homer, after Voltaire, and with the exception of the immediate authorities, is more often referred to than any other writer. But Homer's real influence was exerted not only in his early reading, in the close study recorded in the Journal, but also in that preoccupation with details of

[1] G. M. Young, *Gibbon*, p. 84.

epic construction, common to Gibbon and his contemporaries, which are to us of so remote interest.

Gibbon's art never attains to that pitch where it conceals itself. Every movement is conscious and he has been accused more than once of displaying himself rather than his subject. Yet 'Julian discovers his own character with that naïveté, that unconscious simplicity, which always constitutes genuine humour'.[1] So does Gibbon. This trait has the singular effect of putting the several parts of a variegated world in their place. They are valued impartially in the scale of the historian's favourite epithets. Le Nain de Tillemont's accuracy is 'incomparable'; what of the cherry trees which 'produce our incomparable marasquin'?[2] One of the most musical sentences of the whole work is devoted to a fish, a very important fish:

> 'The endless exportation of salt fish and caviar is annually renewed by the enormous sturgeons that are caught at the mouth of the Don or Tanais, in their last station of the rich mud and shallow water of the Maeotis.'

Moreover, they earn a note on their length, weight and yield, ending with an irrelevant reminder that the Bosphorus had supplied the Athenians with corn in the time of Demosthenes.[3] This is the very spirit of Herodotus and the essence of Gibbon's leisurely and irresponsible procedure. There is something very salutary about this tribute to a fish. Julian himself could receive no more.

Attempts are made to place Gibbon in honourable retirement. If he is read, it is as literature, or as a typical figure of the eighteenth century. Some ulterior motives are to be suspected in this kind of criticism. Its weakness should be apparent. To be a typical man of the age

[1] *The Decline and Fall*, c. xxiii. n. iii. [2] *Op. cit.* c. lx. n. 46.
[3] *Op. cit.* c. lxiii. (7-407) and n. 46.

is a poor guarantee of being read, and those whose literary qualities predominate over their subject generally do cease to be read except by the dilettante.

It may be enough to ask such critics if they think that Gibbon would still be read if he had not written with the substantial accuracy with which he did. Amid the enormous accessions of knowledge and the widening of the curiosity about the past which goes with the expansion of modern life, Gibbon's bridge between the ancient and modern worlds remains remarkably safe. Moreover, the journey is unfailingly entertaining. No more masterly skill in holding the reader's attention over so vast a theme has ever been known. At the heart of it is the informing spirit of the creator with his conception of the unity of history, his suggestive judgments and unsleeping scepticism, and his truly humane outlook. This expresses itself partly in his roguish wit and his unflagging gusto, no less also in his sober recognition that mankind goes its way never much better and never much worse. What changes there may be, must be evolved by ourselves. There is no other help.

Nothing is extolled more often by Gibbon than freedom. But freedom, either political or personal, is beset with equivocations. Nevertheless his most insistent lesson—for in the end there is a lesson—is that the freedom of the mind is 'the source of every generous and rational sentiment'. His still timely warning is that it may be destroyed by 'habits of credulity and submission'.[1]

[1] *The Decline and Fall,* c. xxxvii. (4-313).

Chapter 25

'GIBBON CASTLE'

1788–1793

THE autumnal felicity which should now have been Gibbon's, began well with a visit from Fox. From 'the bloody tumult of the Westminster Election' he arrived at the Lyon d'Or with Mrs Armitstead. There is a lyrical quality in Gibbon's description of a memorable day:

> 'I have eat and drank and conversed and sat up all night with Fox in England; but it never has happened, perhaps it never can happen again that I should enjoy him as I did that day, alone, for his fair Companion was a cypher, from ten in the morning till ten at night.'

In the wide range of that long talk Fox did not forget to flatter his host on his book, to take an interest in his garden, and to let him think he envied him. His reward was to watch Gibbon pacing up and down the room as he talked, with many complacent glances at the Reynolds portrait over the chimney-piece.[1] The portrait was soon to be sent away in exchange for Sheffield's by the same artist. Sheffield had coveted it before; but according to Gibbon, Deyverdun had objected to its removal.

But Deyverdun was fast declining beyond such cares. The one blot on this wonderful day was his inability to be of the party. Strokes of thundering apoplexy had

1 *Rogers's Table Talk*, p. 78.

failed to cure him of his indulgent habits, and early in 1789 the doctors said he could not live. As a final resource he was sent 'to the mineral waters at Aix in Savoy'. An express announced that he had died there on the 4th July, and the lawyers came to seal up his apartment. 'Je croyais être préparé', Gibbon wrote to Madame de Sévery, 'mais ce coup m'a bouleversé. . . . Après trente-trois ans . . . Adieu.'

Deyverdun, foreseeing his end, had taken precautions in his will to secure the use of La Grotte for his friend. Gibbon had the option of buying the property at an advantageous price or of renting it for life. But the Swiss laws introduced an unexpected risk, since the heirs-at-law also had the option of buying it and at the same advantageous price. There were other difficulties on the side of renting. But after some anxious pondering and negotiation with M. de Montagny, the ultimate legatee, an agreement was made by which Gibbon was left in possession for life, with a free hand to improve the property as he liked.

Grief for Deyverdun was no transitory emotion. Every walk and bench in the garden reminded Gibbon of conversations never to be resumed, and he especially felt the return of an evening to the lonely house. For some months he was in a depression of spirits which alarmed Sheffield. Other friends were at hand. Whereas in his first period at La Grotte Gibbon had only slept one night from home, he now began to pay regular visits to the pleasant country houses of his friends, de Sévery at Mex and Rolle, and later to the Neckers at Coppet. The vintage and he became welcome concomitants.

But how about filling the empty rooms at La Grotte? Gibbon could not venture on the suggestion of inviting an agreeable couple to share it. He turned to his own family. His cousin Charlotte Porten had lately lost her father, Sir Stanier, and the family were poor. Should he

Brandoin del. *Lith de C. Constans*

EDWARD GIBBON

From a contemporary drawing

adopt this charming child and mould her like wax to Swiss habits, that is to say, his own? He threw out hints; but the widow would not part with her child. Marriage once more? A remedy for loneliness that might cure too much. Mme Necker, perhaps a little jealous, certainly very wise, counselled him to refrain. 'Vous êtes marié avec la gloire', she said. But her friend had already prudently dismissed the idea. 'I am not in love with any of the Hyaenas,' he told Sheffield, 'though there are some who keep their claws tolerably well pared.'

It was better to rule alone over 'Gibbon Castle'. His servants are said to have adored him, and he was never out of humour with them even in his frequent illnesses.[1] But the greatest exactitude was required. A hairdresser was dismissed for being after seven in the morning, and his successor, who arrived some minutes beforehand, met the same fate.[2] The house was arranged with taste and without ostentation. Gibbon had the art of sending away his visitors pleased with themselves, and never showed *ennui*. His enemies never upset him, and he forgot any slights *d'une manière si douce et si facile* that one doubted if he had noticed them.[3] For intimate company he relied more and more on the family de Sévery. Mme de Sévery helped him with the elegant entertainments which he gave, often on a large scale. He was spending freely on them and on improvements to the house.

For a turn at last had come in his fortunes, though Sheffield still had cause to remark 'there seems to be something supernatural attending all your worldly concerns'. Buriton had at last been sold in 1789, but only for £16,000. Yet the completion dragged on for two

[1] The Chanoinesse de Polier's obituary notice in *Journal Littéraire de Lausanne*, 1794.
[2] *Briefe von Friedrich Matthisson* (Zürich, 1792), pp. 43-8.
[3] Mlle de Polier, *op. cit.*

years while the lawyers haggled over the title. A painful resemblance to the old Lenborough business. Finally, after nearly twenty years of unflagging devotion, Lord Sheffield had delivered his friend from the burdens of a landed gentleman. Before this achievement Aunt Hester had died. A legacy from her of £1000 was cut down in a codicil to £100. Gibbon pretended to no grievance; he had neglected his aunt when last in England. But an estate at Newhaven now devolved to him bringing in some £225 a year. This Gibbon very naturally wished to sell. An essential deed, once more, was missing, and once more Sheffield came to the rescue, this time as the purchaser under arrangements which nearly doubled the income. It being then a period of cheap money, the laying-out of so much liquid assets was difficult, especially as Sheffield had a preference for mortgages over the funds. Gibbon followed his transactions insistently and clamoured for information, only to be called a damned Jew or a Tabby for his pains. But his anxiety is understandable. At last after many minor hitches he had some £20,000 well laid out, not including other resources, and could be called 'a rich old fellow'. His income must have been over £1200 a year.

It is only for this period that any number of Lord Sheffield's letters have survived. They afford the expected contrast with his friend's. Energetic and playfully abusive they nevertheless betray a real and tender regard. Amid an increasingly busy life the member for Bristol, the successful adversary of Pitt over the Corn Laws, could find time to look after Gibbon's concerns great and small from Madeira to mortgages. 'In truth a wise active indefatigable and inestimable friend.'

Gibbon showed his gratitude by insistently demanding a visit to Lausanne. Although Sheffield swore he had not a shilling, the ladies forced a surrender, so that the whole family set out in June 1791, crossed revolutionary France and were royally entertained from July to October by Gibbon. He was indeed known as 'The King of the Place', and reigned, in Sheffield's words, over 'all the society, I mean all the best society that Lausanne afforded'. But behind the dignified peer, conscious of his position as a literary man's friend, was a quizzing daughter.[1]

Maria Holroyd voted Swiss society dull, tame and absurdly obsequious. When the little round mouth opened, as it generally did some moments before the sentence was ready to issue, an awful silence ensued. There was no one to meet Gibbon on equal terms, and she could not understand how much pleasure flattery gave the most sensible people. Yet Gibbon would not stand any joking about the Lausannois and gave Maria a 'scouting' several times.

The truth in part was that Maria's eyes were set on the French refugees, the truly pitiable fragments of the most brilliant Parisian society, great ladies like the Princesse de Bouillon and the Princesse d'Hénin. But the French and the Swiss were not taking to one another, and Gibbon entirely shared the prejudices of his fellow citizens. Describing an entertainment of the exiles at the Château he says, 'J'étais le seul Suisse à table'.[2] A time was coming when he was more anxious to glory in the name of Englishman.

Salomon de Sévery was a dying man, and it was unkind of Maria to judge him *ennuyeux*. She thought the whole family was frigid and dignified, the more so because of the historian's attentions. For he doted upon them, and they were known, so she says, as 'Gibbon's Adopted'. Next a scratch at Mme Necker: 'She is rather a fine

[1] This chapter and the next depend for much valuable information on J. H. Adeane's *The Girlhood of Maria Josepha Holroyd*.

[2] *M. et Mme de Sévery*, ii. 68.

woman; much painted, and when she is not painted, very yellow'. She was very learned, and liked to hold Mr Gibbon in long literary conversations. But Mr Gibbon was wont to waddle across the room to the side of a pretty Portuguese lady with whom he was 'desperately in love', and sit looking at her, 'till his round eyes ran down with water—not Tears of Love—for poor man, he could not help it, as they are not of the strongest, and if you fix the Sun, you will weep, in spite of yourself'. Mme de Silva had a husband and, what was more, a cicisbeo who spiked Gibbon's guns by giving him a hogshead of Madeira—he was said to own half the island.

In one of the many letters of flat adoration which Mme Necker could write to Gibbon in these days without trespassing the bounds of a lifelong propriety, she tells how time is annihilated as she sits by him and he is at once the historian and the young man of twenty, *son premier et son dernier ami*. Did she ever reflect how doubly right she was? As the incorrigible old flirt goggled at his pretty Portuguese, did she see him once more in a corner with La Petite Femme? Laugh at his amorousness as you may, the ladies liked him. Even the irrepressible Maria was sincerely fond of him, and his latest flame, Madame de Silva, was one of the last four or five persons to see him alive in his melancholy London lodgings.

In the year after Maria, came a more impressionable observer.[1] Sophie Laroche was full of *Schwärmerei* and respect for the prestige of the West. She was almost overcome when she found herself at dinner between Sir John Macpherson and Gibbon;[2] and still more when

[1] Sophie Laroche, *Erinnerungen aus meiner dritten Schweizerreise* (Offenbach, 1793); also *Revue Suisse*, 1858, pp. 243 *sqq.*, 323 *sqq.*, 378 *sqq.*, and E. H. Gaullieur, *La Suisse française en 1792*.

[2] She was more interested in Macpherson as the bearer of a name connected with the romantic Hebrides. A similar enthusiasm for Richardson's Lord

in the historian's library, almost as great a show as himself, she heard the Chevalier de Boufflers give Gibbon an account of the races of Senegal and of the remains of the Roman occupation in Africa. But her greatest scene was set in a building which still survives.

Near the west door of the Cathedral, at the head of and in fact bridging the Escalier du Marché, is a wooden pavilion once belonging to Gibbon's friend, the pastor David Levade.[1] A small wooden room, with slatted windows commanding a view of the lake towards Geneva, is surrounded by a verandah. It is adapted to making the best of all weathers, and the interior is appropriately decorated with paintings of the four seasons. Here a *déjeuner* was given amid exotic plants and a *volière* full of canaries. The chief guests were a number of French ladies, some of whom were yet to return to France and lose their heads, Mme de Silva who recited her ailments to Sophie, the de Séverys and Gibbon. After lunch the ladies turned over Lavater's *Physiognomie* in Levade's library and Sophie observed Gibbon's face, intently, as he examined a print of the newly discovered tomb of Scipio and discoursed on it to Mme d'Aguesseau and her daughters. She did not take to Gibbon particularly, and disapproved of his manner with ladies. But his chief offence seems to have been a bitter attack on Mme de Genlis's works. A good thing too. He also entertained the company with the story of the Sheffields' abigail who gave birth to 'a sea nymph' in mid-Channel.[2] A little scandalising perhaps for Sophie, *pauvre et bonne femme souabe*. Her most interesting observation was

Grandison led her to call on a Mr Grandison at Mon Repos. She found a little copper-coloured man who smoked and spat all day. He was in part redeemed by the habit of calling his servants by the names of flowers.

[1] It had been built for him by a friend who had a similar building in Amsterdam, and the design perhaps comes from the Dutch Indies. G. A. Bridel et E. Bach, *Lausanne, Promenades historiques, etc.* 28. It is mainly through M. Bridel's efforts that this interesting building survives.

[2] See Sheffield's and Maria Holroyd's letters. *Prothero,* ii. 272-3.

that although Gibbon appeared to be naturalised in Lausanne, he was in fact deeply attached to English ideas and habits.

It used to be the fashion to sneer at Gibbon's perturbation over the French Revolution. In the snugness of the last century this may have been very well. In our days it will not do.

Once more, it was not the historian's business to foresee revolution. When people questioned him on the causes of it, he pointed to *The Decline and Fall*—it was a good way of silencing enquirers, and they would at any rate find that human nature, if not history, repeats itself. Gibbon knew too much in that dawn to sympathise with abstract propositions, or to imagine that Utopia would spring from Chaos. On the other hand he shocked Maria by hoping that those Vaudois, on whom suspicion of revolutionary aims had fallen, would have a fair trial. With the development of horrors he lost his philosophic detachment, applauded Burke rather wildly, wrote vehement letters to Sheffield suggesting among other things that the names of Whig and Tory were obsolete in the face of the common foe. A very modern ring about that.

Maria might be amused that he was no longer so eager to be a Suisse. But he was not living on a remote island. Examples of aristocracy reduced to poverty were met daily. His own Neckers had been forced to leave France, and that not a moment too soon. Nor were they out of danger. There came a time in October 1792, when the terraces of Lausanne were alive with telescopes sweeping the other side of the lake for the expected tricolour descending on Evian; when Geneva, a bare forty miles away, seemed already a prey to Montesquiou's army. And what an army! 'The officers, scarcely a

Gentleman among them. . . .' A whole new world dawns in this ingenuous phrase. In Lausanne itself '*Ça ira*' had to be forbidden in the streets, and the suspects, a friend, Colonel Polier, among them, were banished. There was a good chance of the fabric of Gibbon's happiness being swept away. He knew himself to be in no personal danger. If he thought of visiting Italy again, Lady Elizabeth Foster, 'Bess we call her', was the incentive, not fear. Far different was the Neckers' case. They were proscribed names, and retreated from Coppet, too exposed to a raid across the frontier, to Rolle, where they were joined by Mme de Staël, a 'constitutionelle' fresh from Paris and expecting a baby. If Geneva fell they would have to move, perhaps to Zürich for the winter. Gibbon would go with them and their society would make any place agreeable. Meanwhile he would wait also, with two horses and a hundred louis in gold for the emergency.

His coolness was rewarded. The dangers of invasion and revolution passed. Montesquiou surprised the Neckers one night by walking into their house a refugee himself. They returned to Coppet and their daughter went to England; she had already opened an importunate correspondence with the historian.

Mme de Staël's object appears to have been to use Gibbon as an instrument to persuade the Bernese government to receive the 'advanced' *émigrés*, particularly Louis de Narbonne and Mathieu de Montmorency. Gibbon was a most eminent man, he was English and therefore neutral, and he was on very friendly terms with M. d'Erlach, the governor of Lausanne. She continued writing from Juniper Hall, sometimes flattering, sometimes scolding. This lady, whose last weapon was her beauty, had the charming impudence to tell Gibbon that apart from his face he was a hundred times *plus aimable* than herself. Thus spurred on, Gibbon seems to have been successful. At the time that he left Lausanne for ever, his correspondent returned to Switzerland. In December she announced the presence of de Montmorency and de Saucourt under Swedish names. Narbonne was coming as a Spaniard. 'Berne le sait, Berne le tolère.' [1]

To all but himself his health was becoming an anxious concern. Gout was regarded as part of a gentleman's route. It must come, and would go. We hear less of milk and more of Malmsey and Madeira, an essential now of his existence. He had not profited by Deyverdun's lesson. A severe attack of erysipelas in 1790 was borne with fortitude. But he apologised to Sheffield for the disgusting details and seemed as anxious to dismiss the subject from his own thoughts. He would not see a doctor. There must have been some deep-seated prudery and impulse to blink at physical facts; they derived possibly from his upbringing as an infant. Perhaps too he was deceived by his unflagging mental energy.

The pleasures of study were inexhaustible, and he had revelled in his new liberty. But he must draw the pen again. Deyverdun's death hastened Gibbon's return to writing.[2] An incautious letter to Cadell led to rumours of a seventh volume. He was probably wise to draw back. Another scheme—a series of biographical portraits of famous Englishmen—did not seem too arduous. He instructed Sheffield to open negotiations, which would need the dexterity of an Auckland or a Malmesbury. It was essential that the booksellers should do the soliciting. If Nichols rose to the bait, Sheffield was to lead him on with hesitations; he must say:

[1] P. Kohler, *Mme. de Staël et Gibbon avec des lettres inédites, Bibliothèque Universelle*, avr. 1912, and *Mme. de Staël et La Suisse*, pp. 125-38, by the same author. The letters are in Add. MSS. 34886.

[2] In the Antiquities of the House of Brunswick and the essay on the supposed circumnavigation of Africa by the ancients, he showed that he had lost none of his old power and charm. He contemplated a volume of such pieces.

1753 June — 1754 December 132

1 Journey to L. — Eliot. — Chesterfield

2 First aspect horrid — house, slavery, ignorance (exile)

3 Benefits — separation, language — health
study — exercises.

4. Pavillard character — use — lectures — conversation
French and Latin — double translations — Logic

5. Return to the Protestant Church.

1755. Jan — December.

6. Mental puberty — voluntary study — habits —
Cicero — my gratitude to him and Xenophon —

7. Greek grammar and Testament

8. Rational reading — common place —

9 Tour of Switzerland.

1756. Jan. — 1758. April.

10. My series of Latin Classics — criticisms, Greek
fragment.

11. Mathematics — metaphysics — Ethics public and
private.

12. Correspondence, with Breitinger Allamand &c

13. Taste and compositions — seeds of the Essay —

14. Love. 15 Friendship and society.

16. Voltaire — Theatre — 17. The World. 18 Recall and Estimate

Page of Manuscript Notes for the Autobiography

'I am afraid, Mr. Nichols, that we shall hardly persuade my friend to engage in so great a work. Gibbon is old, and rich, and lazy. However, you may make the tryal, and if you have a mind to write to Lausanne (as I do not know when he will be in England), I will send the application.'

Many such vivid and artful strokes in the Letters make one think what an admirable novelist or playwright Gibbon might have been.

But that scheme too was dropped, and the historian turned in on himself. Rolling the inimitable phrases over on his palate like good Madeira, he drafted and redrafted his Memoirs. He surveyed his past with complacence and mellow wit, and found no place for resentment and little for regret. The idea may have matured for years, and we can discern some of the famous sentences in their nebular phase if we search the Letters and even *The Decline and Fall*.[1] Sheffield probably alone was in the secret, and he was full of enthusiasm, wisely warning his friend of the possible difference between an immediate and a posthumous publication.

[1] 'The barefoot friars of St. Francis occupy the temple of Jupiter' (*Decline and Fall*, c. lxix, n. 36).

Chapter 26

LAST DAYS

1793–1794

1793 CAME and Gibbon would be called on to pay his promised visit to England, which had been put off in the troubles of the previous year. The Sheffields hoped that it might be the end of this whim of living abroad. Gibbon seemed reluctant to move and was divided between the discomforts of a route through Germany and the dangers of France. He inclined towards the latter, and even thought of going by Paris 'to assist at the debates of the Pandaemonium, to seek an introduction to the principal Devils, and to contemplate a new form of public and private life'. He hoped it was a transitory phenomenon. Had his imagination been fired by Mme de Staël?

Sheffield crushed the wild scheme sternly. There was probably no need. In February Gibbon was at Coppet for the last time and witnessed Mme Necker's prostration after the murder of the King of France. He was stirred to a vehement outburst, although, as the leading Englishman in Lausanne, he had thought it proper not to wear mourning. Sheffield said he was 'a damned temporising son of a bitch'. A private blow was added to support delay. Salomon de Sévery died after a long illness, and Gibbon devoted himself to comforting his family. The weeks and months passed. Mme de Sévery and Mme Necker were both counselling him to stay. These two ladies had been drawn together over their common concern for the historian, just as a bond had been formed between the de Séverys and the Sheffields. Only a powerful impulse, it might be hazarded, would move him now. It came with overwhelming suddenness.

Lady Sheffield died on 3rd April after four days' illness and in the absence of her family. It was a stroke of the revolution, for she had been looking after sick *émigrés* at Guy's Hospital. It was one of them, Lally Tollendal, who conveyed to Gibbon in a letter wild with grief the news that truly struck him to the heart. 'I love her better than any woman in the world; indeed I do', he had told her husband two years before, and his letters for over twenty years had never varied in his affection for her, but only in his constant invention of endearing names.

His decision was immediate and irrevocable. He would start at once, and not all the imploring of the Swiss ladies could stop him. After his death Mme Necker could say that she could not reproach herself for having neglected any means to make him give up that horrible journey. The news had come on the 27th April. Certain preparations and dispositions had to be made. By this time England was at war with France, and there was no choice of route. It was arranged to start on the 9th May. The de Séverys had full powers to look after and use his house. He gave Mme de Sévery his will amid the usual pleasantries. The day before he was to start, his fifty-sixth birthday, he spent the evening with her and the children, and complained that there had been little time to finish his business. 'Pourquoi ne pas rester encore un jour', he said suddenly, 'il sera pour l'amitié.' Accordingly another day was consecrated to friendship. On the 10th he came round in his coach to say good-bye. In spite of what each might say, there must have been forebodings that this would be a last meeting. From her window on the rue du Bourg Mme de Sévery watched him get into his coach followed by Wilhelm.

They were handsomely entertained on the way at Berne and other places by friends and Wilhelm's numerous relations. Bâle and Karlsruhe were passed, and they skirted behind the war. At Frankfort could be heard the cannonade of the siege of Maintz twenty miles away. Here Prince Reusse XIII of Offenbach invited them to dinner and sent his coach for them. Wilhelm went no further. The rest of the route was finished without difficulty or danger. Gibbon reached Downing Street 'not in the least affected by the fatigue of a rough and tedious journey'. He found Sheffield very wisely immersed in public business; but he was philosopher enough to appreciate an irony other than his own. 'In truth', Gibbon wrote to Mme de Sévery, 'the patient was almost cured before the arrival of the doctor.' He added: 'the storm is over, he is weary of the calm. I think he will put to sea again.' A prophecy fulfilled four years after Gibbon's death.

But we must not discount Sheffield's gratitude for an act which he confessed to have expected. And if nothing else, Mrs Gibbon's joy was a reward for the journey. 'I never felt myself happier,' she wrote 'because I never was so miserable, as from the time those vile miscreants the French Democrats was within forty miles of Lausanne, till you arrived safe in England.' She humbly invited him to Bath.

A long summer was spent at Sheffield Place. Holroyd says that his guest's conversation was as entertaining as ever. But the deterioration of his health could not avoid notice, and Maria's franker details are ominous. Gibbon's temper was not what it was. There was querulousness because a turtle was not ordered, and grumpiness because Papa made him stay a fortnight longer than he intended. 'You know he is clockwork.' Worse still, the peer and the historian began to weary of the long *tête-à-tête* after dinner, Gibbon being 'a mortal enemy to any persons taking a walk'. Add to that his insistence on a good fire in the middle of July.

It was a relief when Mr Douglas[1] came with his Greek and Latin, and Fred North full of talk about Ithaca and Corfu.[2] These put Gibbon in a good humour again, and Maria says the three were very entertaining, whether serious or trifling. Good Mr Thomas Bowdler also came for a night, but we do not know if it was anything that was said then that led him to suppose that Gibbon would not have objected to his mutilation of *The Decline and Fall*.[3] Arthur Young was there too. In August and September there were many other visitors and they sometimes sat down seventeen to dinner. The Militia was once more in being, and to see a review the old veteran with the ladies was dragged over the field in the coach with the help of Lord Pelham's cart-horse.

In spite of failing health he performed his last act for scholarship during these months. He agreed to write a general preface and introductions for Pinkerton's projected edition of early English historians. He was to read them himself at Lausanne. He wrote a prospectus for Pinkerton which appeared on the day he died.

In October he left on a round of visits. Bath first, where a *tête-à-tête* of eight or nine hours a day was difficult to support. Then Althorp. But in November

[1] Sylvester Douglas, 1743–1823, later Lord Glenbervie. He had married Lady Katherine North whose sister Sheffield was to marry in 1798.

[2] Frederick North, 1766–1835, youngest son of the prime minister, eventually 5th Earl of Guilford, was a good Greek scholar and an enthusiastic Philhellene. He had travelled in Greece, and studied the modern dialects. He was later founder and chancellor of the University of Corfu, and astonished people by wearing at all times the ancient Greek dress which he had prescribed as academic costume. He seems to have been in the true vein of the old English eccentrics.

[3] Bowdler reduced it to 50 chapters by cutting out all those on church history. He died in 1825, and his son published the work in 1826.

he was in London again in lodgings over Elmsley's shop at 76 St. James's Street. He could no longer conceal from himself or his friends that he was unwell. Yet he was dining out still; in a chair to Lord Lucan's; with Gilly Williams, the one as amusing as the other, at the Douglases';[1] and thinking even of going to the Prince of Wales'. But the rational voluptuary had unwittingly prophesied his own end. 'He indulged himself in a vain confidence which deferred the remedies of the approaching evil without deferring the evil itself.'[2]

He astounded Sheffield, as he astounds us in a different way, by asking him for the first time if he had ever noticed his complaint, while Malone tells us that when Gibbon used to occupy his vantage point before the fire and give a preliminary rap on his box, the ladies did not know which way to look. The hydrocele had brought him to a dropsical state for which tapping was necessary. He asked Sheffield to be with him and Maria feared some risk. But the operation was a success, too much so. For with Dr. Farquhar's approval Gibbon was living as usual and dining out again. Even a second operation close on the first made no difference, and there were people eager to entertain him. He passed a delightful day with Burke, and an odd one with Monsignor Erskine, the Papal Nuncio, and staying at Eden Farm with Lord Auckland increased his liking for Pitt whom he had recently met at Lord Loughborough's. Christmas was spent at Sheffield Place and he was in brilliant conversational form. But Maria noted that going up and down stairs was a great effort for him. 'Poor Historian!'

In January the swelling had increased again and it was a grave sign when he could not enjoy his breakfast. His condition was septic. Sheffield advised him to return to town. The journey over the frozen roads half

[1] *The Glenbervie Journals*, p. 58. [2] *The Decline and Fall*, c. xiv. (2-130).

killed him, yet he persisted that he was not seriously feverish or ill.

> 'I found a dinner invitation from Lord Lucan; but what are dinners to me? I wish they did not know of my departure. I catch the flying post. What an effort! Adieu, till Thursday or Friday.'

It was his last note.

Sheffield followed him to town and was with him on the 13th when a third tapping was made. The next day he felt able to leave his friend 'as the medical gentlemen expressed no fears for his life'. On the same afternoon Gibbon saw his old friends Lady Lucan and her daughter Lady Spencer, and on the next day the seductive Mme de Silva and Craufurd of Auchinames saw him.[1] Sheffield had a good account of him on the morning of the 16th, but later came an express of the most serious import. He left immediately and, reaching town about midnight, learnt that Gibbon had died about a quarter to one that afternoon, the 16th of January 1794.

In the whole of this rapidly fatal illness Gibbon was never treated as being seriously ill. It does not appear that he spent a day in bed. His valet Dussaut sent to the Chanoinesse de Polier an account of his end, fuller than Sheffield's narrative and differing in some ways. It is a grim revelation of the way a gentleman might die in St. James's in the latter end of the age of enlightenment.

On the day before Gibbon died, Dr. Farquhar was pleased with his condition and ordered him some meat; he had not had any for several days. Dussaut had a chicken roasted, and brought him a wing (for he would not look at it whole) and cut it up for him. Gibbon crumbled some bread and ate the food bit by bit. The first morsel

[1] Farington mentions that Horace Walpole, now Lord Orford, was said to have been with Gibbon two days before he died. I suspect a confusion with a servant of Sheffield's called Walpole. *Farington Diary*, i. p. 34.

caused him a terrible effort; but he ate it all, continually asking if he had not finished, as he took the pieces from the plate. He enjoyed three small glasses of Madeira. After this he said he was very uncomfortable in his chair, but would wait until Dussaut had had his dinner. Dussaut made him comfortable at once, and Gibbon remained dozing in his chair, having given orders that if someone called he was to be put off till the next day. He went to bed at nine and took a sedative. But from the time he got into bed until he died he could not close his eyes. He would not have anyone in the room but Dussaut. But as it was impossible to hold him up alone, Dussaut fetched his English servant when he wanted a drink. 'Then Monsieur being unable to speak any more, grasped my hand with his left, looking at me, and drawing his right hand from the bed to signal the other to leave the room; and I was to see him expire, alone and without a soul in the house.'

During the night Gibbon said 'Mon pauvre Dussaut, vous avez un service bien pénible avec moi. Je crains que vous ne deveniez aussi malade.' He never asked to see anyone. But in the morning Dussaut sent for the doctor. He did not come till eleven. Gibbon's only response to his enquiries was 'What is it?' The doctor went out and told Dussaut he had lost his master. Dussaut went in again, and Gibbon took him by the hand, saying, 'Dussaut, vous me laissez'. He was conscious to the end, and, two minutes before it, put out his tongue, at his servant's request. Poor Dussaut was doing his best to the last.[1]

[1] Dussaut's statement in *M. et Mme de Sévery*, ii. 38. There is another one by him in Add. MSS. 34887 on which Lord Sheffield's narrative is based. It adds a number of details which depict both Gibbon's suffering and his fortitude during his last night. It has been suggested that the immediate cause of death was streptococcic peritonitis, in which collapse supervenes rapidly, the patient's mind remaining clear to the last. C. MacLaurin, *Post Mortem*, pp. 180-189.

The funeral was of the utmost simplicity, such as Sheffield had known his friend to desire. On the 23rd of January the coffin was laid in the north transept of Fletching Church, which had been appropriated for the Holroyds' family tomb. On the Gothic stone screen which seals the transept Gibbon's name holds pride of place in the centre. Above him are those of Lord Sheffield and his first wife. The long Latin inscription was composed by Dr. Parr. The historian's merits were recited and, with an exactitude which would have pleased him, the length of his life is given as fifty-six years seven months twenty-eight days.

In London the celebrated Mr Gibbon was dead. Hannah More gave thanks that she had escaped undefiled by his acquaintance. In Switzerland an affectionate friend was mourned. Mme de Staël said that the only link that held her to that country was gone. Her mother's grief was passionate and she took what consolation there was in reflecting that she had always been against the journey to England. Her own health was failing rapidly and she died in the same year.

In his will, drafted and written by himself, Gibbon still spoke to his friends in the familiar style. His dispositions were a little disconcerting. He left no legacies to his executors, mentioning that to Lord Sheffield he owed a debt which could never be repaid. With a last glance at an old grievance, he remarked that his nearest relations—the Eliots—were already sufficiently endowed. He therefore left the bulk of his property—Malone heard it was about £26,000—to his cousins Charlotte and Stanier James Porten. To Wilhelm de Sévery, a comparatively recent friend whom nevertheless he styled by the endearing name of 'son', he left his household effects in Lausanne together with £3000. To Lady Sheffield and Maria he had left small legacies on the same scale as to a number of other people. But of Mrs Gibbon there was no mention at all.

The only explanation of this appears to be that suggested by Maria Holroyd. Gibbon had omitted her name on making a new will, being convinced that she could not live much longer. Mrs Gibbon took the slight—for so it could not but be felt—with great restraint and dignity. 'Not angry', said Maria, 'but affectionately grieved.' She survived another two years, until February 1796.

The testator adhered to an old intention that his library should be sold. Sheffield had in vain admonished him that the books should be left to him to be installed at Sheffield Place as a lasting monument to his genius.

In the summer of 1794 Sheffield and his elder daughter were deep in 'the poor fellow's' papers, and Maria reflected upon the use a Boswell would have made of them. The history of their famous editing lies beyond our scope. With his unfailing energy and loyalty, Sheffield devoted himself for many years to sustaining his friend's memory according to the current notions of dignity. He took liberties which would be heinous in a modern editor. But gratitude far outweighs any other feeling about his work. He himself died in 1821, at the age of eighty-six.

FINIS

APPENDICES

THE FAMILY OF GIBBON

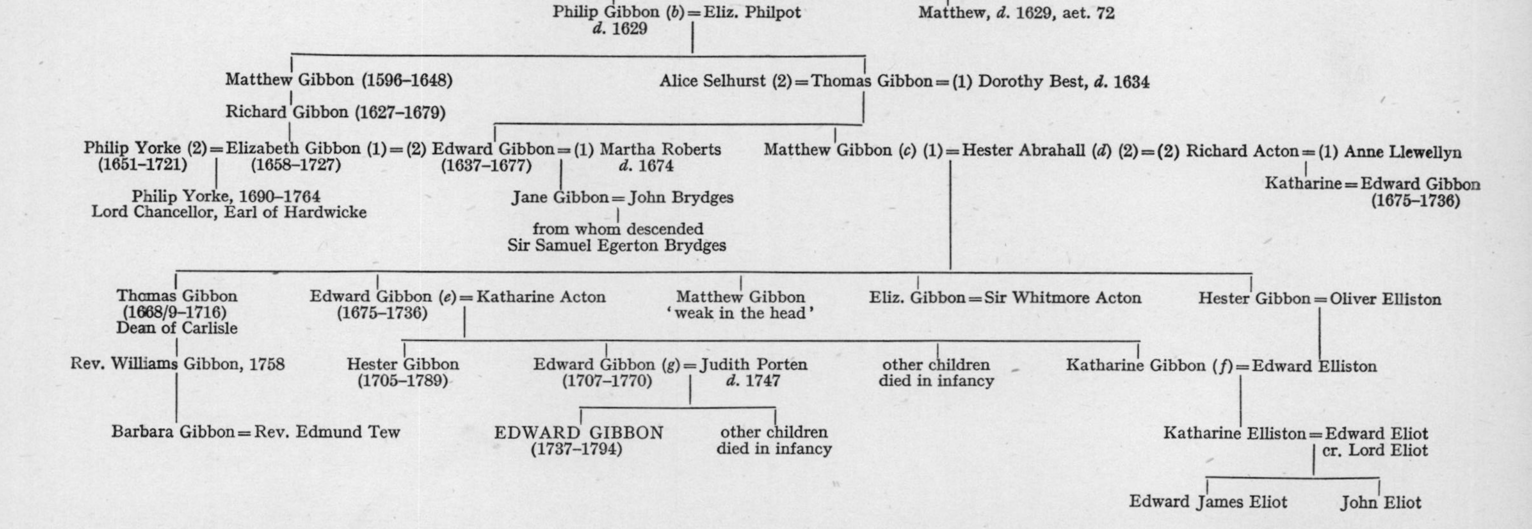

Appendix I

THE FAMILY OF GIBBON

'A LIVELY desire of knowing and recording our ancestors' was dormant in Gibbon until his last years. His father and grandfather had been equally indifferent. Lord Sheffield described his friend's ignorance as distinguished, and had to apply to Mrs Gibbon for information even about recent family portraits which had been rolled up when Gibbon left Buriton. They did not fit in with his scheme of decoration at Bentinck Street.

His interest was aroused about 1788 by receiving from a German correspondent John Gibbon's *Introductio ad Latinam Blasoniam.* Gibbon rashly assumed that the herald was a brother of his great-grandfather and adopted his ancestry in his Memoirs. In December of that year J. C. Brooke, Somerset Herald, was also reporting to Sheffield on his researches into the historian's tree. Meanwhile Sir Samuel Egerton Brydges, a distant cousin, had contributed anonymously to the *Gentleman's Magazine* some notes on the Gibbon family. These seem to have first come to Gibbon's notice in 1792, and on his return to England he advertised for the author in the Magazine. A correspondence then began between him and Brydges. Gibbon was actively interested and borrowed some books on Kent. But he died before he could revise his MS., which he had left in Lausanne. His editor printed the account he had written of his family without comment, although he had a mass of papers on the subject which are now in Add. MSS. 34887. Among them was a tree in Gibbon's autograph based on Brydges' information. Sheffield gave this to Lord Hardwicke; Add. MSS. 36248, f. 9.

The tree given in this appendix follows Brydges and is supplemented from the usual sources of registers, marriage licences and wills in P.C.C. For Brydges' notes and correspondence with Gibbon, see *Gent. Mag.* lviii. 698, lix. 584, lxii. 523, lxiv. 5, lxvi. 272 and 459; Nichol's *Literary Anecdotes*, viii. 557; Brydges' *Autobiography* and *Lex Terrae*. See also papers and correspondence in Add. MSS. 34887, and *Particulars and Inventory of Edward Gibbon Esq.*, 1720.

NOTES

(*a*) Thomas Gibbon is said to have descended from the Gibbons of Rolvenden, *i.e.* ultimately the same line as John Gibbon the herald. He bought the Westcliffe estate from Lord Borough in Queen Elizabeth's reign.

(*b*) Philip Gibbon married 1585 Elizabeth Philpot, an heiress whom Brydges conjectured to be a sister of an ancestress of Swift.

(*c*) Mathew Gibbon, bachelor, about 25, married Hester Abrahall of Allhallows Barking, 17th October 1667. St. Helen's Bishopsgate Reg. and London Marriage Licences (Harleian Society).

(*d*) Hester Gibbon, widow, married Richard Acton 27 October 1698. Faculty Office Marriage Licences.

(*e*) Edward Gibbon, bachelor, 30, married Katharine Acton, spinster, 16, in St. Paul's Cathedral, 9th May 1705. St. Paul's Reg. and Lon. Mar. Lic. (Harleian Society).

(*f*) Katharine Gibbon married her cousin Edward Elliston of St. Peter's Cornhill and Overhall, Guestingthorpe, Essex, in St. Paul's, 2nd December 1733. For the intermarrying here see *Herald and Genealogist*, v. 424-6.

(*g*) Edward Gibbon married Judith Porten at St. Christopher le Stocks, 3rd June 1736, by William Law.

APPENDIX II

THE FAMILY OF PORTEN

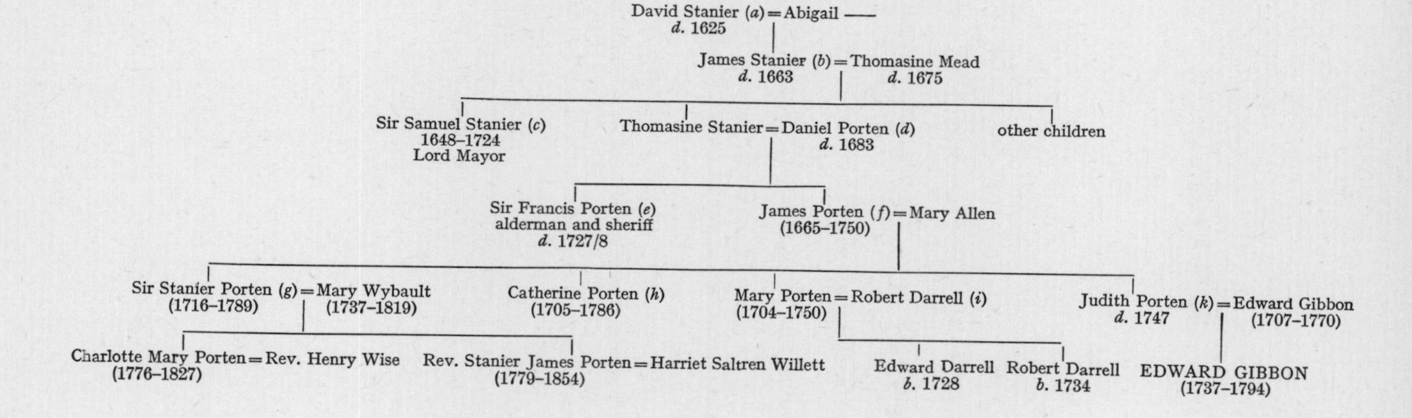

Appendix II

THE FAMILY OF PORTEN

(*a*) David Stanier, born at Cologne, received certificate of denization 13th November 1604; merchant; buried at Great St. Helen's, Bishopsgate, 1625. W. A. Shaw, *Letters of Denization*, etc., Huguenot Society of London, xviii. 6 and 35, and R. E. G. Kirk and E. F. Kirk, *Returns of Aliens*, etc., *ibid.* x. iii. 45.

(*b*) James Stanier, merchant, married 1638; buried in north aisle of Great St. Helen's.

(*c*) Samuel Stanier, merchant of Bishopsgate and Wanstead, Essex, alderman; knighted as sheriff 1705, Lord Mayor 1716; colonel of the Blue Regt. of Militia; buried at Great St. Helen's.

(*d*) Daniel Porten, merchant of St. Catherine Cree. No doubt also of German or Dutch origin. Godfrey Porten, butcher, 'borne under the Duke of Cleve', was a free denizen of some twenty years' standing at the end of the sixteenth century. He married an Englishwoman and had three children, Roger, Abram and Isaac. There is some probability that Daniel Porten was connected with him. For Godfrey Porten and many others of the name see Kirk's *Returns of Aliens*, Hug. Soc. Lon. x. i. 307, 317, ii. 78, 189, 277, iii. 392, and Index in pt. iv. *sub nomine*. The name is often spelt Porteen and Portaine and should be pronounced with the last syllable stressed.

(*e*) Francis Porten, alderman, knighted as sheriff 1725–6; Director of the Bank of England, left money to the poor of St. Andrew Undershaft.

(*f*) James Porten, merchant, Lieut.-Col. the Blue Regt. of Militia; buried at Putney.

(*g*) Stanier Porten, *b.* 26th June 1716(?); *m.* Mary Wybault, 29th December 1774; *d.* 7th June 1789, and was buried at Putney. Consul-General Madrid 1760; secretary diplomatic mission to France 1766; Under-Secretary of State 1768–82; knighted 1772; Keeper of the King's Records 1774; Commissioner of Customs 1782–87. See *D.N.B.* His wife (1737–1819) was d. of James Wybault, engineer-ordinary to the King's Ordnance, and Governor of St. John's, Newfoundland.

(*h*) Catherine Porten, *b.* 6th December 1705, *d.* 23rd April 1786, and was buried at Putney.

(*i*) Robert Darrell, *m.* Mary Porten at Putney 17th December 1724. His sons Robert and Edward Darrell are often mentioned by Gibbon, chiefly over business; Edward was one of his executors.

(*k*) Judith Porten, date of birth unknown, *m.* Edward Gibbon by licence 3rd June 1736 at St. Christopher-le-Stocks; *d.* 23rd February 1747.

Appendix III

THE CLUB

THE following table is compiled from information in Sir M. E. G. Duff's *The Club, 1764–1905*, 2nd edition:

	Year and Number of Dinners												
	'75, 6	'76, 15	'77, 15	'78, 15	'79, 18	'80, 18	'81, 16	'82, 16	'83, 18	'84,* 18	'87, 15	'88, 15	Total
Reynolds	6	14	12	12	17	14	12	14	16	14	13	8	152
Gibbon	6	14	8	8	11	7	11	9	6	0	1	7	88
Johnson	2	3	3	9	3	2	0	3	3	3	..	..	31
Boswell	2	2	0	1	2	0	3	0	3	2	7	5	27
Fox .	2	3	4	0	4	1	0	1	1	0	0	1	17
Smith .	1	6	8	0	0	0	0	6	0	0	1	0	22
Garrick .	..	4	4	4	..	..	..	..	..	..	..	..	12
Burke .	..	1	4	1	2	1	0	3	0	1	1	2	16
Sheridan	..	..	6	8	4	3	0	0	0	0	0	0	21
Malone .	..	..	..	..	..	..	..	..	8	9	..	..	17

* Gibbon was abroad in 1784–5–6. Johnson died 1784.

Other members of the Club in Gibbon's time: (1) *Original members*—Reynolds, Johnson, Burke, Nugent, Langton, Beauclerk, Goldsmith, Chamier. (2) *Elected before Gibbon*—Hawkins, Dyer, Percy, R. Chambers, Colman, Lord Charlemont, Garrick, W. Jones, Vesey, Boswell, Fox, Sir Charles Bunbury, Fordyce, Steevens. (3) *Subsequent elections*—1775: Adam Smith, Barnard. 1777: J. Warton, Sheridan, Lord Ossory, R. Marley, John Dunning, Lord Ashburton. 1778: Sir Joseph Banks, W. Windham, Lord Stowell, Earl Spencer. 1780: Bishop Shipley. 1782: E. Eliot, Gibbon's cousin; Malone, Thos. Warton, Lord Lucan, R. Burke. 1784: Sir W. Hamilton, Lord Palmerston, C. Burney, R. Warren. 1786: Macartney. 1788: J. Courtenay. 1792: J. Hinchliffe, Duke of Leeds, J. Douglas.

In 1777 the numbers were to be limited to 26; on 27th November 1778 the limit was raised to 30. Three members had died, Nugent 1776, Goldsmith 1774, and Dyer; and Hawkins had withdrawn. On 9th May 1780, at an extraordinary meeting, Sir William Jones in the chair, the numbers were raised to 35 and not more than 40. Gibbon supported this motion.

Down to 1783 they met at Turk's Head, Gerrard Street, then moved to Prince's in Sackville Street; later to a place in Dover Street, and finally to the Thatched House.

INDEX

INDEX

INDEX

[1] The N. referred to on p. 318 may possibly be Gray's friend, the Rev. Norton Nichols, who was a visitor at Sheffield Place.

INDEX

Printed in Great Britain by R. & R. Clark, Limited, *Edinburgh*

WITHDRAWN